JOHN DALY

The Biography

Gavin Newsham

For Ann

CONTENTS

Gavin Newsham is the Associate Editor of *Golf Punk* magazine, having previously been the Features Writer at *FHM*, Senior Writer at *90 Minutes* football magazine and a Contributing Editor at *Maxim*. He is also a regular contributor to *The Sunday Times* and *The Observer's Sport Monthly* magazine. He lives in Brighton with his wife, Ann, and his two children, Betsy and Frank.

ACKNOWLEDGMENTS

Originally, this book started life as a magazine feature, but it quickly got out of control. Just days into my research I came to realise that 3,000 words would not be enough to cover John Daly's lunch break, let alone the span of his turbulent career. It was then that I approached Virgin Books with the idea for the biography, and met Jonathan Taylor. Throughout the writing process, Jonathan has always been on hand to lend advice and support and I would like to thank him, and everybody else at Virgin, most notably Vanessa Daubney and Becke Parker for everything they've done.

I would like to express my gratitude to all those who made themselves available for interview. Special thanks are reserved for Ray Hentges and Jim Rackers at Helias High School, Jim Daly, Jane Witherall, Jay Fox at the ASGA, Dave Beighle, Tom Chiarella, Shanae Chandler, Sir Michael Bonallack, Stephen Hamblin and everyone at the AJGA, Scott Cain at the *Arkansas Democrat Gazette*, Steve Loy, Rick Ross and Bill Woodley. To everyone else who offered their time and their opinions, or even just a phone number or an email address, I thank you.

There are also several people who have helped me throughout my career and it would be remiss of me not to mention them. So, many thanks to Paul Hawksbee, Ed Needham, Dennis Winters and Mike O'Hare for all the opportunities they have given me. Thanks also to everyone at KYN for their help and patience, most notably Tim Southwell, Iestyn George, Steve Read, Neil Thomson, Danny Crouch, Sophie Powell, and Dan Owen.

Thanks also to the following: David Willis at the National Sporting Club, Matt Tench, Alan English, Eleanor Levy, Andy Strickland, Dan Davies, Michael Harris, Stephen Brown, Michael Hodges, Tony Milton, Sharon Cunningham, Graeme Thomson, Andrew Woods, Martin Daubney, Ben Raworth, Damian Wilkinson, Adam Boyle, Graham Sharpe, Graham Wray, Dave Cottrell, Mark Leigh and Neil Smith. Also, Bill Borrows and Gordon Thomson for their never-ending advice and encouragement.

On the family front, I would like to thank Bernadette and Adrian Mullen; Betty Farragher; Mum, Dad and Darren; and, of course, my daughter Betsy and my son Frank for their endless entertaining. Finally, a huge debt of gratitude is due to my wife, Ann, for all her unstinting patience, support and love. This is for you, darling.

Gavin Newsham
January 2005

INTRODUCTION

It was the haircut that first caught my eye. A mullet *par excellence*, it was big, blond and deeply unfashionable. It sat there on his head like a bale of hay, the strands running down his heavyweight's neck and over the collar of his snug-fitting polo shirt. On a lesser man, it would have looked ugly, ridiculous even. On John Daly, though, it seemed somehow right.

Trouble was, professional golfers just didn't have haircuts like that. They had sensible, low-maintenance styles that didn't interfere with their swing or discourage potential sponsors. Look at Nick Faldo. Same hairstyle throughout his entire career, and he won six majors. And Ben Crenshaw. Smooth swing, even smoother hairdo.

In the short-back-and-sides world of the PGA Tour, Daly stood out like Seve Ballesteros in the middle of the fairway. There was something quite unique about his heavy-metal haircut, and the fledgling, almost adolescent moustache he wore with it. It was more than male grooming gone wrong; it was a clear and visible symbol of everything John Daly stood for. It was an all-American mission statement that said: 'I'm from Arkansas and I don't give a shit.'

1. I'M THE ONLY HELL MAMA EVER RAISED

'People ask me how I coached John Daly. Truth is, I just drove him to meets.'

Ray Hentges, Helias High School golf coach

It had been a hell of a year for Jerry Pate. As a 22-year-old rookie on the PGA Tour he had hit the ground running, capturing the 1976 US Open Championship with the kind of jaw-on-the-floor shot you only ever saw in the movies. Needing a par at the last for victory, Pate had stiffed his second shot, a five-iron from 194 yards, knocked in the birdie putt and left the 18th green at the Atlanta Athletic Club a fully fledged member of golf's elite band of major winners.

As unexpected as it was spectacular, Pate's victory came in the wake of his triumph in the US Amateur Championship at New Jersey's Ridgewood Country Club, and it sent the game's stats gatherers scurrying for their record books. They soon discovered there was plenty to get excited about. After the legendary Jack Nicklaus in 1962, Pate had become the youngest winner of the US Open since Bobby Jones in 1923. Like Nicklaus, he had now managed to earn more prize money in his first year on tour than any other rookie in the history of the game. And by taking the title he had also become the first player since Nicklaus to win both the US Amateur and US Open titles.

Commentators and golf fans all agreed: here was a star in the making, a golfer of genuine class, maybe even someone who could break the hegemony of Nicklaus. Whether Pate truly believed he could get anywhere near Nicklaus is another matter entirely, but the hullabaloo surrounding the young pro from Macon, Georgia, was so intense, so utterly convincing, that by the time he arrived at the PGA Championship at Maryland's Congressional course two months later, he found galleries ten times the size of what he was used to following his every move around the course – even on his practice round.

Among the throng was a chubby little country boy from Virginia. Ten-year-old John Daly had made the trip from his home in Locust Grove armed with a pen and a notebook, desperate to secure the autograph of his idol, Jack Nicklaus. But Big Jack was out of reach. As golf's biggest draw, he always was. Nicklaus's galleries dwarfed those of every other player on tour; they made Pate's look positively sparse. Faced with fans twice his height and three, four, five times his age, all of them clamouring to get to the Golden Bear, John Daly stood little or no chance of getting a signature.

Unperturbed, he turned his attention to the next best thing. He had watched Pate take the US Open and had liked what he'd seen, and all those Golden Bear comparisons he kept hearing must count for something. With renewed vigour, Daly stalked his man, noting how he freely gave of his time, and, more importantly, his autograph. As Pate reached the turn, he surrendered to the call of nature and dashed into a nearby portable toilet. Daly waited outside, pacing back and forth like a husband in a labour ward, going over and over in his head exactly what he was going to say to Pate when the two came face to face.

Flush. Click. The door opened, and there, standing in front of him, was the US Open champion adjusting his zipper. Daly froze. He stared at Pate for what seemed like an eternity. In turn, Pate looked at this little kid with the awkward grin and the cornflower hair and smiled. It was now or never, figured John. But then the fear gripped him and, unable to speak, he scuttled off, crippled by a sudden sense of unworthiness. He had bottled it, like Doug Sanders at St Andrews. Well and truly choked.

The youngest of three children, John Daly was born in Carmichael, California, on 28 April 1966, and as an autograph hunter he was unequivocally useless. Stick a putter in his hands, though, and the boy could drain twenty-footers like the other kids guzzled sodas. Quite where he got his talent from was a mystery. Certainly he didn't inherit it from his father. Sure, big Jim Daly liked a hack-around with the boys at the weekend, and on a good day he could even break 90, but it was just knockabout stuff, where birdies came around about as often as public holidays and where the only shots worth remembering were the ones they sank in the clubhouse.

Jim was in construction. Over the years, he had fallen into building and revamping power stations as the USA gradually embraced the idea of nuclear energy. With demand for new plants outstripping supply, Jim, along with his wife Lou and his three kids Julia, Jamie and little John, traversed the country, going wherever the work was. It was hard graft with long, irregular hours, but it paid the bills and the kids wanted for nothing.

Whenever he had some time on his hands, Jim would dust down his golf clubs and hook up with his work buddies for nine holes and more than a few beers. Occasionally, John would tag along too, and sit in the golf cart as his old man topped it down the fairway with all the grace of a lumberjack chopping wood for the winter. Soon, John would want to have a go himself so, eager to please, Jim cut down an eight-iron and presented it to his son. In the garden, Jim showed John the correct way to grip the club, and then put a ball down and told him to try to hit it. John swung the club with gusto and, much to the surprise of his father, smacked the ball fully 30 yards, straight through the living-room window. He was just three years old.

In 1971, Jim Daly got a job at the Arkansas One Nuclear Plant, so the Dalys left California and moved east to Dardanelle, a small, blink-and-you'll-miss-it town at the foot of the Ozark mountains. It was a move that made sense. The Dalys had a long association with the self-styled 'Land of Opportunity' state as Jim's ancestors had emigrated there from Dublin in the late nineteenth century. Moreover, Jim's father had grown up in Arkansas and several of his relatives already lived there, including his brother Ben and his wife Ann, and his cousins Deward and Wanda Ferguson.

Nothing much ever happened in Dardanelle. With a tad under 4,000 people living there, it was the type of town where the men brought home the bacon and the women cooked it. It was a tiny, tight-knit community where everyone knew one another's business, and if they didn't they soon would, and where the cut of your suit was less important then the cut of your jib. Located on the south bank of the Arkansas River some 75 miles or so to the east of the state capital, Little Rock, Dardanelle's chief employers were Arkansas Nuclear One, the power plant where Jim would earn his living, and the Tyson poultry plant, where luckless chickens were 'processed'.

The Dalys made their home in a valley called Wildcat Hollow. It was pretty and secluded, but for a young, inquisitive mind like John's there was nowhere near enough to keep him occupied. Faced with the prospect of kicking his heels around the garden for days on end, he would often wander down Highway 22 and pass the hours wading around for lost balls in the 7th-hole pond at the Bay Ridge Boat and Golf Club, a modest nine-hole course that sat next to Lake Dardanelle. Occasionally he would hook up with his friend from the first grade, Donnie Crabtree, and together they would pretend they were playing for the Arkansas Razorbacks football team. Invariably, one of them would catch a touchdown pass in the dying seconds of some imaginary game against Texas to win the match and take the plaudits from the huge crowd.

By the age of five, Daly had been bitten by the golf bug and Jim was soon beginning to regret giving his son that sawn-off eight-iron. Morning, noon and night, young John would be out in the yard, whacking anything that passed for a golf ball. And when Jim told him to quit John would just come indoors and study Jack Nicklaus's tips in *Golf Digest* instead, just so he could get back out the following day and do it better. There was no doubting it: the boy loved his golf.

With John's sixth birthday looming, Jim Daly figured it was high time his youngest son stopped scraping his irons on the driveway and got some clubs of his own. But a new set was out of the question. First, they were just too expensive; second, what if this golf thing was just a passing phase? It would be $200 straight down the pan. It was then that his friend Clete Doyel came to the rescue. Clete was a colleague of Jim's at the nuclear plant and was getting rid of some clubs. Fifty bucks was all he wanted, so Jim, sensing a bargain, handed over the cash. And so what if they were men's clubs; the boy would soon grow into them, just as he had grown into his brother's clothes. Of course Jim wasn't to know, but as investments go, it was up there with giving Bill Gates a few bucks to get his little computer business up and running.

It is difficult to disguise a golf bag, let alone encase it in wrapping paper, so when John bounded into the living room on 28 April 1972 and found his birthday presents spread out in front of him, he knew exactly what was waiting for him. A moment later, John laid his hands on his first clubs – a set of full-size Jack Nicklaus Golden Bears. 'I asked John, "You want me to cut these off?" ' Jim recalled. 'But John said no. Instead, he merely set about manufacturing a swing all of his own, even if the clubs were as big as he was. He'd bring that club behind his back and would have to lift it up to get it around. It generated a pretty good swing.'

It's a moment Daly recalls with fondness. 'There I was, age six, trying to swing a man-sized driver. Not only was the club far too long for me, but it was far too heavy for me, too. It would be about the same as an adult trying to swing a driver that is 60 inches long instead of 43 inches, and that weighs something like 30 ounces instead of 13. The result was, these clubs were so long and heavy that they swung me ... The length of the shaft and weight of the club head carried my wrists, hands, arms and shoulders around so much further that I must have looked like a real lemon! It was ridiculous, because at the top of my six-year-old's swing, sometimes the club head would even hit the ground next to my left foot.' Inadvertently, John Daly's killer swing had been born. The more he swung the clubs (or they swung him), the more his body adapted to his huge backswing, stretching the muscles in his torso, his upper back and his hips to the maximum. 'I became used to the feeling of that heavy club head cocking my wrists and pulling my entire upper body way around,' he said. 'Swinging a club was pretty tiring back then, but I didn't know it wasn't supposed to be so tiring. I was just having a lot of fun.'

So it wasn't really his pop or the papers that created John Daly's unique swing, it was John Daly himself, albeit with a little help from Jack Nicklaus. Like any young boy, John had his idols, and in his eyes there was only one professional golfer in the world worthy of the name, and that was Nicklaus. Sure, other players like Lee Trevino and Fuzzy Zoeller would catch his eye from time to time, but it was the Golden Bear that captured John's imagination. With an incomparable record in major championships – he bagged eighteen, all told – and superstar status in the sporting world, he was everything little John aspired to be.

It is easy to see what Daly saw in Nicklaus. In his early years in the professional game, Nicklaus, while undoubtedly gifted, looked more like a wrestler than a pro golfer. He was fat of face and wide of waist, living, breathing proof that you didn't need a six-pack to make it in sport. Indeed, Daly was so smitten that he set about replicating the set-up and swing of Nicklaus, imitating each and every detail right down to the interlocking grip. 'Ever since I was maybe six years old,' he would explain, 'I have tried to do everything the way my golfing idol, Jack Nicklaus, does it.'

If Nicklaus was playing on TV, there weren't enough cookies in the world to tempt John away from the screen. He would be mesmerised, studying the Nicklaus technique with decidedly more fervour than he ever did his school books. Marvelling at Jack's length off the tee, he would note how long and flowing the arc of his swing was and then take what he had picked up out into the garden or on to the golf course and do his utmost to replicate it. He was a fast learner. By the age of nine, John was routinely beating his father in their games together and outdriving golfers twenty years his senior at club competitions.

Every day, when he got out of school, John would have his mama Lou drop him off at the home of Shirley Witherell, an elderly family friend who lived next to the 1st green at Bay Ridge. Shirley's daughter, Jane, was a teaching professional at the club and was in the privileged position of owning her own electric golf cart, which John and Shirley would commandeer on a regular basis. Arriving at 3.30 p.m., John would leap into the cart and scoot off down the fairway like Evel Knievel, with Shirley hanging on for dear life and the clubs rattling around in the back. By 5.15 he would be back home in time for his dinner, having squeezed in another eighteen holes.

But just as Daly had finally managed to birdie all of the par-fives at Bay Ridge, much to the amazement of the Witherells, it was time for the family to hit the road again. This time, their destination was Locust Grove, Virginia, and they set up home near the Lake of the Woods (LoW) golf club where John would become a junior member.

It wouldn't be long before the LoW members were suffering the same fate as the players at Bay Ridge. In the 1979 Spring Championship – seniors, not juniors – John, still just twelve, promptly dispatched the very best players the club threw at him to land the title. For the club elders it was one humiliation too many, and soon afterwards they changed the rules to prevent under-eighteens, especially gifted ones with the initials J.D., from entering their serious grown-up competitions. It's a decision that still rankles with Daly. 'They wouldn't give me the trophy,' he complains with a shrug.

Ellen Blain was a member at LoW and a regular partner of Daly's. 'I'd play golf with him every day when he was about twelve,' she recalled. 'He was the nicest little kid, so carefree and happy when he was out there on the course. He'd play eighteen holes with someone else and eighteen with me, and at night – our house is on the 14th tee of the Lake of the Woods golf course – I'd see him hitting shots to the 13th green. Once he told me he'd played nine holes in the moonlight.'

But golf wasn't the only thing John Daly had taken an active interest in. As he had grown up, he had watched his father come home from his backbreaking shifts at the power plant and relax in the only way he knew how – with a good stiff drink. Like any kids with time to kill and noses for trouble, John and his brother Jamie would wait until their old man was out of sight and then go and see what he had in his special cupboard. At eight, John tried his first beer, followed soon after by a pint of Jim's home-made wine, which he shared with Jamie. Though it made him violently sick, John would always remember just how drinking made him feel. He liked the warm sensation as the liquid slid into his stomach and the sense of invincibility it gave him. He could do anything when he had had one of his dad's drinks.

Midway through John's tenth grade, the Dalys were on the road again, and after a brief stay in Zachary, Louisiana, they loaded up the car and made tracks for Jefferson City, Missouri. Jim Daly had been hired to help build a new nuclear plant in the town of Reform, some 40 miles south of their new home, but with their youngest son now showing such an aptitude for golf the family's priorities had changed. Now, whenever they went looking for a new house, they had to ensure there was a course nearby. 'It was always the first thing we looked for,' Lou Daly confirmed, 'how far the house was from the golf course.'

Compared to Dardanelle, Jefferson City was a vast metropolis, even though it had a population of only 34,000. Named after Thomas Jefferson, the third President of the United States, it was a pretty little town that had started life as a trading post. By 1821 it had succeeded St Charles as the state capital. The Dalys bought a house on the western edge of the city on Joseph Road, and Jim and Lou Daly enrolled their boys in a nearby school, Jefferson

City High. With nearly 2,500 students, there were almost as many kids there as there were people in Dardanelle, and it was too big for John's liking. He was used to a smaller, more intimate atmosphere where the pace of life was less frantic and where you could hear yourself think occasionally. Indeed, within the week John had kicked up such an unholy fuss that Lou decided to take her sons out of Jefferson City and, despite the family's Episcopalian background, enrol them at the local Catholic school, Helias High.

That weekend, Ray Hentges, coach of the Helias High School's golf team, met with his counterpart at Jefferson City High who, unaware that John had already slipped through his fingers, announced with a mile-wide smile that a new boy had arrived at his school who was said to be the best young golfer in the state. 'He was telling me about this transfer kid he'd got in from Arkansas and, of course, it was John,' Hentges recalled. 'I said to him, "That's just what you need," and I didn't think anything more of it.' The following Monday, Helias principal Jim Rackers made a beeline for Hentges as he strolled down the corridor. He was grinning like a madman. He asked the coach what the regulations were if a kid went to a school for just three days, transferred to a different one and then wanted to represent the new school at sports. 'I said, "Well, he's ineligible to participate for a year." He [Rackers] said, "Are you sure?" and I said, "I'm sure." So he said, "There's a kid and his mother up in my office. He went to school for three days and it was too big and they want to get him in a smaller environment. I think he plays golf."'

At that, Hentges did a double-take. 'Where's he from?' he enquired.

'Arkansas,' came Rackers' reply.

'Oh, Jim. That's the kid the Jefferson City golf coach told me about. He finished second in the state down there.'

'I'll take your class,' Rackers said without hesitating, 'you go upstairs and meet him.'

As Hentges entered the principal's office, he found Lou Daly and her sons waiting patiently for him and found it hard to believe that this little kid with the shock of blond hair and the cartoon smile was the best junior golfer in Missouri. 'John wasn't a physical specimen,' Hentges recalled with a laugh. 'He was just a little undeveloped freshman. I even said to myself, "This kid plays golf?" But he could play, and he was our number one man.'

9

While landing the best junior player in the state was undoubtedly a huge coup for a school as small as Helias, Hentges still had to find out whether John Daly would have to sit out that year's golf and wait for his turn to represent the school. He contacted the Missouri State High School Activities Association, and after some deliberation they ruled that as John had been at Jefferson City High for just three days he need miss only the first three matches of 1982. For Daly, Hentges and Helias High School, it was the best possible result.

Ask any new kid in school and they'll tell you those first few weeks are a living hell. There's that uneasy feeling that everyone is watching you (which they are); you're permanently on guard, suspecting that the world and his wife are judging your hair, your shoes and your clothes (which they are); and you feel like nobody is ever going to talk to you. Beat you up, steal your lunch maybe, but engage you in conversation? Forget it.

Withdrawn at the best of times, John Daly's only hope at Helias High School was that his reputation for being the best junior player in the state would win him some new friends. By the time his first practice session with Helias's Crusaders golf team arrived, the word had spread that there was a big shot in their midst, a kid with a golf game sent from above who could shoot par with his eyes closed.

The 1st tee. It's what separates the men from the boys, the kings from the jokers. Daly stepped up, reached into his bag and picked out his driver. Give them what they want, he figured, let the big dog eat. Bending down, he jammed a tee peg into the turf and balanced his ball on top. Hentges watched on, secretly praying that he was about to witness this tubby wunderkind beat the bejesus out of the ball and hit it halfway across state. John drew back the club, his hands high and handsome, and in a flash brought it crashing down on the ball. But something wasn't right. That familiar whistle as the ball ripped through the air, that unmistakable fizz, was absent. Instead, John came out of his swing to see his ball scuttling along the grass and coming to rest less than 100 yards away. He shook his head and laughed to himself. Topped it, like some half-cut plumber on a municipal course.

As a statement of intent to his new team-mates, it was only marginally less embarrassing than running naked on to the tee box, singing 'Star Spangled Banner' and playing an air shot. But nobody said anything. No brickbats. No barracking. No nothing.

The fact that Daly had made such a miserable mess of his first shot didn't mean a jot to Hentges. He had seen it a thousand times before. And anyway, there was something extraordinary about his new student, something he had never seen before. It was that swing, that massive, cavalier overswing.

Ideally, when a player swings a club, the shaft should be parallel to the ground and pointing towards the target at the very end of the backswing; in Daly's case, the shaft went way beyond that limit, pointing at the ground and very nearly clipping his left heel when he drew it back. It was unorthodox, even reckless, and Hentges was staggered by it. 'He had that long, extended swing and it hasn't changed much over the years,' he said. 'Back in the old days I could stay with him [off the tee], but I don't think I could now somehow.'

Hentges wasn't the only one bowled over by Daly's swing. His son, Chris, was also taken aback. Chris was everything John Daly wasn't. Tall, handsome and built like a Buick, he was the kind of kid dads dream of. Not only was he the mainstay of the Crusaders golf team, he was also the star full-back in the school football team and a wrestler of no mean ability. Indeed, when he graduated from Helias, it came as no great surprise when Chris was named Missouri High School Athlete of the Year. He was that kind of guy. But when he laid eyes on the swing of John Daly he was dumbfounded. Under the tutelage of his father, he had been brought up trying to perfect the classic golf swing – the smooth takeaway, the club staring down at the target at the top of the backswing, the elegant finishing position. And here in front of him was a kid with a swing so wild, so fearless, that when he hit through the ball and wrapped the club around his neck on the follow-through he nearly lost his footing. 'He'd say, "Daddy! He's going past parallel!" ' Hentges said. 'I replied, "I don't care. If it's not broke, don't fix it!" '

Chris Hentges needn't have worried. The kid who could shoot par with his eyes closed and one hand tied behind his back didn't shoot par on his first outing with the team. He went one better. 'I'd never seen anybody hit a ball like that. My goodness, I couldn't believe it,' Jim Rackers recalled. 'Of course, Ray had told me, "You gotta come and watch this kid hit the tee ball," and I did. It was hard to believe.'

'People ask me how I coached John Daly,' Hentges said. 'Truth is, I just drove him to meets.' Hentges underplays his part in

Daly's high school golfing success, but one need only examine Daly's performances to realise just how exceptional the standard of his golf was. By the end of Daly's junior year – the equivalent to the lower-sixth form in the UK – the Helias Crusaders team had won the State Championship in their division with a 66–9 individual win–loss record. Moreover, John was collecting records like other kids collected baseball cards. Over the course of the year, he was just one over par after 243 holes of competitive golf. This remains a Helias record, and he still holds every other golf record at the school, including those for lowest average (35.01 per nine holes) and lowest score (a five-under over nine holes at Fulton Country Club, Mississippi).

When schools played one another at golf, it was customary for the respective coaches to bring up the rear and play a round together. Whenever Ray Hentges played, he would tell his boys that if any of them could better his score then he would pick up the tab for that player's meal when they stopped off at McDonald's on their journey home. Before John Daly arrived at Helias, it wasn't a problem. Very occasionally, one of the boys would claim their free meal and the coach was happy to cough up, but as soon as Daly showed up, complete with voracious appetite, Hentges found himself out of pocket a little too often for his liking. Within months, he had changed the rules, capping his contribution to just three dollars per student. It was either that or face financial ruin. And boy, could Daly eat. In his three years at Helias he piled on nearly 50lb (three and a half stones) in weight, primarily because of an almost overwhelming compulsion for fast food and a fondness for his mother's speciality, a super-rich chocolate sauce – or 'chocolate gravy', as Daly calls it – that he spread on everything from biscuits to breakfast.

Despite his initial diffidence, John had struck up firm friendships with his Crusaders' team-mates Chris Hentges and Brad Struttmann. The three of them had junior memberships at Jefferson City Country Club and would spend their spare time there avoiding inconsequential matters like homework and household chores and putting the wind up the slow players in front of them by belting drives over their heads or into their golf carts. During the summer vacation in 1982, while Chris and Brad were working, Daly would play 36 holes a day there, and if he wasn't too full after Mama Lou's dinner he'd go out again in the evening to hit buckets of balls down the range. Some days he would play alone, other days he would tag along with any of the adult members who didn't mind being embarrassed by a schoolkid.

Despite his supremacy on the golf course, Daly's academic performance was less than spectacular. According to his teachers, he was certainly serious about his education, but nowhere near as serious as he was about his golf. 'He was a C student, average, about the middle,' Rackers summed up. 'I don't think he was real enthusiastic all the time, but then a whole lot of the kids aren't that enthusiastic about coming to school. But [John was] very convivial and easy to work with.'

In one class Ray Hentges held, the kids were asked to give presentations on what they wanted to do with their lives when they left school and entered the real world. Predictably, there was a clutch dreaming of becoming astronauts and fighter pilots, but it was John who dominated proceedings. Standing at the front of the class, without any notes, he informed everyone, matter of factly, that he was going to play on the PGA Tour. There were a few barely concealed giggles, a 'Yeah, right!' here and there, but there was no disputing John's passion for the game or, for that matter, his detailed knowledge of exactly what he had to do to fulfil his destiny. By the end of his speech he'd spoken for an entire hour, answered the many questions posed by his classmates and convinced everyone that he would one day be wearing the famous green jacket awarded to the winner of the US Masters tournament. 'Some people laughed,' Hentges recalled, 'but I really did think he could make it. The kid had a lot of talent. I could see that.' Rackers agreed. 'He talked about how he hoped to go professional on more than one occasion, and the attraction for him, most definitely, was that green jacket.'

Daly's attendance and disciplinary records at Helias High were exemplary, but his extracurricular activities were going unnoticed. Unbeknown to the staff, he was discovering the perils of alcohol, much like his father had done and his paternal grandmother, too. Indeed, it seemed as though drinking was not so much in the family blood as virtually welded to the Daly DNA. Part of the problem was the absence of his parents. From time to time, Jim would be called on to work further afield in Ottawa or New Hampshire, and Lou would go with him, leaving John and his older brother Jamie to their own devices. Before leaving, Lou would give her sons money to buy provisions while they were away, money which the boys invariably took straight to the liquor store. With no parents on hand to call a halt to proceedings, the Daly boys revelled in their fleeting freedom, hosting party after party at their home in Joseph Road. By the age of sixteen, John Daly was quite capable of consuming a case of beer on his own.

It was a situation made all the more difficult by the amount of time he was spending at the country club. Lou always imagined he was out of harm's reach whenever he went to play golf, but she was unaware that by the time her son was in his senior year he was being corralled into four-balls with adult members, many of whom thought nothing of buying him a beer or two when their round was finished. 'We always figured he was safe there,' Lou reflected some years later. 'Looking back, I don't think it was such a great place for a young boy to be.'

By the summer of 1983, John Daly was feeling invincible. He was the undisputed, record-breaking star of the Helias Crusaders side, and the kids had a new nickname for him: 'The Lion'. His performance in the American Junior Golf Association (AJGA) events had been impressive, too. The AJGA was a nationwide organisation for golfers aged between thirteen and eighteen who were looking to go to college on golf sponsorships; eager to raise his profile and test himself against the best kids in the country, John had thrown himself headlong into their contests. He'd won the Hudson Junior Invitational in Hudson, Ohio, taken fifth at the Six Flags Junior Invitational and at the AJGA Tournament of Champions, and then claimed seventh place at the Future Legends of Golf Championship. Now the executive director at the AJGA, Stephen Hamblin recalled seeing the young Daly in action. 'He was just one of those guys who would just hit it, find it, hit it, find it. There wasn't a lot of emotion to John, even at an early age. I mean he would swing as hard as he could off the tee, go find it and hit again. The other unique feature about him was that once it was his turn to putt he never marked the ball [on the green]. He putted until the ball went into the hole. That was it. It didn't matter if he hit it twenty feet by, he was hitting it again and again until he finished, and that was it.'

In July 1983, John Daly decided to go for the Missouri State Championship, an event open to any amateur resident in the state. With his friend Chris Hentges carrying his bag, he progressed to the final and found himself up against a college player from Kansas City. It was no contest. After thirteen holes, the Kansas kid was two under par and Daly was eight under. John Daly was state champion at seventeen.

They take school sport very seriously in the States. You can tell that because they have golf coaches at high school. In Ray Hentges, Helias had a man who knew his sport inside out. He had been doing the job for the best part of twenty years, and in John Daly he had chanced upon the most gifted kid he had ever worked with. Yet Daly's sporting prowess wasn't limited to the fairways and the greens. Despite the marked increase in his weight, John could still hold his own in basketball shoot-outs against the guys and, unbeknown to Hentges, was an undiscovered star on the football field.

In his junior year, Hentges had taken his star pupil north to Kirksville for a tournament, which Daly had duly won. As the pair prepared to leave for home, Daly turned to his coach and a smile broke across his round face. 'I've now got as many golf trophies as I have football trophies,' he said excitedly. Hentges was intrigued. 'What kind of trophies?' he enquired. Daly explained that once when he was eight, and again when he was nine, he had made the semi-finals of the NFL-sponsored Punt-Pass-and-Kick Championship in Washington and then in New Orleans, but that he had given it up in the tenth grade in order to concentrate on golf. Hentges asked John whether he could still kick a football. Sure, said John, 50 yards in his tennis shoes if he caught it just right. Here was an opportunity too good to miss. As well as being the Crusader's full-back, Hentges' son Chris was also responsible for all the kicking and punting on the team, and in Daly he saw a way not just to improve his football team's results but also to ease the burden on his son. 'I said, "Why don't you come out and kick for us?" but he said, "No, my future's in golf, not in football, and I don't want to get hurt." I understood.'

The coach thought no more of it, until Daly, having been badgered by Chris, approached him one morning and announced that if he still wanted him he would be only too happy to kick for the Crusaders, as long as he didn't have to get involved in any of the rough stuff. Even then, Daly knew that if he did sustain an injury it could mean a premature end to his golfing career. 'We needed a kicker,' Hentges added, 'so I told him, "You gotta come to every practice, you gotta do all the callisthenics and stretching, and when we're through I'll keep you out of the contact stuff and we'll work on kicking."'

It was an inspired move by Hentges. Daly, so long the butt of people's jokes as a result of his ever-expanding waistline, was a revelation, never missing one field goal inside 40 yards and making all but two extra points which a couple of plucky opponents had had the temerity to block. In one game against their arch rivals Rock Bridge High School, the undefeated Helias team took a 6–0 lead thanks to two field goals from Daly. Then, with only minutes left on the clock, the Rock Bridge wide receiver caught the ball and broke down the field, avoiding tackles with all the agility of a chimpanzee. With less than twenty yards to the end zone, and as a cruel defeat loomed for Helias, the Rock Bridge whippet was left with just one player between him and the vital touchdown – John Daly.

When Daly had decided to play football for his school he had agreed with Hentges that he would be spared any potentially injurious challenges and, true to his word, the coach had ensured that in the entire season Daly had not had to make a single tackle. Now, though, Daly was faced with a dilemma: did he try to stop this kid and put his golf career on the line, or did he think of his future, risk the wrath of his team-mates and let the kid through? Daly made his mind up, and hurled his huge, hulking frame at his opponent, flattening him like a bus hitting a cyclist. 'John just threw his body at him and turned him upside down,' Hentges recalled. He had saved the day. With his two field goals and that all-important tackle, the Crusaders secured another victory; if they could have lifted him, his team-mates would surely have carried him off the pitch. 'He came off the field jumping up and down,' Hentges added, smiling. 'He was really excited about making his first and only tackle in his high school football career.'

The Rock Bridge football coach, John Henage, had an altogether different nickname to 'The Lion' for the thickset kicker who had deprived his team of a win. When he was quizzed by the local press about the game, he concluded that his side had been beaten by 'the Pilsbury Doughboy in pads'.

2. TOO MANY PARTIES AND TOO MANY PALS

'I have taken more out of alcohol than alcohol has taken out of me.'

Sir Winston Churchill (1874–1965)

In February 1984, the University of Arkansas offered John Daly the golf scholarship he had long been expecting. Going to college, however, would cost thousands, even with a scholarship, and it was money Jim and Lou Daly simply didn't have. Faced with a dilemma, Daly discovered that if he could prove he was still an Arkansas resident he would qualify for the lowest rate of tuition, or a 'full in-state ride' as Ray Hentges called it. Despite the years spent on the road, Jim and Lou had kept the house in Dardanelle with the intention of one day using it as a retirement home when Jim called it a day, so the family hatched a plan: John would move back to the house in Wildcat Hollow with his brother Jamie and the pair of them would live there until John headed off to college. Moving back to Dardanelle meant leaving his friends in Jefferson City, but there was simply no other way, and on 1 March Daly packed his bags, grabbed his clubs, and said his goodbyes to everyone at Helias High School, pledging, yet again, that one day they would see him on the PGA Tour. For once, nobody doubted it.

For the last three months of his senior year, Daly enrolled at Dardanelle High School, but he might as well not have bothered for all the time he spent there. With a scholarship in the bag and few friends to make his attendance worth his while, Daly's final weeks were rendered virtually meaningless. Despite his indifference, he would still get his diploma from Dardanelle High, though with an important game lined up on the same day as the graduation ceremony he opted to play golf rather than share in the celebrations with his fellow students. Unsurprised by his absence, the school put his certificate in the post. 'I didn't care about wearing one of those gowns and that funny-looking hat on my head,' he announced.

With nothing to do but look forward to college, Daly spent the summer doing as he pleased – which meant eating, drinking and some Olympic-standard larking around. His gold-medal-winning performance came when he and Jamie purloined a trampoline, set it up in the front yard and then took turns to climb on to the roof of the house and jump on to it. With their folks hundreds of miles away, they could do what they wanted, when they wanted. And more often than not, they did. Of course, Daly also had the freedom to play golf to his heart's content at Bay Ridge. They liked him down there and he could always find a game, so long as he promised to go easy on his opponent.

Bay Ridge was a simple club. With just nine holes and a modest single-storey wooden clubhouse, it had been built on an old cow field and was the kind of club where rules were largely peripheral, where jeans were almost mandatory and where you could take your shirt off in the summer and nobody would give a damn. For the men from the power plant, a round at Bay Ridge was the perfect way to wind down after a long shift. Riding around in carts with a half-set and a six-pack, they would play for a dollar a hole and then drink in the clubhouse until the bar staff decided they had had enough.

Don 'Dandy' Cline was a regular partner of Daly's at Bay Ridge. A retired hospital administrator, Cline helped 'look after' him during his senior year – which, if Lou Daly is to be believed, meant showing her son the ropes when it came to the manly things in life like gambling and drinking. It's an allegation Cline refutes. 'I love John like my own son. I'd do anything for him,' said the father of three, or four if you include Daly. 'By the time I met John he was a senior in high school, and from what I've read a person's basic personality is formed by the age of six.'

Certainly the evidence suggests that John Daly had always been his own man, even when he was just a boy. On the one hand he could be kind and loving, on the other, impetuous and wanton. His mother recalled her son's first tantrum, at the age of three. John had been playing outside one afternoon and had come indoors and ordered a glass of water. 'Wait just a minute, honey,' Lou told her son. 'I've got to finish up dinner.' Little John didn't like having to wait. In a flash, he was flailing around on the floor, kicking and screaming and demanding his mother drop everything and get him his drink. Lou duly walked over to the sink, filled a glass and threw the contents straight in John's face. Wiping his face, John looked at his mother and whined, 'Why'd you do that?' Lou explained that he simply couldn't get what he wanted whenever he wanted it; he would have to ask politely and learn the virtue of patience. It would be a lesson he would struggle to comprehend. 'John always wanted everything immediately,' Lou added, 'and you could never tell him to do anything.' He was equally impatient with his father. 'John always hated to be told what to do,' Jim recalled. 'When he was growing up, if he didn't get his way, he'd butt his head on the floor.' On one occasion, when Jim returned home after a long trip, he asked John to mow the lawn. The reply? *You* mow the lawn. And when his parents advised him to practise his parallel parking before his driving test, he ignored them, then returned home a couple of hours later without a licence. 'Messed up on that parallel parking,' he explained with a shrug.

In the years to come, this intransigence, this 'I know best' attitude, would prove to be much more of a problem, but for now it seemed like typical teenage obstinacy. But then, what did anyone expect? John and his brother had been left to fend for themselves far too often for them to care about petty matters like a varied diet and a sound education.

During his junior year at Helias High School, Daly's weight, so long the bugbear of his adolescence, had gradually increased as his love affair with beer and burgers blossomed. Now, as a new chapter in his life opened, he was woefully out of shape and the people around town were beginning to notice. As usual, though, the quality of his golf hadn't suffered in the slightest. The heavier he got, the further the ball went. His style of play hadn't changed either. It was still hit it, find it, hit it again. It was brash, fearless and verging on the arrogant.

That summer of 1984, Daly added the Arkansas State Championship to the title he'd picked up in Missouri the previous year, and tried his hand in some more AJGA events with no small measure of success. Paired with Brian Watts, he won the Future Legends of Golf event at Onion Creek in Austin, Texas, then claimed sixth in the Oklahoma Junior event. That said, his progress wasn't entirely without incident. At one AJGA event, the Tournament of Champions at Horseshoe Bend, the association's home course, tournament director Chris Haack received word that Daly had been seen drinking from a bottle of Jack Daniels that he'd secreted in his bag. Jumping into a golf cart, Haack drove out on to the course to confront him. When he finally located him, Daly was reeking of alcohol. 'I went out and found his group, asked him about it, and he confirmed it,' explained Haack, now the golf coach at the University of Georgia. 'I had no choice but to disqualify him.' After Haack had driven Daly back to the clubhouse, the saga ended as it would so many times in the future, with John spending hours 'throwing up in a bathroom'.

At this time Daly hooked up with Rick Ross, a local golf coach who having missed out on a place on the PGA Tour was now dividing his time between giving lessons at Bay Ridge and coaching the Arkansas Technical College's golf team in Russellville. When the two met on the range, Daly told Ross what he had been telling everyone since he was barely out of short trousers, that he was going to play on the PGA Tour. Like Daly, Ross was self-taught, and he saw a lot of himself in John's determination to do everything better. 'John is one of those personalities who if you give him a challenge, especially in golf, he'll definitely give it his best shot and try and do it,' Ross said. 'That's the way we started out coaching. Can you do this? Can you do that? How do you hit a cut shot? And his backswing would go and the club would touch his left ankle. [I'd say] "You don't hit one like that," and he'd say, "Well, that's the way I do it." '

Ross wasn't the only coach interested in Daly. Steve Loy's track record spoke for itself. As the golf coach at Scottsdale Community College, Arizona, his teams had claimed two National Junior College Athletic Association titles. It was the kind of success that an under-performing institution like the University of Arkansas badly needed, and it was enough to convince athletic director Frank Broyles that this was the man to make their golf team something to shout about.

Broyles liked the cut of Loy's jib. He was meticulous, dedicated, and ran his teams like he was a drill sergeant at a boot camp. When it came to golf, his word was God; you either did as you were told or you could go and play golf elsewhere. Loy was the antithesis of Daly. John was the eat-anything, drink-anything kid from the sticks who just picked up a club and swung the damn thing, usually with astonishing results; Loy was the original tough cookie, a coach who believed that technique and application were every bit as important as natural talent.

Fastidious as ever, Loy had done his homework on Daly. He had first encountered him at a National Junior Championship event at the Rolex Tournament of Champions in Innisbrook, Florida. Daly was just fifteen at the time, and because he hailed from Arkansas he had Loy's 'undivided attention'. '[His swing was] very long and flowing. Just typical John,' Loy recalled. 'You know, he loved to play golf, and he had a great attitude about playing golf. He was just one of those kids that you loved to watch.' Loy monitored Daly's progress, and as other golf schools came sniffing around he set about persuading him that the University of Arkansas was where he belonged. 'I used the state and the traditions of the University of Arkansas as the real asset in recruiting him,' explained Loy, now the president and CEO of Gaylord Sports Management, an agency that handles the interests of pro golfers including Phil Mickelson, Mark Calcavecchia and Rich Beem. 'He was the biggest recruit we ever had.'

And then some. When Daly finally arrived at the Fayetteville campus in August 1984 he was five foot eleven and weighed in at a colossal 235lb (nearly seventeen stones). The idea that he needn't do any work, academic or physical, over the long summer months had wreaked havoc on his waistline; the Doughboy bounced into college looking like he had won a scholarship in sumo wrestling, not golf. For a coach with Loy's disciplinarian principles, it was too much. No student of his, no matter how talented, could represent the university in the condition Daly was in. John, Loy decided, needed to shape up or ship out. That meant no more of Mama Lou's chocolate gravy, no more McDonald's and absolutely no beer. Welcome to college, John Daly.

Seeing someone as gifted as Daly wasting his talent rankled with Steve Loy. In his first year at Arkansas, Loy had won the Southwest Conference Coach of the Year award for rejuvenating a golf team that had previously been viewed as something of a joke. Now, as they stood on the verge of some long-awaited success, they found that the player everyone thought would take them on to the next level had arrived at school with more chins than the rest of the squad combined.

With the permission of Daly's parents, Loy formulated a strict diet and exercise programme that would have tested the resolution of a heavyweight title contender, let alone a fat kid with a penchant for biscuits and Budweiser. 'He [Loy] said, "You're gonna lose 60lb if you're going to play for me," ' Daly remembered. 'I was working on the golf course for him, putting the signs up and stuff, doing everything. I felt like I was working for him instead of playing golf for him. My whole freshman year he never let me play.'

Restricting Daly to noncompetitive golf was just one of Loy's devices to get him to comply. The daily weigh-in was another, with each pound John gained punishable with extra fitness work. 'He [Daly] and the golf coach didn't get along,' said Jay Fox, who witnessed John's rapid transformation from stout to slimline. 'John wasn't much of a physical fitness nut in those days and the story was [Loy] had him up three days a week running bleachers in Razorbacks stadium at six o'clock in the morning. John did it, but he didn't agree with the philosophy.' According to Daly, though, Loy had another, more brutal way of persuading his students to do what they were told. When Daly duffed a bunker shot in a round during his freshman year, for instance, he alleges that Loy marched over, picked up his sand wedge and smacked it against Daly's leg. He still has the scar to this day.

Today, Loy is diplomatic when asked about his time with Daly, wishing him nothing but success in his career and insisting 'he can win on any given day'. That said, it's patently clear that the two are not on each other's Christmas card lists. Daly is less reticent. 'Loy made me hate myself,' he said.

But the crash diet worked, although perhaps not in the way Loy had intended. From August to November, Daly shed an astonishing 65lb (four and a half stones). The guys started to call him 'Skinny'. But Daly had his own secret diet plan: 'I said, "If I'm going to have to eat rabbit food, I might as well just drink." ' Which he did to excess. He even ditched the beer and switched to his daddy's drink, Jack Daniels. Daly had first encountered the bourbon when, aged fourteen, he had guzzled a ton of the stuff at his sister Julia's wedding and had to be driven home by his dad, stopping every now and then so he could throw up. Now, faced with a 1,200-calorie-a-day diet, he found that Uncle Jack was the perfect way around his beer ban.

To his credit, Daly stuck to his new regime and swallowed all the lettuce leaves Steve Loy could throw at him. For a country boy raised on a diet of carbohydrates and cookies, it was hell. 'I came close to being anorexic,' he admitted. 'I couldn't eat. I didn't feel like it. I didn't want to get fat again.' What coach Loy didn't know, however, was that the rest of Daly's daily intake consisted of nothing but Coke – Diet, obviously – black coffee, bourbon and a packet or two of Marlboros. As a weight-loss programme, it was ideal. As a lifestyle choice, it was nigh on fatal.

A slimline Daly was a different proposition to his portly alter ego. With his newly discovered cheekbones and a bucket-load of confidence, John Daly became the party king of Fayetteville. The girls liked his new look too, and he indulged himself with the ladies as he did with the JD. One of Daly's favourite methods of attracting the opposite sex was to persuade liquor store clerks to change the price tags on $2.50 bottles of wine to $99.95 just so he could walk into a party and impress the girls with his supposed sophistication.

Much as he disliked Loy and his draconian methods, there was no denying his diet plan had given Daly not only a tidy new figure but a whole new lease of life around campus too. Typically, though, Daly took his new-found status as the university's drinking champion too far; it fast became impossible for him to enjoy a social drink with his buddies without the evening descending into the kind of heavy session guys usually reserve for stag nights. Even 'quiet' nights at a Razorbacks football game would turn ugly, as Daly and his pals would secrete bottles of Jack Daniels in their cowboy boots just to get them past the doormen. On one occasion, Daly drank until he was sick. It was no great shock; it was part and parcel of student life. And anyway, his team-mates had seen him puke before, only to pick himself up and get straight back on the bottle. But this time it was different. By his own admission, Daly hadn't eaten for three days and had done 'four fifths of Jack'. Not surprisingly, he collapsed. When his friends found him they thought he had swung his last seven-iron. He lay there lifeless. Trouble was, you could have written what his mates knew about first aid on the back of a scorecard. Between them they bundled Daly's (thankfully lighter) frame into the back of a car and rushed him to Washington Hospital in Fayetteville. The doctors immediately did the necessary introductions: John, meet the stomach pump; stomach pump, this is John. The pair would become close friends over the years to come.

Three days passed as Daly lay there with an intravenous drip in his arm. When he was eventually given the all clear, he found that word of his dalliance with death had spread and the advice came thick and fast: quit drinking, buckle down, concentrate on your golf. Daly listened. It was the least he owed everyone. But the reality, in Daly's mind at least, was that the occasional trip to casualty and the shame of having a huge tube suck out the contents of your stomach from time to time was just an occupational hazard of being a professional drunk. As far as Daly was concerned, it was carry on drinking. 'I was never able to just have three or four beers; one was too many and ten was never enough,' he would say later. 'Whiskey is what really did it by my junior year in college. I either passed out or did something crazy. It made me mean, not to other people but to myself.'

Remarkably, Daly still found time for a little golf in between his hectic college schedule of drinking, partying and his trips to hospital. Whatever Daly felt or still feels about Loy's coaching ideals, there can be little argument that the quality of his golf didn't suffer in the slightest. Despite the tension between the two, Loy, to his credit, never tried to work on Daly's swing, primarily because there was nothing to work on. 'We put all our golf swings against a certain criterion on film and tape ... This helped us make a few changes,' the coach explained. 'When we got to Daly, he was doing everything right. When we checked his position throughout his swing, he was correct at every step, just naturally.'

So, in spite of his phenomenal extracurricular activities, Daly seemed able to play golf to his usual exceptional standards. With his weight in check and coach Loy making him the mainstay of the university's five-man team, Daly bagged three top-ten finishes in his sophomore year, including a fourth place in the South-West Conference. He also shot a course record 65 at the National College Athletic Association on his way to a fourteenth-place finish. He even gained one of the few places available to amateurs at the 1986 US Open at Shinnecock Hills, New York, by virtue of some sterling showings in the qualifying tournaments.

The US Open. The pinnacle of any American professional's career, let alone that of a fresh-faced country boy who had never earned a bean in the game. Here was twenty-year-old John Daly, the college boy who boomed it, the first Arkansan to play in the US Open for sixteen years, going head-to-head with Jack and Arnie. 'I've always dreamed of playing the Open, but I didn't think I'd do it this early,' Daly told the *Arkansas Democrat-Gazette* on 11 June. 'This is an honour, to be going to the Open. I just want to go out and not worry about anything. I just want to play golf. I have nothing to lose.'

Situated two miles from the coast on Long Island, Shinnecock Hills is the second oldest golf club in the United States. Opened in 1891, it was built by fabled course designer Willie Dunn, with the help of some local native Americans, and then later remoulded by Flynn and Toomey in 1931. It is a course steeped in history. In July 1896 it played host to the second-ever US Open Championship, won by James Foulis, but then had to wait another 90 years before it staged another major. Of course, such rich tradition doesn't come cheap: today it will cost you $250 for a round at Shinnecock Hills. You can get a game for a tenth of that at Bay Ridge. And you can wear jeans.

Not surprisingly, John felt a mite awkward as he took his place on the practice range at Shinnecock Hills. So many people, so many famous faces. As he thrashed a few balls around under the watchful gaze of a mass of golf fans, he noticed a familiar figure walk by, all the time waving and acknowledging the vast crowds. It was Jack Nicklaus. And what's this? He's just looked right at John and said 'Hi', like he knew who he was. Time to finally meet his idol, thought Daly. But rather than summon up the courage to go over, introduce himself and generally suck up to the great man, Daly did what he had done all those years ago when confronted by Jerry Pate. He bottled it. 'When he spoke to me, I was so shook, so in awe, I couldn't say a word back,' he told reporters. Instead of talking to Nicklaus, Daly simply stood nearby and watched him practise. 'He does everything so right. He is so slow and deliberate,' he observed. 'He does the same things before every practice shot that he does in a round, that's the main thing I noticed.' But though Daly had spent his childhood studying Nicklaus, he admitted that his pre-shot routine differed greatly from that of his idol. 'Three looks, three waggles and I'm hitting it,' he added. 'On the green, two quick practice strokes and I'm putting.'

Back home, Daly's appearance in the US Open was all the news. The state newspaper, the *Arkansas Gazette*, had been in touch and wanted to track his progress as he went head-to-head with the biggest names in the game, and Daly, eager to please, had agreed to phone in with a report each evening. It was an irresistible story. Surely this college kid from Arkansas couldn't overcome the odds and win the biggest golf tournament in the world? Surely the Doughboy couldn't land a major at his first attempt?

Of course he couldn't. As Mr Nobody from Dardanelle, Arkansas, Daly teed off at 3.00 p.m. when virtually everyone else was back in the locker room enjoying a hot shower and a rubdown. It was a truly miserable day for golf, the kind of day when if you were meeting the guys for a four-ball you would all look at one another, shake your heads and make haste for the comfort of the clubhouse instead. Cold, wet and blustery, it had proved tough going for everyone, not just John Daly. Even the top dogs had struggled. Trevino hit a 74, Crenshaw took 76, and even Jack – yes, Jack – had come in with a 77. To compound matters, there were precious few people there to share in John's misery, let alone offer him a damp shoulder to cry on.

And what misery. By the time Daly finished his round with the two PGA nontour pros Michael Malaska and Michael Colandro, he looked at his scorecard and saw two fat ladies staring back at him. There were lost balls, dropped balls, three-putts and duffed shots. Eighty-eight. A disaster. He couldn't remember for the life of him the last time he had nudged 90. When he was ten years old, perhaps, maybe eleven? 'I just hope I didn't let the state down,' he told the *Arkansas Gazette* that night. 'I'm glad I stayed with it and never gave up. I think I got a lot of respect from a lot of people by not giving up . . . I just want the state to know I tried up here and never gave up.' At eighteen over par there was more chance of his mother winning the competition than there was of Daly making the cut. Faced with a humiliating exit from his first major championship, John decided to go out in his second round and at least try to show the watching world just what he could do. The result, a face-saving 76, was a major fillip for the kid from the sticks.

In the locker room afterwards, Daly was minding his own business when one of the game's legends walked over and sat next to him. 'Lee Trevino told me that I should never have made that [the US Open] my first big tournament appearance,' said Daly. ' "Never start in the Open, because a low score is almost impossible and the experience can set you back," he said. Actually, I don't mind, because that's behind me, and I just want to get back in it.'

Although Daly's performance at Shinnecock Hills would help him land the title of Arkansas State Golf Association Golfer of the Year for 1986, he was unaware, blissfully so, that this would be the beginning of a turbulent relationship with the US Open.

Steve Loy left in the spring of 1987 and moved west to Arizona State University. His replacement was Bill Woodley, who had arrived from Texas Christian University (TCU) and had already met Daly when his TCU team had defeated Arkansas at the Conference meet the year before. 'Although playing for Arkansas, with the tournament being held in Arkansas [John] was the first one to come over and greet me,' recalled Woodley. 'I didn't know him particularly well at the time, except that he was a good player on another team. What did stick out though was that he was the first one to come over and offer congratulations. [He was a] tough competitor and hated to lose, but "Way to go," he said. "Congratulations." '

Loy and Woodley had markedly different approaches to golf coaching. Loy, to all intents and purposes, was a percentage golf man who believed that if you could minimise the mistakes, the birdies would come in due course. Woodley, meanwhile, chose to concentrate not on swing planes and coils and arcs, but on taking what talent a player had and making the most of it. It was a technique that struck a chord with Daly, especially after the rigorous, disciplined and overly physical regime of Loy.

When Woodley watched Daly play he knew he was a PGA Tour pro in the making. 'I've been coaching since 1979 and the ones that have made it in that time – the Tigers, the Mickelsons – are the guys who make a lot of birdies. It's those guys that can continue to play for a living,' he explained. 'Par sucks if you're a pro. You gotta make tons and tons of birdies, and it was quite evident that John was a birdie machine.' The more he watched Daly, the more Woodley realised that coaching this prodigious talent was futile. In his eyes, the kid had everything in abundance. He had the length, he had the short game (he even used to practise pitch shots one-handed) and, despite his antics off the golf course, he certainly had the big-match temperament. 'I never coached him on the mechanics of the game. I mean, if you were to change that swing, what would happen? He'd go to hell. I've got several [of my] former players on the PGA Tour [including J.L. Lewis, Pete Jordan and the Pappas brothers] and twice that many on the Buy.Com [now the Nike Tour, a feeder to the PGA Tour]. They're all talented in their own ways but John, when he's right, it's just ridiculous what he can do.'

After the unyielding, regimented reign of Steve Loy, Woodley's approach seemed almost laid back. Individuality was positively encouraged. The team was told to think for themselves, to make their own decisions and to live and die by them. After all, there was going to be nobody there to hold their hand when they made it on the PGA Tour. OK, so it was hardly *Dead Poets Society*, but at least it was, well, different.

There was a mutual respect between Daly and Woodley, even though they might not have shown it. John enjoyed the coach's informal practice sessions and Woodley, knowing full well that he had a potential future major winner under his instruction, gave Daly the room to develop his own golf game. Indeed, Daly would show his appreciation of Woodley's efforts when, having made his mark on the pro game, he rang his old coach. 'He called up one day and said, "Coach, y'all need a van." I said we don't need a van, we fly everywhere. So he said, "Well, hell, y'all need a van to get to and from the airport." So he had a custom van delivered to me, and on the side of it was GRIP IT AND RIP IT. He gave us that $40,000 van – just gave the golf team a van.'

Woodley's way was Daly's kind of tuition – heavy on the golf and light on the lecturing – and it did little to curb his social shenanigans. There were too many parties and too many pals, so he carried on drinking. After all, Loy was gone now, and what was the worst that could happen, apart from another visit to casualty? Sure enough, that hospital visit came just one month into Woodley's tenure at the university. 'From what I gather he [Daly] wouldn't eat a lot and then he would party and it would get the best of him,' said Woodley, who took the job of head golf coach at the University of Southwest Texas in September 2001. 'I didn't see anything. If I had I would have done something.'

Still, a combination of Daly's latest excursion to hospital and his seemingly endless exuberance was enough to set the alarm bells ringing in Woodley's head. It was in the coach's power to grant Daly's scholarship for his final year at college, but if he was going to give John the opportunity to graduate there was going to have to be a marked improvement in his behaviour. 'I said, "OK, here's what you're gonna have to do. You gotta stop drinking and smoking, you gonna have to go to class," and all this kind of stuff. And he thought that was OK until the summer and then he realised that, hell, school is going to start pretty soon.' The thought of another year with mind-numbing pursuits like reading books and attending class didn't appeal to Daly. 'I couldn't get past world lit., reading about things that did or didn't happen 5,000 years ago,' he would say. 'It talks about death too much.' If he couldn't enjoy student life on his terms, he figured, there was little point in being there. At the end of July 1987, shortly after he had won the Longhills Individual Golf Tournament in record-breaking style, John Daly announced that he would not be returning to the University of Arkansas. Moreover, he would be turning professional at the end of the summer.

In a phone call to the *Arkansas Gazette*, Daly confirmed that he was quitting college. 'This is just a decision I made,' he said. 'It's just time. I need the time now. I feel like I was put on this earth to play golf. I have so many goals; I didn't set any goals in college. I played to help Arkansas out. I had no goals to win a golf tournament in college.' Despite his numerous disputes with Loy, Daly had words of commendation for his university coaches, even though he had yet to tell Bill Woodley of his decision. 'I learned an awful lot from coach Loy. I learned everything from him. And coach Woodley helped me out a lot this spring. I feel like I've done pretty good for the U of A, but I think maybe they can probably do better without me. Instead of concentrating on me, they can concentrate on themselves. I wish them the best.'

When Woodley eventually learned that Daly was leaving, he was 'disappointed but not surprised'. Any coach who has just lost their star player would be. But, in time, he came to understand Daly's decision to quit. 'John just hated school. He wasn't in it for scholarly endeavour, he was there to play golf.' Which was true to a point. 'People say college is supposed to be the best four years of your life,' Daly said. 'I made sure I packed four years into three.'

3. YOU ARE MY SUNSHINE

'It's a town full of losers and I'm pulling out of here to win . . .'

'Thunder Road' by Bruce Springsteen

As Bill Woodley and the Razorbacks golf team reeled from his premature departure, Daly announced that the Missouri Open at the end of August 1987 would be his first tournament as a professional golfer, providing he could scrape together the $300 entrance fee. When he had left college, John had told the local press that his parents were 'backing me 100 per cent'. Now, as a personal liquidity crisis threatened to scupper his professional ambitions, he found himself indebted to his mother, Lou, who stepped in and gave him the cash on the condition that he pay it back just as soon as he started making some money of his own.

Daly spent the remaining few weeks of his amateur career cementing his position at the top of the table for the Arkansas Player of the Year award. With one eye on his pro debut, he had also hooked up again with Rick Ross, now the assistant professional at Pine Bluff's Rosswood Country Club, and discussed with him just what it would take to make it on to the tour. In turn, Ross, whom Daly described as 'like a brother', accompanied him as he played in his Arkansas State Golf Association (ASGA) events, carrying his bag and helping to iron out some of the minor flaws in his game. 'Rick tells me to be patient and play smart. He knows my golf game better than anybody,' claimed Daly. 'My lesson with him is two or three minutes, then I'll work it out. I probably won't ever have anybody else coach me. If I make it on the PGA Tour, he'll be with me. It's his decision, but I hope to God he will.'

While he waited for his professional bow, Daly took his talents around the state and, according to Jay Fox, himself a two-time Arkansas Player of the Year and a regular sparring partner of Daly's, his golf that summer was off the scale. In one competition at Morrilton Country Club, Fox played with Daly in the final pairing and as the two reached the 1st tee he noticed John sizing up the hole ahead, a straight 360-yard par-four with out of bounds directly behind the green. As the group ahead stalked the putting surface, Daly bent down, teed his ball up and pulled his Taylor Made Brassey from his bag. Fearing for their safety, Fox alerted his playing partner to the group in front. 'You know, John,' he said, 'you might want to wait if you're going for the green.' Daly was having none of it. 'Oh, I don't think I can get there,' he replied, 'but I'll see how close I can get it.'

Wallop. 'John hit his shot and we watched it take a couple of hops and run up on to the green,' recalled Fox, now the ASGA director of operations. 'All the players in the group ahead turned and watched as it rolled over the green, across the street and out of bounds.'

Three off the tee. It's a test of any player's mettle. Lesser men hold up their hands, accept defeat, put the driver away and dolly one down the fairway with an iron. For Daly, though, there was only one thing to do: keep hitting that ball until it damn well did what it was told. John shrugged his shoulders and reached for another ball. 'He never flinched, never uttered a foul word,' added Fox. 'He just teed up another ball, knocked it on to the green and made the putt for four.'

On the Arkansas mini-tour, Daly racked up victories like he was the only guy teeing it up. Perhaps in his mind he was. He would win five designated events that year, as well as the 1987 Arkansas State Championship for strokeplay, and it was a formality that he would retain his title as the state's Player of the Year. It was on one of these victorious outings that Daly met someone who would change his life, and not always for the good.

Daly had ventured northeast to Blytheville, a small town near the Missouri border that was once home to the National Cotton Picking Contest. For Daly, the Blytheville Invitational Stroke, a 36-hole medal-play event with a field of nearly 50 players from around Arkansas, was just another amateur competition that wasn't the PGA Tour. Still, at least he wasn't in college. In the first round Daly bludgeoned a four-under-par 67 which gave him a two-stroke lead going into the final round. His verdict was typical Daly: 'It was OK,' as if he knew the title was already in the bag. It was a similar story on the Sunday. Nobody came close to challenging Daly, and he breezed to a comfortable victory.

Intent on celebrating, Daly headed into the centre of Blytheville, but it was a quiet Sunday night and the only place he could find open was the Holiday Inn on Main Street. He went in and lined them up. As the beers disappeared, he noticed a woman in the distance, a dainty little thing with a pretty face and a prickly haircut. Soon, they began talking. He told her that he was in town for a golf competition at the country club, but that he would soon be a professional on the PGA Tour. Sure, it sounded far-fetched, but at least it was more impressive than saying he'd just dropped out of college and that his favourite pastime was drinking. In turn, she told him her name was Dale Crafton, that she was a local girl and that her grandmother was Ethelyn Dunlap, winner of the Arkansas Senior Women's Golf Association title way back when. It meant nothing to Daly.

Dale Crafton was the only daughter of an affluent Blytheville family. She was a couple of years older than Daly and worked as a hand model in Memphis. She was well groomed and said please and thank you like she meant it. She was quite a catch. Daly was flummoxed. What did a classy lady like Dale want with a diffident Dardanelle boy with a gawky grin and a permanent thirst? Surely she couldn't really like him? But she did, she really did, and the couple soon became inseparable. As Daly put the wheels in motion to turn pro, Dale offered her support, joining him at his final few events as an amateur and cheering him on from the sidelines. John liked the stability Dale gave him, while Dale enjoyed John's generous nature and his sense of humour. And if he drank a little too much, well, it never really got out of hand, did it? Within six months, and much to the surprise of their families, the couple had announced their intention to be married. It was the archetypal case of young love, with neither party displaying anything approaching common sense or restraint. Dale had fallen for the young golf pro with his eyes on the big time, while John was waylaid by his hormones, confusing strong physical attraction and sex on tap with the real deal.

Not that John was unduly concerned. Everything in his life was going to plan, and the fact that he had found a wife along the way was an added bonus. Soon, Daly and Dale were doing the rounds, meeting everyone who mattered in John's life. The folks, the family, even his old coach at Helias, Ray Hentges, was granted a reception. They all smiled, too chicken to point out that John should maybe wait a while before getting hitched.

It would be a grand wedding in Blytheville, and, truth be told, Daly was a little uncomfortable about the scale of it all. Everything about the bash was big, perhaps too big. The dresses, the guest list, the bar bill – it was all too much for the 21-year-old. But still he went along with it. 'I did it to please her,' he would explain later. 'I wanted to make her happy.' Dale's happiness was also at the heart of John's decision to accept her family's offer of a house in Blytheville, free of charge. The couple had been living in a modest place in the state capital, Little Rock, and Dale, desperate to be closer to her family, badgered her new husband into moving. 'Her grandparents gave us a house to live in, but I felt like a cheap person,' said Daly. 'I didn't want anybody giving me anything.'

As Daly wound up his amateur career, Dale's presence alongside him gave him such a lift that when he finally made his professional debut at the Missouri Open his confidence was sky high. Held at the Country Club of Missouri, the Open was a 54-hole event and there was a $6,000 cheque awaiting the winner. Compared to the riches of the PGA Tour, it was peanuts, but for Daly, flat broke and still in debt to his mother, it meant everything. On the first day, Daly hit the ground running, carding a seven-under-par 65 in his inaugural professional round. After surviving 'a few bad holes' in Friday's rough winds, he posted a respectable 73. Going into the final round, Daly was tied for the lead at 138 with little-known Scottish pro David Hunter. What followed was typical of the kind of phenomenal, fearless form Daly was in. Faced with a stiff challenge not from Hunter but from reigning champion Stan Utley, Daly produced three consecutive birdies at ten, eleven and twelve and pulled away from his rivals, eventually finishing four shots clear of the field. In his first event as a professional, 21-year-old John Daly from Dardanelle, Arkansas, had emerged triumphant, and that $6,000 felt like $600,000.

Daly found life as a golf pro to his liking. In less than two months he banked over $17,000, second-place finishes in the

Yamaha Arkansas Open at North Little Rock's Burns Park (worth £2,062.50) and the Elks Invitational in Duncan, Oklahoma ($2,500) the highlights of his endeavours. Buoyed by the ease with which he had established himself in the professional game, albeit at a level much lower than where he wanted to be, Daly set his sights on qualifying for the big time, the PGA Tour.

The PGA's Qualifying Tournament, or 'Q-School' as it's known, is where the satellite tour players and those professionals who have screwed up on the main tour and lost their card challenge for the right to win their place on the blue-riband circuit. Those players who have endured the event will tell you that it is an immeasurably more daunting prospect than, say, challenging for the lead in a bona fide tour event. It is a competition where reputations and livelihoods are put on the line, where dreams are dashed and careers ruined. That said, for the few that win their card it is a passport to riches untold: you can earn more in a week on the PGA Tour than you can in a couple of years slogging around on one of the minor tours.

In 1987, 800 players applied to the PGA's annual bun fight, chasing just 54 tour cards. There were three qualifying stages. Daly, chasing his childhood dream, cruised through the first two with few problems. Everything was going to plan. One more solid showing at the finals and he would have his card. The final rounds of qualifying, all six of them, were to be held at Matanzas Woods Golf Club in Palm Coast, Florida. With the original field now cut to 183 people, Daly's chance of landing one of the places on offer was greatly enhanced. Confident and relaxed, he had convinced himself that he was about to join the elite of the professional game and that his and Dale's future was assured.

He was wrong. The one thing Daly hadn't banked on was failure, and as he trudged away from Palm Coast with the 128 other players who had missed the cut, he was back where he started. With his hopes dashed for another year at least, a despairing Daly headed back to Arkansas, all the time wondering whether he really was as good at this game as everyone kept telling him.

After the encouraging start to his professional career, missing out at Q-School hurt Daly more than he could have imagined. Of course, Rick Ross had tried to tell him how he would feel if the unthinkable happened, but John, being John, had given the idea of failure short shrift. 'We knew we had the talent, but we also knew that Q-School was a long and arduous process and one or two bad rounds can really hurt you,' explained Ross, himself a victim of the Q-School experience. 'When you have to play three separate tournaments and end up with a six-day gruelling test in the final, and one or two strokes here and there determine what you do for the next twelve months, [it's] quite depressing.'

Now that the worst-case scenario had transpired, however, everything in Daly's life was thrown into confusion. He had craved the soft verges of the PGA Tour but had been given the hard shoulder, and all those days spent dreaming of wildly enthusiastic galleries, network TV exposure and fat cheques were now put on hold. Not even Daly was sure just when he would claim his place in the game's elite. With a heavy heart, he returned to the mini-tour and thought of what might have been. Of course, toiling away in the small-time events meant surviving on the comparatively meagre prize funds these competitions offered, which was fine if you were performing well week in, week out, but less so if you were returning home each week without a dollar to your name.

After the letdown of Q-School, the first real hiccup in his golfing career, Daly's form collapsed and his relationship with Dale took a distinct turn for the worse. Where once she would accompany John as he set about enacting his plans for global golf domination, now she would stay behind in Blytheville, letting Daly drive to and from events on his own and awaiting his return, more often than not without a cent. This wasn't the way he had planned it. Driving hundreds of miles each week, sleeping in the car and with barely enough to cover his expenses, Daly's experience of professional golf in the wake of his disaster at qualifying was as far removed from the PGA Tour as anything he could have imagined. Now, as he trawled the country in search of a pay cheque, away from his friends and family, there was nothing else Daly could do but seek the company and consolation offered by the only buddy that never talked back, Jack Daniels. He counted down the days as he waited for the next PGA Qualifying Tournament. It would prove to be a taxing time. With precious little money coming in, Dale grew tired not just of her husband's drinking but of his repeated claims that everything would be all right just as soon as he made it on to the tour. But when was that going to happen?

When the competition arrived in the autumn of 1988, it seemed as though everything in Daly's life, not just his golf career, was riding on his success. Once more he progressed to the final rounds, this time held at La Quinta, California, with customary ease, but yet again he came up short. If the first failure at Q-School had been like a kick in the teeth, this latest setback was like a six-iron through the heart. 'As far as I'm concerned, Q-School is the fifth major,' Daly would later claim. 'It's the most nerve-racking tournament I ever played . . . You're so focused on every shot. By the time you get to the finals, you're physically and mentally stressed out to the max. It's just so hard on your body and your head.'

After the misery of 1987, Daly had decided that if he missed out again he would try his hand overseas in South Africa. Daly had heard about the Sunshine Tour, which ran from December to February, during his time at the University of Arkansas and had earmarked it as a potential training ground for the PGA Tour. Now it was time to put Plan B into operation, but getting to South Africa was not going to be easy, not least because Dale would not be making the trip with him. Aside from the initial outlay to get there, there was also the not inconsiderable matter of his living expenses for the duration of the trip. If he was going to survive while he was halfway across the world, he would need bankroll- ing. Using his country boy charm, and playing on his reputation for being the best player in the state, Daly approached twelve people from friends and family to local businesses and persuaded them that if each of them purchased a $1,000 share in him he would make it worth their while. There was no shortage of takers.

Away from home and the seemingly never-ending wrangles with Dale and her family, Daly managed to recapture some of the form that had given him such a promising start to his professional career. Playing in front of sizeable galleries, the kind he had only really experienced at the US Open, Daly finished second in the Swaziland Classic, where he also won the long-drive contest. He took fourth in the Dewars White Label Trophy and in the Lexington PGA. There was an eleventh placing in the Protea Assurance South African Open and in the AECI Charity Classic, and a twelfth place in the Tournament of Champions. By the time he returned home to Arkansas in early 1989, Daly had achieved a stroke average of 70.12 from his eight events, and while he hadn't won a tournament he had finished eleventh on the Sunshine

Tour Order of Merit. More importantly, he had won over $23,000. Just as he had done in the past, Daly called the *Arkansas Gazette* to report on the relative success of his South African sojourn. 'I was pretty pleased with my play for it to be the first time to be that far from the States,' he enthused. 'I had the chance to win three tournaments. I shot 68s and 67s, but somebody always came in at 63 or 64.'

Clearly, the trip had worked wonders for Daly's attitude. He had returned with a new positivity and, having found some much-needed consistency, his golf game was showing real signs of improvement. Moreover, he had nothing but praise for his South African hosts. 'I think South Africa's the best foreign tour anybody could play except maybe Europe,' he said, even though he had no experience of playing on the European Tour. 'All the tournaments are televised there. We had probably 8,000 to 10,000 watching on Saturday and Sunday every week. It's the closest thing to the big time here.'

Daly's golf career was apparently back on track, but his marriage to Dale was very much on the ropes. He had been away from his wife for two months and had found that not only was his golf game better than it had been for a year, but he hadn't missed Dale half as much as he thought he would. Something would have to give.

4. I DON'T KNOW WHETHER TO KILL MYSELF OR GO BOWLING

'Beer was never a problem with John. JD's problem was JD.'

Dave Beighle, John Daly's former caddie

Jim Daly hammered the signpost into the ground and took a step back to admire his handiwork. The notice read WILDCAT HOLLOW DRIVING RANGE. PRO – JOHN DALY.

After the comparative success of his trip overseas, Daly had, with the help of his old man, turned the cow field down the hill from the family home in Dardanelle into his very own driving range. The pair had already constructed their own putting green on which Daly would spend endless hours honing his putting technique; now they had gone one step further and built a range, complete with floodlights and Bermuda grass tees, that Jim would manage and at which John would teach – when he could get away from Blytheville, of course.

Aside from the material gains of the South Africa adventure, Daly had also found some much-needed focus in his career. No longer was it necessary to blitz his way on to the PGA Tour and win every event he entered. Now, with some higher-quality tournament play under his belt, he had learned that when you were playing for your livelihood it was imperative to keep going, even if your A-game had stayed at home. Moreover, Daly now had a clear idea of what he was going to do before his next crack at Q-School, and announced his intention to qualify for individual PGA events. But with up to 200 golfers chasing just four spots for each tournament, that wasn't going to be easy. 'Last year I didn't want to, but now I think it's a smart thing to do,' he explained. 'I'll probably try eight or nine, maybe ten. The chances are very slim, but there's always that chance you might get in and maybe win, and then be set for two or three years. It looks good on your résumé.' Daly duly made it into a couple of PGA Tour events that spring of 1989, but missed cuts at both the GTE Byron Nelson Classic and the BellSouth Atlanta Golf Classic suggested that perhaps he wasn't ready to make the step up to the big time. Still, imbued with a greater sense of determination, Daly persevered and succeeded in his quest to qualify for the US Open.

Unusually, John and Dale were still on speaking terms as Daly set off with his wife for Rochester's Oak Hill Country Club. After what he had euphemistically called 'a character-building exercise' at Shinnecock Hills three years earlier, Daly arrived for his second major championship believing, with some justification, that he was a markedly better player than he was in 1986, but even he didn't know just how good he really was. If any tournament could show Daly how much progress he had made since turning professional, it was the US Open. He need not have worried. A first-round 74 followed by a 67 on the Friday (bettered only by eventual winner Curtis Strange's 64) guaranteed Daly's place in the weekend line-up. He had made his first cut in a major. Though his disappointing weekend performance of an 80 and a 79 left him 20 over par and tied for 69th, there was still a sense of satisfaction as he left Rochester on Sunday evening and headed off on the long drive to St Louis for the Bogey Hills Invitational event the following week. 'He's chalking it up to experience,' explained Dale. 'He's just glad he made the cut.'

Later, Daly revealed that the highlight of his week at Oak Hill had not been his 67 in the second round or the fact that he had banked his first, admittedly meagre, cheque from a genuine PGA Tour event, it was that Jack Nicklaus had winked at him, twice. 'A lot of people wink at everybody, but he's been my idol since I was four. On the range he winked at me, and when he got done hitting balls, he watched me hit. I haven't even introduced myself to him. I'm too nervous. I can't introduce myself to my idol.' Like an adolescent girl confronted by the Backstreet Boys, or a grown man in the company of Kylie Minogue, Daly had once more found himself unable to remember even the most basic elements of speech, and had yet again passed up another gilt-edged opportunity to meet his idol.

In August, Daly was offered two sponsor's exemptions to play in the FedEx St Jude Classic in Memphis and the Chattanooga Classic in Tennessee. These kind of invitations were comparatively rare, and for Daly to gain two was a sure sign that his stock in golfing circles was on the up. He made the cut in both events and earned close to $11,000 for his efforts. 'I figured one PGA event would be nice this summer, just to see what it was like, but heck,' he said in his trademark country drawl, 'I feel almost like a tour player now.' Indeed, Daly was in such demand that when he returned to Blytheville on the Sunday evening after the St Jude Classic he took a call at 11.30 p.m. offering him a place in the 21st Insurance Youth Golf Classic in Texarkana. Trouble was, it was starting the following morning and Daly was over 300 miles away. Undaunted, he accepted the offer, and at 3.00 a.m. set out for the Texarkana Country Club.

The Insurance Youth Golf Classic was an unusual event in that it paired 20 professionals and 60 junior golfers from around the States; Daly found himself in a four-ball with three whippersnappers intent on bringing the professional to his knees. Top of the pile was a thirteen-year-old called Eldrick Woods. His parents called him 'Tiger'.The kid was good, very good. By the turn, Woods, who had clocked his first score in the sixties the year before, was three under, four shots ahead of Daly. Fearful of losing to a thirteen-year-old and the damage that would do to his growing reputation, Daly birdied four of the inward nine to finish on 70 while Woods slipped with three bogeys to an even-par 72. With a sigh of relief almost as big as his thirst, Daly paid due credit to his young opponent. 'That kid is great. Everybody was applauding him, and nobody applauded me. Of course, I didn't do much to applaud. I had heard a lot of good things about him, but he's better than I'd heard.' Little did Daly know that he had just defeated a boy who would become arguably the greatest golfer ever to play the game. Woods' verdict was less glowing. 'He wasn't a smart player,' he said. 'He would take a driver and go over trees and would hit sand wedges to par-fives.'

While the invitations to PGA events were welcome, there was a distressing trend developing in Daly's tournament play. In too many events he was starting like a bullet and blazing scores in the sixties, only to fade away in the final rounds. A case in point was the Chattanooga Classic. After rounds of 65, 66 and 63 Daly was in real contention for the first time in a PGA competition, but he faded badly in the final round with a 74 and had to settle for a tie for fourteenth place. Despite his highest finish in a PGA Tour event, he was irritated by the way he'd thrown away his chance of victory and decided to handle the disappointment in the one and only way he knew how.

By now, Daly's drinking was reaching prodigious levels, but, typically, his golf never suffered any adverse effects. His occasional coach, Rick Ross, used to pray that when John had been drinking he would go out and shoot 85, just so he didn't get the idea in his head that he could do what the hell he wanted and still play the kind of golf that would render most spectators speechless. But he never did. He nearly always went out and shot 68. 'It's all right, I guess, to sow your wild oats once in a while,' said Ross, 'but when it gets to be very, very consistent then everybody wants you to slow down a bit and take a good look at life.' Clearly, Daly was labouring under some absurd misapprehension that his golf game was bulletproof and that even with the mother of all hangovers he could beat anyone who dared to tee it up with him. This perceived invincibility in his professional life also filtered through to his personal life, and on several occasions Daly would come perilously close to ending his career before it had really begun. At the heart of this problem was a seemingly voracious appetite for self-destruction, Daly displaying a frightening disregard not just for his own safety but for that of anyone who ventured out with him, and that included those closest to him.

Bored of the bickering with Dale, John grabbed his brother Jamie and the two spent the evening drinking heavily and shooting pool in a bar in the nondescript town of Centerville, a few miles from Dardanelle. It was a big session, even by the Daly boys' standards. Then, foolishly, John decided to drive. He started up his ageing open-top Chevy Blazer and headed back home. Some six miles out of Dardanelle, Daly was racing along Highway 7 and fiddling with the stereo, trying to find something, anything, that he could sing along with. The road was clear and the speedometer was nudging 80. Ahead of him was a tight bend in the road. The signs at the side of the road told him to slow down; anything more than 30 and he was in real trouble. But he had left it too late. As he approached the bend, he hit the brakes and the Chevy skidded off the side of the road and into a drainage ditch, before hitting a cement post, rolling over three times and coming to rest 160 feet from where it left the road. Jamie had been thrown out of the car and had landed in a farmer's field while John had ended up in the passenger seat, wondering how the hell he had got there.

When John regained his senses he jumped out of the car and went to find Jamie. To their amazement, the two of them were unharmed, not even a single scratch. Counting their blessings, the brothers ditched the Chevy and decided to walk home before anyone turned up to see what the commotion was all about. Later, Daly would admit that if they had been wearing seat belts that night the two of them would, in all probability, have been dead, adding, 'I've had an angel on my shoulder for a long time.' And a devil on the other. The live fast, die young attitude so beloved by those in the rock fraternity had clearly struck a chord with Daly, even though he might have been experiencing problems mastering the latter part. In the years to come, several more stories of what Daly called 'crazy' behaviour would emerge. There was the occasion when he almost killed himself and a companion when he deliberately ran seventeen consecutive red lights, without even thinking about the consequences. *Sports Illustrated*'s Rick Reilly called it 'the record for failed suicide attempts'. He smashed windscreens and wing mirrors with his fists, and once even ripped a seat clean out of a friend's car.

The common thread running through these episodes, of course, was alcohol, and more specifically, whiskey. If Daly stuck to beer he was rarely a problem, but whenever he switched to hard liquor it was as if that first shot unlocked a whole new side to his character, an alter ego consumed with rage and hellbent on carnage. Some time later, Daly attempted to explain just how overwhelming this mind-set was during his early twenties. 'Seems I used to do everything like I was on a mission,' he said. 'If it was alcohol, I wanted to drink till I couldn't see straight. If it was golf, I wanted to beat everybody's brains out. If it was driving, I can get there faster'n you can. It's not anybody's fault, I guess. I was stubborn as hell. I had no direction.'

While Daly viewed his heady social life as harmless high jinks without intent or consequence, his wife plainly saw it as more than just goofing around. For Dale, it was an abdication of all

John's marital duties and immaturity on a life-threatening scale. By the autumn of 1989 she had decided that there was little point in continuing with a marriage so clearly going nowhere, and filed for divorce. Her intention to annul their two-year marriage came as no real surprise to Daly. After those first few months together when they were apparently joined at the hip, relations between the couple had gone from bad to worse to irreconcilable. The conversation had gone beyond laboured, all the plans they had once hatched had been discarded, and the passion, well, that had long since left town. 'When we signed the paper to get married, she was like, "You ain't getting no more sex," ' he would complain.

Daly dealt with the news the same way he dealt with any news, be it good, bad or wholly irrelevant. This time, however, he somehow managed to up the ante, savaging bottles of Jack Daniels like they were cans of Coke and drinking until he couldn't see, speak or stand. The problem, according to Rick Ross, was that Daly didn't feel 'the buzz or the high most people feel as a warning signal that we've had one too many', adding, 'There's no warning by his system until it's too late. Then it's alcohol poison and seizure.' By December, even Daly, the country kid who always knew best, had to accept he had some serious issues with alcohol and he checked himself into Dardanelle Hospital to seek help.

According to the American Medical Association, if a person has a blood alcohol concentration (BAC) of ten grams per decilitre, then he or she is equal to or in excess of the legal definition of intoxication in all 50 states. When Daly's test results came back his BAC level was 27 grams. His nurse told him she had never seen a reading anywhere near that high. 'Things looked bleak,' he admitted later. Two days later, Daly checked out of hospital, feeling weak but with a better idea of what he should do with his life and career.

Desperate to get away from the unending demands of divorce lawyers, Daly signed up once more for the South African Sunshine Tour, only this time he needed some company. Step forward Blake Allison, a drinking buddy of Daly's from Morrilton, Arkansas, who, as luck would have it, also ran a liquor store. He was a big guy, bigger than John, and when the marriage to Dale had crumbled he had given Daly somewhere to crash while he sorted himself out. As a token of his appreciation, John had asked Blake if he wanted to come along for the ride. Bowled over by the offer, Blake said yes.

Having someone close by to talk to (and drink with) clearly suited Daly's golf game, and with Allison on his bag he claimed three top-30 finishes in his first three events. When the pair reached Johannesburg's Rand Park Golf Club for the AECI Charity Classic in February 1990, Daly's mood was more positive than it had been in some time. He had warmed to the reception he had been given by the local fans, who remembered him as that big-hitting blond American from his previous visit. His form, too, was approaching something resembling his best, and by the time he reached the final hole of the tournament he was tied for the lead and required a twelve-foot birdie putt to land the $16,000 winner's cheque. Needless to say, Daly, with his customary two short practice swings, stepped up and drained it. Things were going better than he could have imagined.

After two years of pettiness and penury, Daly arrived at the Hollard Royal Swaziland Sun Classic as a single man again. He had received word from home that his divorce from Dale had come through, and after a first-round 66 he decided to mark the occasion by repairing to the local casino. That night, Daly bombed at the blackjack tables. As the Jack Daniels disappeared, so too did his money, and by the early hours of the morning he had squandered virtually all of his winner's cheque from Rand Park. Alone in his hotel room, Daly succumbed to the same whiskey-fuelled rage that had possessed him so many times before and set about reorganising his room as if he were Keith Moon.

By and large, professional golfers are not the kind of creatures to trash their hotel rooms. Scrub the bath and dust the coffee table, maybe, but engage in gratuitous destruction? Not likely. Top of Daly's wanted list that night was the television set. The only problem, however, was that the damned thing chose to fight back; as he tried to put his fist through it – never the cleverest of ideas – he succeeded only in fracturing his right hand and breaking his little finger. Fortunately, Daly had enough money left after his splurge at the casino to pay for the $600 damage to his room – 'After the hotel room was paid off I broke about even,' he remarked – and no more would come of it, but by the time he teed it up the following day his stitched right hand was covered in so many bandages it looked like he was wearing an oven glove. The doctors advised Daly against playing, and ordinarily he would have withdrawn, but now he really needed the cash so with incredulous players and officials looking on he continued, after announcing to Allison, 'I think I'll just win this damned tournament.' True to his word, Daly did as he intended. With a busted hand he eased to a three-stroke victory and pocketed another cheque for $16,000, which went some way towards easing the pain of his hand and his night in the casino.

With two victories under his belt, the latter seemingly scripted by the writers of *Rocky*, Daly suddenly became the story of the Sunshine Tour, and with his self-confidence running high he scored two more third-place finishes. As one of the new personalities on the tour, Daly also received an invitation to the South African Skins Game, one of those fill-your-pockets events he had only ever watched on TV. By the time Daly and Allison stepped on to the plane for the journey home at the end of March, Daly had banked another $48,000, and as there were no shareholders to look after this time around the money was his to spend as he saw fit. Broken hand aside, it had been a successful trip.

Before Daly had set off for South Africa, he had finished top of the pile in a qualifying competition for the Ben Hogan Tour, a new league set up by the PGA and sponsored by Cosmo World of Japan, the parent company of Hogan's golf equipment and clothing company. The concept was simple. The Hogan Tour would operate one level below the main PGA Tour and the events would be staged in 30 cities that did not host a PGA Tour event already. Clearly, it wasn't the money that appealed to most of the 132 hopefuls busting a gut on the new tour. With a prize fund of just $100,000 at each 54-hole tournament, $20,000 of which went to the winner, the purses were less than 10 per cent of those on the PGA Tour and substantially less than those on offer for tours in Europe and Asia, where many young American professionals went for the experience. Moreover, with weekly expenses approaching $1,000 to set against what money the players earned, only the very best could expect to live off their winnings. The main pull of the new tour was that it offered a quick ticket to the big time, each of the year's top-five money winners receiving a one-year exemption on the PGA Tour. Those that finished in positions 6 through to 20, meanwhile, would be eligible for a bye through to the final round of the PGA Q-School, while those who claimed a place between 21 and 50 would get to miss the first stage.

When the Hogan Tour began in Salt Lake City at the beginning of April 1990, Daly was one of the bookies' favourites to steamroller his way on to the PGA Tour. Predictably, however, things didn't quite pan out as many had anticipated. By the end of his first month on the tour Daly had shown only glimpses of his true potential, the highlight being a tie for second place at the Gateway Open in Fort Myers, Florida. By the time the players arrived in Macon, Georgia, Daly had earned a little over $10,500 from his first three outings, $9,750 of which had come from the performance in Florida. Compared to most of the other guys it was a decent return, but it had dawned on Daly, as it had on other players, that to make any real money on the Hogan Tour you needed to win tournaments.

As he prepared for the Macon Open, Daly's attention was taken by a attractive woman who was working at the course as a convention sales executive for Radisson Hotels. Her name was Bettye Fulford. When the two hooked up, she told John she was 29, single, and, like John, had one failed marriage behind her. She was a graduate of Mercer University in Macon and had been a cheerleader at Georgia Southern College in Statesboro. Daly liked that, and Lord knows he needed some fun in his life. This professional golf career of his was proving to be extremely hard work, harder than he could ever have imagined. There was the endless driving, the cheap motels, the fast food and the frayed nerves. You had to watch each cent because for all you knew it could be weeks before you next saw a pay cheque. It was a tough life built on Darwinian principles of natural selection, and one which Daly didn't want to spend another season having to endure. So when a pretty girl like Bettye suddenly shows an interest and gives you the opportunity to forget about everything for a few hours, what is a normal, red-blooded country boy supposed to do? As Daly would later explain, 'It was sort of a sexual thing at first sight.'

Just as Dale Crafton had accompanied John as he set out on his professional career, now Bettye took up the vacancy, joining Daly as he tried to make his mark on the Hogan Tour. Occasionally, some of Daly's closer friends would nudge him and ask whether Bettye was really thirty, but John would laugh it off. But there was something about her, something not quite as it seemed. Not that

John cared. After the bitter end to his first marriage, he had found a woman who didn't give him grief about his drinking and who didn't have a family on 24-hour call, eager to offer their opinions at the drop of a hat. He was having fun, something he hadn't had for years, and nobody was going to stop him.

Aside from the company of Bettye, virtually the only other thing that made the Hogan Tour in any way bearable for Daly was the camaraderie between the players. Spending week after tiresome week driving around the country, struggling to make ends meet and sharing in one another's joy and, more often than not, misery had created a special bond between the professionals, one that went far beyond the confines of whatever course they were playing that week. At the New Haven Open, some five months into the tour, Daly spoke of the stresses aspiring professionals had to cope with. 'Basically, I'm starving,' he sighed. 'You've got to win tournaments to make any money. But that's the test of whether you are ready to play with the best. Some of us are going to make it, and some aren't. But nobody is living the superstar life out here. We are all trying to beat the other guy, but it's a struggle for everybody. And that makes you close.'

Daly's week at the New Haven Open provides a good illustration of just how insecure the financial position of the Hogan Tour professionals could be. Taking into account average weekly expenses of close to $1,000, his finishing position of tied 35th earned him just $626.66. Fortunately, Daly could always rely on his trademark power to earn a few extra bucks when the chance arose. At the New Haven Open, for example, he took the $500 first prize for winning the longest-drive competition when he blasted one out over 340 yards. It took him into profit for the week, but only just.

While those around Daly knew he was becoming increasingly agitated by his failure to capitalise on the promise he had shown in South Africa, nobody could really gauge just how depressed he had become. When the Hogan Tour reached Falmouth, Maine, for the New England Classic in July, Daly was driving along with a golf buddy of his, Brent Everson, when he turned to him and with an expressionless face asked, 'Do you ever think about just running off the road and straight into a tree?' It should have been a warning sign, an all-too-obvious indicator that Daly was on the edge and in danger of falling off. Clearly he was in no mood for another tournament of indifferent golf and scant reward, and the last thing he needed was a missed cut. But miss the cut he did, shooting an unthinkable 91 in his second round. It was the kind of mortifying score his old man would shoot when he was carving his way around Bay Ridge with the boys from the nuclear plant, not the score of a young professional with one eye on the PGA Tour.

Downhearted, Daly grabbed his fellow tour player Roger Rowland and dragged him to a local bar. Once inside, he pulled up a stool and began lining up the JD and Cokes, ordering a triple for himself at a time. Concerned at the speed with which Daly was downing his drinks, the young bartender slapped a one-drink-at-a-time deal on him, although Daly soon found a way around the newly imposed restriction. As she served him his drink, Daly would simply down it in one and then ask for another, and when that arrived he would down that too. By the end of the evening Daly had seen off fifteen triple JD and Cokes – that's 45 shots – and had drunk himself unconscious.

Rowland was scared. He had known his friend had been down of late, but he had never realised just how low he had sank. Try as he might, he couldn't revive Daly. Even though he had been drinking too, there was no other option but to load John into his car and drive off in search of the nearest hospital. Indeed, at one stage Rowland would become so scared for Daly that he even pulled over a cop to ask for directions, his breath still stinking of liquor. When they finally reached the hospital, the doctors discovered that John had fallen into an alcohol-induced coma, which explained why Rowland couldn't revive him. The following morning, Daly woke up in intensive care. Another day, another overdose. Rowland, meanwhile, was a relieved man. 'I really thought he was going to die,' he said. Rick Ross recalled that night only too vividly. 'The doctor said he didn't know how in the world he made it through. That scared the hell out of John. That was his last dance with Jack.'

Sheepishly, Daly phoned Bettye in Georgia and told her what had happened. Ever since they'd met she had turned a blind eye to his drinking, but clearly she wasn't aware of the staggering stupidity her new man was capable of. Bettye suggested a break, and Daly agreed. The two escaped to Hilton Head Island in South Carolina and between them arrived at some difficult decisions. Bettye enjoyed her job, but she was willing to give it up and join John full-time on tour providing he quit drinking whiskey, which was always at the root of his problems. ('I don't drink the whiskey any more,' he would say later, 'but I still want to have fun. I just drink light beer. It's protein. You can wash your hair with that stuff.') Her plan was to keep John on the straight and narrow by pulling him away from any temptation he encountered. She had him play golf all day and then tennis at night, anything to wear him out and take his mind off the liquor.

Initially, it seemed to work. Bettye's lifestyle changes were paying dividends. Daly's weight steadied at a svelte 175lb (twelve and a half stones), the lowest it had been since Steve Loy had run the pounds off him at university, and if John wanted a drink he could have one, so long as it was nothing stronger than a beer. Suddenly, his game returned and golf no longer seemed like a burden.

Away from the Hogan Tour, Daly was granted another sponsor's exemption to the FedEx St Jude Classic in Memphis. A year after he had tied for 64th in the same event, Daly improved to claim a tie for 21st. It was a consistent display with a round of 69 and three rounds of 70 giving him $9,387.50, and although the prize money didn't count towards his position in the Order of Merit for the Hogan Tour, it would nevertheless pay for a tank of gas and a few welcome nights out with Bettye.

Finally, Daly also began to make a long overdue charge up the Hogan Tour money list, too. In September he bagged runners-up spots at the Texarkana Open and the Amarillo Open, and then, at last, he won an event, taking the $20,000 first prize in the Utah Classic at Provo's Riverside Country Club. 'I made one bogey for 54 holes,' he reflected. 'I played really solid. I think I'm 35 under par the last three tournaments. This is the ninth straight round in the sixties in tournament play.' It was the kind of hot streak Daly and his fellow professionals always knew he was capable of. Prior to the Texarkana event, Daly had stood at 51st on the money list; now, having taken just short of $40,000 in three weeks, he had moved up to ninth and was finally making a claim for one of the all-important top-five positions. According to Daly's old friend Don Cline, the improvement was down to Bettye's intervention. 'John pulled himself up by his bootstraps,' he explained. 'Bettye helped. She is very mature. She's done wonders for John. I think she understands his potential, and that things take time.'

But Daly had left his challenge too late. The top five players were streets ahead of their rivals and he had to settle for ninth place on the end-of-season list. Though he had missed out on an automatic card for the PGA Tour, Daly remained positive, consoled by the fact that as one of the top-twenty finishers on the Hogan Tour he could now proceed straight through to the final round of the PGA's dreaded Q-School at La Quinta, California.

5. SEND IN THE CLOWN

'I have never led the tour in money winnings, but I have many times in alcohol consumption.'

Fuzzy Zoeller

Without the rigmarole of the first two stages of Q-School to distract him, Daly arrived at the PGA West Course at La Quinta in early December 1990 knowing that just six rounds of golf stood between him and that elusive ticket to the PGA Tour. Displaying all of the skill, guile and composure he had shown during his successful September, Daly eventually tied for fourteenth place and comfortably claimed his place among the game's elite.

It was a blessed relief. After three years in which he had battled poverty, his ex-wife and that dangerous drinking problem, Daly had fulfilled his dream and was about to tee it up with the game's royalty. But winning his card meant so much more than just the occasional round with Jack Nicklaus or Tom Watson. It meant a guaranteed place in the field of practically any PGA competition in 1991, a huge increase in his profile and, he hoped, a queue of wealthy sponsors lining up to get his signature.

With nothing to do until his first event of the new season, the Northern Telecom Open, Daly spent his spare time house-hunting with Bettye, eventually settling on a $120,000 home in the Memphis suburb of Cordova. It was almost twice as much as Daly had earned in the past year on the Hogan Tour, but it was a calculated risk. After all, even average players on the PGA Tour earned a couple of hundred thousand a year, and that was before the Pings, the Wilsons and the Reeboks of this world had handed over any cash for using their clubs or wearing their clothes. And the very fact that Daly had purchased the house with Bettye in mind was conclusive proof that he had gone and fallen in love again, that the woman he had only ever wanted a bit of fun with had now become a central part of his life.

The house in Cordova would not be the only real estate Daly would invest in. Deciding to set his mum up in business, he snapped up a wooden shack down on Highway 22 and soon afterwards opened the John Daly Convenience and Golf Shop. To his young eyes, it was the perfect business idea. People could come in for a carton of milk and get some tee pegs or fishing bait while they were there. What more could you want from a shop?

As their new home underwent some essential refurbishment – John was having a trophy cabinet made – Daly decided to take Bettye with him as he tried his hand once more on the courses and casinos of the Sunshine Tour. While his previous visits to South Africa had been driven by a need to test himself against better players and a desire, or rather necessity, to make some money, this time the golf took a back seat as Daly enjoyed his time away with Bettye. In many ways it was just like those carefree final days at Dardanelle High when Daly didn't really care what would happen because he already had a scholarship in the bag, only this time he had a place on the world's premier golf tour to look forward to.

Daly's golf in South Africa was OK, nothing more. It was his performance in the casino that gave Bettye the most cause for concern. The evening before the final round of a tournament in Sun City, Daly had gone to the casino to play a little blackjack, leaving Bettye to get a early night. At dawn, Bettye awoke to find her man standing there with $40,000 in cash. It was more than he had ever won in any golf tournament. Concerned that if he didn't do something with the money he would just hand it back to the croupiers that night, Daly gave the cash to Bettye and told her to take it to a bank and convert it into a cheque that he couldn't squander before he got back home. As Daly completed his final round, Bettye was left walking the local streets, desperately trying to find a bank to take all that money off her hands. 'The thing is, he'd lost almost that much before he won,' Bettye later told *Sports Illustrated*. 'He was all the way down and then climbed back. It took him all night.'

In a world where the occasional misplaced expletive or the wrong kind of collar, both sartorially and economically, can mark you down as one of the game's reprobates, it doesn't take a whole lot to gain yourself a reputation. For the most part, golf professionals are clean-living, clean-shaven, middle-class men with steady backgrounds, identikit wives and the manners of a butler. They say 'appreciate it' when you wish them well, as if they're genuinely touched by your concern. They're not, obviously, but at least they have a way of making you feel, well, good about yourself. Everyone, but everyone, tows the line. If they're ever asked about the condition of the golf course they have just played on, they say 'it's in great shape' even if what they really want to say is that it looks like the Battle of the Somme out there. Phil Mickelson is a case in point. Nice chap and everything, but he even calls journalists at press conferences 'sir' and 'ma'am' and he's a thirty-something with a wife and a couple of kids.

The unwritten rules of being a modern-day golf pro are simple, really. First, be considerate to your fellow players. It doesn't pay to bad-mouth anyone. Second, be generous with your time for the all-important, all-powerful media. Finally, say nice things, say really nice things, about the sponsors. Follow these rules and your life will be easy. Step out of line and you will soon find yourself on the outside looking in.

There have been precious few bad boys in the history of golf. While the tabloids are full of footballers who have been led astray by champagne and cocaine, by lager and lapdancers, it is rare to read of a golfer who has been caught in flagrante delicto. Arguably the first rogue to make a mark in the game was Walter Hagen. Famed for his lavish lifestyle as well as his astonishing talent – he won eleven majors – Hagen was as flamboyant as they came in the 1920s, dressing way ahead of his time and using his limousine as his personal changing room at tournaments. His mantra was simple, and it spoke volumes about his approach to life: 'I didn't want to be a millionaire, I just wanted to live like one.' And boy, did he. When his second wife Edna filed for divorce, she sighed, 'The only place I can find him is on the sports pages.'

More recently, there was the English professional Brian Barnes, a man so addled by booze that on the final green of the 1981

Scottish Open he actually marked his ball with a beer can. In a career spanning thirty years, Barnes claimed sixteen tour victories and was also the only man ever to beat Jack Nicklaus twice in a day, 'man to man', during the 1975 Ryder Cup at Laurel Valley, Pennsylvania. At the culmination of a Barnes round it would be a close call as to which was lower, his score or his drinks tally. During a game he would wet his whistle with two thirds of a bottle of vodka topped up with orange juice, just to make it look like the kind of healthy, vitamin-packed drink professional sportsmen should be seen with. Yet he was an exceptional golfer. In a competition at Dalmahoy in 1981, for example, he played the final nine holes in just 28 strokes while drinking a six-pint cooler of beer, and then consumed another eight pints in the 90 minutes that passed before he was called on to take part in a play-off. Needless to say, he won. During a five-year spell in the late 1980s and early 1990s, Barnes admitted to being 'completely rat-arsed, 24 hours, every day' and had even drunk himself to the verge of suicide. He drove his car, drunk of course, to the top of the South Downs and decided that things would be a mite better for all concerned if he just stuck it in first and drove the thing off the edge. Mercifully, he chose not to. He 'didn't have the guts'. Instead, he quit drinking and turned his attentions to the Seniors Tour. It was a prudent move. When he won the 1995 Senior British Open at Royal Portrush, Northern Ireland, he won £58,330 – more than he had ever won in a single season on the regular European Tour.

It's unclear how much Daly knew about Brian Barnes when he embarked on his first season on the PGA Tour – apart from his victories over Nicklaus, of course – but he need only have asked around the pro circuit to garner some kind of opinion on just what chronic alcoholism can do, not just to a man's golf game but to his life, too. But he didn't. Instead he struck up a close friendship with Fuzzy Zoeller, the two-time major winner and self-appointed social secretary of the PGA Tour. The pair had first met during a practice round they had played with Hubert Green at the St Jude Classic in August 1989, and John had warmed to his easy-going, wisecracking nature. So when Daly finally secured his tour card, the first thing the 24-year-old did was call Zoeller, twelve years his senior, and ask him whether he would look after him in his first year on tour. In retrospect, it was like ringing the Samaritans and finding Keith Richards on the other end of the line.

Zoeller was intrigued. After all, he was hardly the sage of the pro game. But the more he thought about it, the more he liked the idea of being Daly's de facto big brother on tour. He felt flattered that some wet-behind-the-ears kid had seen fit to ask him for help as he found his feet in the big time. 'Hubert Green and I kind of corrupted his little brain that week [at the St Jude Classic],' joked Zoeller, unaware that that particular operation had been carried out many years before. 'I feel comfortable around him. I think he feels the same with me. It gave me a nice feeling when he called up and asked for my help.'

Daly's debut as a bona fide PGA Tour player, however, would prove to be something of an anticlimax. Surrounded by the kind of seasoned professionals and huge galleries he had watched on TV for years, he surrendered meekly in the Tucson-based Northern Telecom event, posting two unspectacular rounds in the seventies and missing the cut by some distance. So much for taking the PGA Tour by storm. When the trophy was handed out on the Sunday evening, it was a twenty-year-old college junior by the name of Phil Mickelson who lifted it high above his head. To this day, he remains the last amateur to win a PGA Tour event.

Though Daly had emerged from his first tour stop without a cent, the experience had at least served to remind him that now he was just a small fish in a big pond, when just last year it had been the opposite. Moreover, he had realised that reputations counted for very little in the big time. Whatever he had done as a kid or on the mini-tours meant nothing now that he had taken his place on the PGA Tour. Every player on the tour, without exception, was gifted. They had all been college and state champions and they had all wowed their schoolmates with their ability to hit fades and draws and get the ball to spin back. It was no big deal. Of more concern was the final standings. If an amateur five years his junior was stepping up to the plate and whipping Daly's hide, then there was truly an awful lot of work to do if he was to stand any chance of keeping his card for the following year.

A little over a month into the tour, Daly met with Bud Martin, a Pittsburgh agent who had recently started the Cambridge Sports Agency with his friend John Mascatello. Martin was only four years older than Daly but possessed the kind of nonstop business brain that could, theoretically, make John a very wealthy young man. His agency already boasted several golfers on its books, as well as ice hockey and baseball players, and their reputation as being one of the best up-and-coming agencies was spreading fast.

Martin had met Daly the previous year when he'd been playing golf at the Chickasaw Country Club, one of John's many hang-outs in the Memphis area. He had been enjoying a round with Jack White, the PGA Tour administrator, but had noticed Daly nearby and dropped everything to go over and introduce himself. 'We saw John, and Jack said I needed to talk to him,' said Martin. 'I was sort of in a hurry but I thought, "You never know." So I introduced myself.' Seven months later, their paths crossed again while Daly was in California for the San Diego Open. This time, however, things were different. Without a PGA Tour card Daly had been just another young professional with an uncertain future, but now, as a signed-up member of the game's elite, he was an altogether more attractive proposition for sponsors and, for that matter, agents. Taken by Martin's straight talking, Daly happily signed a two-year deal with Cambridge.

Gradually, minor agreements would be struck with sponsors. Club manufacturers Ping agreed to give Daly up to thirty golf shirts each year, although bizarrely he still had to pay for his own trousers, and Maxfli gave him some balls. But these were piecemeal deals, and clearly he was getting frustrated at being the only guy on tour with no endorsement on his golf bag. 'That could bring $50,000 a year. What am I getting? Nothing, absolutely zilch,' he moaned. 'I don't know why no one's called. I've wondered about it. I guess all I can do is wait. I'm sure I'm going to get a good deal one of these days.' Daly's concern that he was missing out on the lucrative pay days his contemporaries all seemed to be enjoying was compounded by the fact that, unlike most other professionals, he had no golf or country club backing him either. Although he played most of his noncompetitive golf at Chickasaw, there was no club waiting in the wings to pick up the occasional tab or offer him free rein in the club shop. He was out on his own. 'I'm out there doing my job, and I like the idea that I keep the money I make,' he said. 'There is no sugar daddy.'

Despite the conspicuous absence of any major endorsement deal, Daly was nevertheless picking up sufficient prize money to more than cover his expenses, and by the end of March he had banked $71,704 in just eight events, and this despite three missed cuts. With Bettye keeping an eye on the costs, the couple traversed the States in Daly's 1989 Dodge Caravan while the likes of Greg

Norman took private jets between each tour stop. The vehicle was only two years old, yet the mileage gauge was nudging 90,000.

Although Daly's form had been steady, his performances had been characterised by that age-old problem of starting each event with a flyer only to fade away as the tournament unfolded. It was only in the Honda Classic at Coral Springs, Florida, in March that he'd finally imposed himself on the tour. Indeed, had it not been for a wretched 76 in his third round he would have been in contention come Sunday evening. Still, a tie for fourth was more than acceptable, as was the cheque for £41,333.33.

For most of the name players, this was the first time they had seen, or perhaps even noticed, John Daly in something approaching full flight. As usual, it was his astonishing length off the tee that attracted the lion's share of the attention; players, commentators and fans all agreed that his swing was something else. As Daly went about his business on the course and the galleries grew in number as word spread of his potent ball striking, Bettye took time out to talk to David Lanier, a journalist from the *Arkansas Gazette*. Asked how Daly was finding life on the PGA Tour, Bettye let it slip that even though John had been playing well and they had both been enjoying his rookie season on the Tour, she was not overly enamoured with some of the company he was keeping, adding that, 'He drinks far too much when he hangs around with fellows like Fuzzy Zoeller.' Sensing a scoop, Lanier pursued the story with John in the press room after his round. Daly, hardly the most savvy of players when it came to dealing with the media, was taken aback at the line of questioning but did his best to play down the extent of his problem, pointing to the fact that he only ever drank because of the turmoil in his personal life. 'I have had some problems with my drinking, but I thought it could help me deal with some things I was going through,' he explained. 'I felt like I was being controlled, being controlled by my ex-wife and then drinking, and I couldn't take it any more. I had to put my priorities in order.' As John and Bettye climbed into the Dodge that Sunday, they thought nothing of the story that was waiting to be written, but the word was out that the new boy on tour liked a drink.

Like a kid in a sweet shop, Daly entered every PGA tournament he could. Virtually every event boasted a purse in excess of a million dollars and he drove from one to the next like some fugitive on the run, desperately trying to grab his share of the loot along the way. And who could blame him? For all he knew this could prove to be his one and only season in the big time and he needed to maximise any opportunities that came his way.

Despite a schedule to rival that of the president, Daly still found time to return to Arkansas late in April, on the way back from missing the cut at the Greater Greensboro Open. He had agreed to play in a charity golf day at the Chenal Country Club in Little Rock to help raise funds for the Centers for Youth and Families and took his place on the practice range to give a clinic to over 200 amateur golfers, all of whom had paid between $150 and $2,500 for the privilege. Coach Frank Broyles had even turned up to take a look. As usual, Daly's meaty drives were met with the kind of oohs and aahs that you tend to hear only at firework displays. As every shot easily cleared the 250-yard marker at the end of the range, each ball still gaining velocity and altitude when it was 200 yards from tee, spectators shook their heads in disbelief. Everyone there wanted to know the same thing: just how did he do it? 'I don't know how I do it,' the star of the show said with a shrug. 'I think it's club-head speed and timing. I've had lots of people analyse my swing, and nobody's really sure why I can hit it so far.'

But while those who had witnessed Daly's awesome drives that day left Chenal happy that they had seen a rare talent at work, the man himself was less pleased. His form since his fourth place at the Honda Classic had taken a pronounced turn for the worse and had left him doubting whether he really had the talent and temperament to make it to the top. Still, there was always Bettye on hand to offer consolation, and she never doubted him. Indeed, as Daly drove around the country from one nondescript golf course to another, he had come to realise that this woman sat next to him, feeding him French fries and fiddling with the radio, was always going to be there for him. It was about time he made her the second Mrs Daly.

When John missed another cut at the Buick Classic, he decided it was high time for a break. After all, he had played seven events in succession and his only reward had been one top-twenty finish, with his new caddie Dave Beighle, at the Kemper Open. He had been promising Bettye a trip to Las Vegas for some time, and with a couple of weeks away from the hubbub of the tour the couple drove to Nevada. What John had failed to tell Bettye was that as well as going to Vegas to gamble he was going there to make her his wife. He had even chosen a little chapel on the Strip. After his champagne-and-vol-au-vents wedding with Dale, a Vegas ceremony was all Daly wanted. It was quick and hassle-free, and he wouldn't be left with a bunch of presents he didn't want and a bar bill the size of the state. Strangely, however, Bettye was less keen on the idea and became uneasy at the very suggestion of tying the knot. John didn't get it. They had been together for over a year now with barely a cross word between them. They had travelled the length and breadth of the country, they had been to South Africa and back, and they had always had a good time together, and now here she was knocking him back. And him a PGA Tour player as well. What was the problem? Bettye did her best to assure John that she really wanted to be with him, that she had always wanted to be Bettye Daly one day, but now was not the right time. Grudgingly, Daly accepted her reasoning but made her agree that when they next came back to Nevada for the Las Vegas Invitational tournament in October they would be married. Bettye agreed, and she left Vegas as John Daly's fiancée.

By the time he arrived back in Memphis for the Federal Express St Jude Classic at the end of June, Daly had missed six of the last eleven cuts and earned just under $33,000. Almost certainly it was the kind of form that would mean missing out on the top 125 on the end-of-season money list and a quick return to the frayed nerves and bitten fingernails of Q-School.

Having moved to Cordova, Daly now lived just ten minutes' drive from the Tournament Players Club at Southwind, and as it was the nearest PGA event to his family back in Dardanelle he had Jim, Lou and a bunch of other friends over to stay for the week. 'We have a houseful, but John loves it,' Bettye told the *Arkansas Gazette*. 'He's having fun. I think it helps him relax.' The presence of those closest to him at Southwind seemed to inspire Daly, and with his parents in hot pursuit, not to mention an army of Arkansan golf fans who had made the trip to watch their state's only PGA Tour player, Daly made his first cut in a month. Predictably, though, Saturday's wayward round rendered Daly's encouraging work worthless. Trees were dented, wildlife was endangered and spectators ran for cover. And just like that first session at Helias High, a tee shot was topped, leaving the PGA's longest hitter trudging red-faced up to a ball that had gone only 110 yards. 'I was teeing the ball up too low,' he explained.

With the round over – he scored 75 – and any chance of a victory extinguished, Daly talked at length about his recent form.

Whether it was the rejection in Las Vegas or the fact that the PGA Tour was proving tougher than he'd anticipated, it was evident he was struggling to keep up. 'This has been my worst month of golf that I can remember,' he reflected. 'I get it going one day, then lose it the next. It's been up and then down.' But mostly down. In fact, Daly's trademark inconsistency was no longer an itch that needed scratching, it was a predicament that was threatening to derail everything he had worked for. If he could just string four decent rounds together, he figured, there would be no stopping him. Vowing to 'stay positive no matter how things went this week', Daly went out on Sunday and shot a respectable 70 for a three-under-par total of 281. It left him in a tie for 32nd place, which, given that some of his recent outings had been verging on the humiliating, was an achievement in itself.

The mere fact that he had finished an event, and in a position nowhere near last, proved to be an enormous fillip for Daly and over the next few weeks the confidence that had so clearly been absent from his game returned. Slowly, he began to turn things around, and on 21 July, with four rounds in the sixties, he bagged his best ever finish in a PGA event, a tie for third in the Chattanooga Classic. He had banked over $70,000 in just three weeks. The smile had returned to his face. The PGA Tour was his for the taking.

6. SEEING STARS

'The only time my prayers are answered is on the golf course.'

Billy Graham

Business as normal. After his wholly unexpected success in July, John Daly's form reverted to type. Despite the blip, however, his progress in his inaugural year had been sufficiently striking that even the walking conglomerates had stopped counting their millions for a moment to take a look at the kid from the country. He wasn't exactly the talk of the tour, but everyone knew him as that big blond guy who could batter the ball into the middle of next week. Indeed, with Daly's 300-yard drives fast becoming the norm and not the exception, it was little surprise that he was now ranked number one in the PGA's long-driving statistics.

With 24 tournaments under his belt in 1991, Daly was gradually adapting to the demands of the PGA Tour, even though his form was still patchy. Thankfully, the returns of July had left him at 72nd on the money list, and barring a collapse of epic proportions – always a possibility when Daly was playing – he was almost assured of finishing in the top 125, thereby guaranteeing his card for the next season. Not that any of this would count for much in his bid to claim a berth in the final major of the year, the PGA Championship.

Organised by the PGA of America and not the PGA Tour itself – the tour was formed in 1968 when the Tournament Players

Division of the PGA broke away – the event differs from the other majors in that it also throws its doors open to 25 club professionals from around the States (the tournament used to allow 40 of its members entry, but in 1995 they cut the number, freeing up 15 slots for foreign players or special cases whom they felt deserved inclusion). For the club pros, then, who survive on comparatively modest earnings on the PGA of America circuit, it is the biggest event of the year. It is their chance to see the Crenshaws and Kites of this world up close and personal, to bask in the media spotlight for a week and maybe take a decent cheque home with them too. But not everybody cares for the event. Although they don't say as much, there has been a feeling among many tour players that the mere presence of the club pros devalues the competition and makes it the runt of the major litter. Needless to say, it is those tour players with most to lose who feel most aggrieved. With the field limited to 150, a sixth of which comprises club professionals, there is always going to be a clutch of players who miss out on an event they would otherwise qualify for. It's as if they've been robbed of a week's wages.

But look at anybody who's won the PGA and you'll soon realise just what it can do for a golfer's career. Make that leap from tour pro to major winner and your market value among potential sponsors increases significantly. Suddenly, you start to get invitations to those big-money made-for-TV events you only ever used to watch from the comfort of your armchair, and when you venture overseas to play you'll find an extra zero or two on the end of your appearance fee. That's right, people will now pay you to play.

And then there's the history of the event. First played in 1916, it is a competition steeped in tradition; the names on the Rodney Wanamaker trophy read like a Who's Who of golf. Check the records of the greats and you will find that from Hogan to Sarazen, Nicklaus to Woods, everyone who is anyone in the game has done their utmost to land the PGA Championship.

In recent years, the PGA of America has worked hard to boost the cachet of their event. The importing of the European Tour's brightest stars has given it a decidedly more cosmopolitan feel, and the prize money is up there with the other majors. In August 2002, Rich Beem, a player who had once quit the pro circuit to sell mobile telephones and car stereos instead, took the title at Hazeltine and received $990,000 for his efforts. In anybody's books, that's a hell of a lot of cellphones. Factor in a ten-year exemption to the PGA Tour and a five-year exemption to all of the majors and it becomes a tournament every bit as valuable as the other three majors.

Of course, none of this mattered to John Daly. He didn't care if there were Martians in the starting line-up, or if the winner's prize was just a fancy rosette and dinner for two at KFC. All he knew was that the PGA was one of the four majors and he wasn't in it. Despite a solid year, Daly was way down the pecking order; his only real chance of landing a spot in the PGA was if someone with an exemption decided to withdraw. Hoping against hope, he signed up, but as ninth reserve, or 'alternate'. The chance of his ever teeing off at Indianapolis's Crooked Stick course was at the very best remote. With a shrug of his broad shoulders, Daly repaired to Memphis, assuming that for this season at least his chance of a decent pay day in the majors had gone. Everyone, it seemed, was going to the ball except John Daly.

With time and increasing amounts of money on his hands, Daly kicked his heels for the week and did his best to forget about what was going on in Indianapolis. On the Monday he had a lie-in before dragging his body out of bed and down to Chickasaw to play a few holes with some friends. Meanwhile, his caddie, 34-year-old Dave Beighle, had made his way to Crooked Stick to see if he could pick up a bag for the week, but with no sign of any work he had returned home to Virginia. On Tuesday, Daly went shopping, returning home with the keys to a brand-new BMW (in Arkansas Razorback red) for Bettye. It was on the never-never but, what the hell, he was going to make millions at this game sooner or later. An uneventful Wednesday was drawing to a close when at 5.00 p.m. Daly's phone rang. It was the PGA. Kenny Perry, Ronnie Black and a bunch of other guys had pulled out. A few had injuries, one had a poorly mother-in-law, and, in Lee Trevino's case, it was just the extreme length of the Crooked Stick course that put him off. Remarkably, Daly was now first alternate. OK, so it wasn't the offer of a place in the competition, but it was the next best thing. All it would take was one more player to withdraw and Daly would be teeing it up in the PGA Championship.

There was only one course of action to take. Booking the first hotel he could find, Daly called the PGA to let them know where he would be staying and threw his clubs in the boot of Bettye's new Beamer. With his fiancée by his side, Daly set out for Crooked Stick; it was over 450 miles away and the tournament started in just 15 hours. If he made the starting line-up, it would mean no practice round and, as Bettye didn't know the first thing about John's yardages let alone about reading stimpmeters, having to find himself a caddie. But it was worth a shot. It had to be.

By the time they arrived at the Radisson Hotel in Carmel, Indiana, John and Bettye were exhausted. The near eight-hour drive had taken its toll, especially on Bettye: caught up in the anticipation of a possible appearance at the PGA Championship, Daly had started drinking soon after leaving Tennessee and had passed out in the back, leaving her to do the driving. The couple checked in and made their way to their room. Daly opened the door and threw his things on the floor. By the bed, a red light flashed on the phone. There was a message. He picked up the receiver, and as he listened his chubby face broke into a grin as wide as the Mississippi. To his amazement, the Zimbabwean Nick Price had withdrawn. His wife Sue had gone into labour with their first child and Price, the dutiful husband, had rushed off to be by her side. The miracle had happened. Daly was in.

At 7,289 yards, Crooked Stick was the second longest course in PGA Championship history. Pete Dye, the Marquis de Sade of golf course design, had prepared the course to typically devilish PGA directives, making the rough penal, the sand traps bigger and uglier, and the greens, which some of the pros had likened to putting on glass table tops, nigh on impossible. After their practice rounds players could be seen shaking their heads, breathing huge sighs of relief and giving thanks to some higher power that the round was over. It was hell with a flagstick. Not that Daly cared. This was the third major of his career, and he reasoned that simply making the cut would be a more than respectable result after his late call-up. Anything else would be a bonus.

When he arrived at the course, Daly met up with his caddie for the week, Jeff Medlen. He was Nick Price's bagman, but now, with nothing to do all week, he'd agreed to do the honours for Daly. The players and caddies called him 'Squeeky' on account of his unusually high-pitched voice, and he insisted on his nickname being spelt with a double 'e' rather than an 'ea'. No one knew why. 'When John Daly phoned me earlier that week, enquiring as to my plans, I told him it didn't look good for me,' Price recalled. 'I then said that if he went to Crooked Stick, Squeeky, my caddie, was there and he would have all the yardages done and I would appreciate it if John used him.'

Lawrence Donegan said it best in *Four-Iron in the Soul*, his laugh-a-minute account of life on the European Tour as a trainee caddie. 'The first thing to understand about caddying is that it's not brain surgery,' he said. 'It is more complicated than that.' He's right, of course. You can't put a figure on the true value of a good caddie. Their role is much more than mere carthorse and rake rat. They can advise and motivate, cajole and console. They are a comedian and a companion, tutor and counsellor. Look at the legends. Arnold Palmer had Creamy Caroline, Nicklaus had Angelo Argea, and Trevino had Herman Mitchell. Even Tiger Woods had to ditch Fluff Cowan in favour of the New Zealander Steve Williams before he really began to fulfil his undoubted potential. It's a crucial, critical part of any player's success.

When Nick Price hired Squeeky Medlen in 1990 he lucked out; the two clicked, and the preposterously talented but perennially underachieving Zimbabwean never looked back. Medlen was a safe pair of hands. He had already worked with Fred Couples, Steve Jones and Jeff Sluman, and was about to enter the most successful spell of his and his employer's career. But for this week and this week alone he was Daly's guide to the evils of Crooked Stick. And boy, did Daly need him. Without time for a practice round and faced with a course he'd never set foot or laid eyes on before, Daly was entering the unknown. On his way to the 1st tee he even stopped and quizzed a few locals about where the real dangers lurked on the course. Just about everywhere, they sniggered.

Daly's tee-off time was 12.58 p.m. By the time he reached the 1st tee, the storm clouds had gathered and were threatening the kind of biblical weather more suited to the North Sea in winter than a summer's day in Indiana. It wasn't long before the rains came down and the players came off. Crooked Stick really had become hell on earth. Tragically, though, not everyone found shelter. At 2.30 p.m., 39-year-old Thomas Weaver from Fisher, Indiana, was struck by lightning as he walked through one of Crooked Stick's parking areas. He died soon afterwards. When play finally resumed, the field soon realised that the second longest course in PGA Championship history had just got even longer.

Despite the valiant efforts of the ground staff, the course was as close to being waterlogged as was allowable. Tee shots stopped dead on the fairways. The greens, already baffling, slowed up markedly. And if you had the misfortune to end up in the bunkers, well, you'd better get yourself a spade.

Back in Virginia, Dave Beighle had just got in from a round of golf with his buddies. He had grabbed a beer from the fridge, turned on the TV and sunk into the sofa, ready to watch the PGA Championship. 'They were running the scores and they got to about the sixth page and I see John Daly, plus-one after six holes,' he recalled. 'I just stood up and went, "What the f*** is that?" I was trying to figure out how the hell they had got all the way down to John.' When Daly eventually completed his first round he was sitting pretty with a three-under-par 69 in a tie for eighth place, just two shots off the lead held by Kenny Knox and the Welshman Ian Woosnam. It was a steady, unspectacular round built on the foundations of some fiendish driving and some spot-on putting. If anything, the deluge had given Daly an edge. His drives had always been long, sometimes ridiculously so, but they also had a tendency to be wayward. But with the course playing so soft and wet, the chances of his tee shots hitting the fairway and scuttling off to find a nasty lie in the rough or up against the face of an unforgiving bunker had dwindled.

When Daly was invited to meet the press pack he assumed that his round must have made a few waves in the media centre. He was wrong, of course. Golf journalists are, for the most part, uninterested in the bit-part players who have the audacity to try to steal the headlines by playing the round of their lives only to follow it up with a score nudging 80, missing the cut and disappearing without trace. Give them a big box-office name, a Faldo or a Norman, and it's standing room only in the interview room; throw them a lesser pro or, God forbid, a rookie, and the likelihood is that unless they have either smashed the course record or decapitated their playing partner with a lob wedge, or maybe both, then the scribes will be more concerned with the endless hospitality the PGA affords them. When Daly sat down he was met with a handful of press boys. For the most part, the Q&A session was just a trawl through a few biographical details for those journalists unfamiliar with John Daly (which was pretty much all of them), just in case this guy with the burgeoning beer gut and the trailer-park haircut actually did anything in the tournament. Name, age, rank. It was like a PoW under the bright lights of the interrogators. It was only when one reporter asked whether Daly had a nickname that his answers attracted anything approaching curiosity. 'My friends call me the Wild Thing,' he replied.

Friday arrived. His first round had proved that when push came to shove Daly really could mix it with the big guys. Not that Daly had any real doubts about that. After all, one of his greatest assets was his self-assurance, especially when his driver was behaving itself. This time out, though, the galleries following him were a little larger. Word had spread that there was some big old redneck cutting up the course and belting the ball into submission. 'Long' John Daly, the fans were calling him.

Throughout that second round, and the competition as a whole, Squeeky, a seven-handicapper, coaxed his new employer round Crooked Stick. His advice was simple and straightforward. Before each shot, he would say just one word: 'Kill!' It was exactly the kind of no-nonsense instruction Daly appreciated. Here's the yardage, here's the club, now kill! Buoyed by his caddie and his new-found army of fans, Daly carded a sparkling 67. It was clear he was enjoying himself. On the 18th, having unloaded a 310-yard drive right down the middle, Daly knocked his approach to 15 feet, walked along the fairway, looked right into a TV camera and smiled, as if he was just out for a country stroll. Despite predictions to the contrary, the kid hadn't crumbled. He hadn't just made the cut, either. Twenty-five-year-old John Daly from Dardanelle, Arkansas, was now leading the PGA Championship. He laughed to himself. 'I'm not even supposed to be here, and I have the lead going into the weekend!'

The numbers had swelled in the interview room, too. It was as if someone somewhere had let it slip that Madonna would be previewing a new strip routine in there. The place was packed. Suddenly, John Daly was the news. 'It's the best I've ever played in my life,' he announced, 'just a great thrill.' Daly insisted that he was treating this as just another competition, which it patently was not, but it was one softly spoken comment that really revealed what was going on inside his head. Surrounded by scores of tape recorders, cameras and microphones, he was asked what it felt like to be leading the PGA Championship. His answer, while truthful, betrayed a clear feeling that not even he believed that (a) he really was leading, and (b) that he was still going to be there when they handed out the gongs on Sunday evening. 'I'll remember this day for the rest of my life,' he said, shaking his head in disbelief.

Saturday is a key day in any tour event. It's the day when you can put yourself in a real position to win or kiss goodbye to any chance you ever had of taking the trophy. While nobody said as much, people were expecting this to be the day when Daly succumbed to the pressure of being the championship leader, when Crooked Stick reared up and knocked the young upstart from Arkansas down a peg or two. But if Daly was feeling the heat, it didn't show. Chatting with fans, signing autographs and with a permanent ear-to-ear smile, it seemed as though he had finally found his place in the game. And you know what? It felt pretty good. With a spring in his step and a high-five for anyone who wanted one, Daly set about his third round.

The strategy was the same: driver, driver, driver. Nobody could talk him out of it. Not Squeeky. Not Jack Nicklaus. Not no one. 'He will not back off on the driver. He will take it out on every hole and hit it as hard as he can,' raved CBS commentator Gary McCord. 'I've never seen an exhibition of strength and power overwhelming a course like this.' Later, McCord would calculate how far he himself would have gone by choosing the same clubs as Daly in the third round. On a course measuring 7,289 yards, the pundit reckoned he would have covered 6,489 of them, which would have left him 143 yards short of the 16th hole. Daly's reliance on his driver was such that there actually seemed little point in putting it back in the bag, let alone slipping the head cover back on it. If there was a par-four or -five laid out in front of him, then there was only one thing to do: take the red and white Razorbacks cover off his driver and let the big dog eat. His drives boomed down the fairways like mortar shells, leaving him 20, 30, sometimes 50 yards ahead of his playing partners. And when he really ripped one, when he really got hold of it, well, the collective gasp from the gallery could be heard in Canada.

Daly's game plan was fast reducing Crooked Stick to a pitch-and-putt. He had breezed into town and hit it like a wrecking ball. The course that had threatened to tame the Wild Thing was cowering like a kitten in a corner. While the other players were knocking long-iron approaches into the greens, Daly was tickling nice 'n' easy short irons up to the pin. The country boy would go on to hit 54 of the 72 greens in regulation that week, prompting Tom Kite to comment, 'He should, when he's hitting eight-irons and the rest are hitting two-irons.'

Of course, the support Daly was getting was worth a couple of shots a round too. Fans had warmed to his big, round, smiling face and his cheerful demeanour. They loved his who-gives-a-shit attitude, his haystack hair and his spare tyre. Hell, he was one of them. As the tournament progressed, Daly rode this tsunami of goodwill safe in the knowledge that if he ever came up short on a hole there was every chance that those nice Indiana folks would all get together and blow that little white ball closer to the hole.

Opinion is divided, but there's enough evidence to suggest that it was here during the PGA at Crooked Stick that the phrase 'You da man!' was first heard at a tour event. And who was it aimed at? Take a guess. Back then, though, it was new and faintly amusing; these days it's up there with 'In the hole!' – irritating and unnecessary. But then Daly was the man, not merely of the moment, but of the whole PGA Championship.

In the high-gloss world of television, an old face was now at the CBS microphone, watching events unfold. Jack Nicklaus had already heard on the grapevine about Daly's respect for him. He had even invited him to his Memorial Tournament held in May, but a pair of 74s followed by a couple of 83s had done little to impress the great man. But this was different. When Nicklaus watched Daly now, he saw a player who was at the top of his game, who was carefree, cavalier even, and who was growing with stature with every monstrous drive. When he studied Daly's swing on the monitors, he shook his head. 'Good gracious,' he exclaimed. 'What a coiling! What an unleashing of power! He's so long it's unbelievable. And straight. I have never seen anybody in my life hit it that long.' Strangely, Nicklaus couldn't resist giving the young whippersnapper a few words of sage advice, even though Daly was four shots clear of the pack. 'John Daly is going to have to learn,' he lectured. 'If he's going to be a good player as well as a long hitter, he's going to have to learn to collect himself and play.' Quite why the game's greatest player saw fit to stick his oar in, especially at a time when Daly was on a roll, is a mystery. Perhaps he was trying to protect him in case of a sudden and catastrophic collapse. Maybe it was just Jack being fatherly. Maybe, just maybe, it was because he really, really wanted him to win.

Daly marched to the scorer's cabin. Another round of 69. Eleven under par. He had a lead of three strokes going into the final day. Time to take stock. Time to keep calm and think things through. There was just one round of golf standing between John Daly and a place in golf's history books, not to mention a big old bag of cash. Maybe tonight he should just share a light meal with Bettye, talk strategy with Squeek and get an early night, ready for the challenge of the new day. Well, maybe. The Indianapolis Colts were sending a limo for him and Bettye and he was to be the guest of honour at their NFL game at the Hoosier Dome. Best seats in the house. Free beer, too.

That night, Daly was lauded as never before. As he was led out on to the pitch, smiling and waving, the crowd exploded into the kind of wild, raucous applause typically reserved for the Chippendales. Then, much to Daly's surprise and amusement, the Dome's giant video screen burst into life and the PGA Championship leader found himself watching an analysis of his golf swing performed by the one and only John Madden, the all-American hero and most famous football pundit in the country. He even used one of those telepointers to draw lines on the screen just like they did in NFL games. Later that year, Daly would be named in the 1991 All-Madden NFL squad. And he was a golfer, not a footballer. 'Daly was a Madden kind of guy,' said director Michael Frank, who worked with the Madden team. 'Daly was a big, heavy guy with a hellbent swing. Madden got all excited about it.'

And he hadn't even won the damn thing yet.

When Daly had arrived at the course on Thursday it was only the fact that he was carrying his own clubs that had identified him as a competitor. Without them, he could have strolled around Crooked Stick all week without anyone giving him so much as a second glance. Now, three days later, he couldn't move for autograph hunters and snap-happy punters. At the beginning of the tournament, Daly's old AJGA friend Chris Haack had run into him by the practice green and the two had joked about their clashes on the AJGA circuit. 'No one knew who John Daly was up there [in Indianapolis],' explained Haack. '[But] by the weekend, I couldn't get within twenty feet of him because the crowds were so big.'

If Daly had thought the reception at the Hoosier Dome was crazy, then pay day at Crooked Stick was something else. From the moment he turned up at the course, he was engulfed by well-wishers. People cheered his name. Some were even screaming. Who did they think he was? David Cassidy? Eventually, he found sanctuary in the locker room. A few of the guys walked by, slapped him on the back and wished him luck for the day. He opened his locker. Inside, he found a rain forest's worth of PGA Tour announcements. Like he was going to read any of it. But as he went to shut the door he discovered a note hiding in the bundle. He opened it up. There were four words and a signature. It read: 'John, go get 'em'. And the signature? None other than Jack Nicklaus.

But Daly was feeling far from great. As usual, he had overindulged at the football game the night before, and it was only the fact that he had the latest tee-off that gave him sufficient time to get his head in order. Thankfully, by the time he teed it up some blood had returned to his alcohol stream and the crowd around the 1st tee were in expectant mood. John Daly, the new people's champion, was among them and getting ready to make their day. It was like happy hour at Hooter's. Make no mistake, there was only one man they wanted to win the PGA, and it wasn't Kenny Knox, Daly's playing partner for the final round. Indeed, Knox, whose average drive was almost 50 yards shorter than Daly's average, knew what his game plan was. 'On the 1st tee,' he said, 'I'll just say, "So long, good luck, see you on eighteen." We play completely different games.'

The self-appointed chief of John's new legion of supporters was local man Jeff Hall. He was so convinced that Daly was destined to triumph that he had a bunch of T-shirts printed up with the legend DALY BELIEVER spread across the chest and had given them to everyone he knew so they could wear them around Crooked Stick. 'I didn't plan on coming out here, but when I saw John on TV on Saturday I had to come out here and support him,' explained Hall. 'Anyway, Saturday night, I called a friend who owns this T-shirt shop and had a bunch of them made up. We bought some tickets, hopped on a bus Sunday morning and followed our guy.'

Amid the ballyhoo, there was the first sign that maybe Daly was feeling the pressure. At the 1st, he surprised everyone by ditching the driver and pulling the one-iron out of the bag. It was a change of tack that was to cost him a shot. One hole down and one shot gone. The whispers had started. Daly was going to fold. He had to. No rookie, no matter how confident, could lead for as long as he had and not feel The Fear. But Jeff Hall and his Daly Believers needn't have worried. Daly immediately reverted to his driver, hitting it on holes where it patently wasn't needed, and by the turn he was sitting pretty at one under for his round. Moreover, no other player had the balls to mount anything resembling a challenge. Knox was falling away, Bruce Lietzke was toiling manfully but to no avail, and Craig Stadler, who had stood just three shots off Daly at the beginning of the round, was on his way to a miserable 76. In the CBS booth, Nicklaus was asked if he thought Daly could close the tournament out. 'What is that saying about going home with the one that brought you?' he asked. 'That's what he is doing. He started out with a driver and blasting it, and he's still blasting it. That's his mentality.'

Daly marched on. Pars at eleven and twelve followed, and while the birdies weren't coming as regularly as in the first three rounds, his putter was doing more than enough to keep his nose in front. Just six holes now stood between John Daly and the PGA title. But it was thirsty work being the tournament leader. On his way from the 12th green to the 13th tee, Daly stopped for a drink and disappeared from the view of the TV cameras. Moments later he was back, clutching a large white cup. 'Having a nice soft drink right there,' said Gary McCord as Daly quaffed away. 'You've got to wet the whistle, you know.' Ben Wright, McCord's CBS colleague, was less convinced. 'Well, I have a feeling that's a beer.' What? A beer? Surely with just a handful of holes left before claiming his maiden tour success and with millions of people witnessing the events live on television Daly wouldn't jeopardise it all by necking a cold one in full view of the watching world? Years later, Daly would admit that he had actually been drunk throughout the entire event, although in his time in Daly's employ Beighle never once saw his boss drinking on the golf course. 'But if you're asking me whether there was some left over [in his system] from the night before,' he added, 'well, that's a different story.'

A birdie followed at thirteen, and out came the magic white cup again. When he reached seventeen, Daly had a seemingly unassailable five-stroke lead. It was turning into a procession. But then the hiccup. A double bogey at the penultimate hole gave cause for concern, but with three shots to play, surely the unthinkable couldn't happen at the last, could it? Truth was that even after the disaster at the 17th, the only way Daly could blow this thing now was if he blocked his drive into the water that lined the right-hand side of the 18th fairway. And even then he would have to do it twice for Lietzke to have an outside chance of victory. 'That's why most of the gallery was stunned when I whipped out the driver instead of playing safe with a long iron,' he said later. 'They thought I was crazy. But I said to myself, "I've hit this fairway three days in a row. There's plenty of room out there, so I'm just going to knock it on the fairway again." I went through my normal visualisation process, gripped it, and ripped it. When I saw that pretty little golf ball heading down the fairway just like I had planned, I knew I had the PGA Championship won.'

It was a hell of a play. After all, you only need fast-forward eight years to see what can happen when bravado gets the better of common sense. At the 1999 Open Championship at a windswept Carnoustie in Scotland, France's Jan Van de Velde also held a three-shot lead as he stood on the 72nd tee. Like Daly, he too chose a driver, but unlike Daly he saw his chance of major success disappear in the most humiliating, self-destructive manner imaginable. Needing just a six to take the claret jug, he finished with a triple-bogey seven and ended up wading in the Barry Burn with his trousers rolled up to his knees, contemplating playing his ball out of the water. Needless to say, he lost out in the ensuing four-hole play-off to Scotland's Paul Lawrie and watched as his name overtook that of Greg Norman as the game's biggest ever choker.

But Daly nailed that final drive, just as he had so many others that week. No fear. His average drive for the championship was now 303 yards, far in excess of any other player. He had hammered the course into complete submission, not to mention a field including 46 of the top 50 players in the world. As he strode up the fairway to the final green, he was greeted by a wall of noise that made the hairs on the back of his neck stand up. He could barely hear himself think, let alone the words of encouragement and congratulation from Squeeky.

Daly left himself a four-footer for his par. He crouched down and gave the putt a cursory glance. Squeeky also took a look, but walked away, knowing full well that there was only one place this ball was going to end up. He took a couple of practice putts and steadied himself for one last time. Dead centre.

It's always interesting to watch a winner to see how they celebrate when that final putt drops. Multiple champions like Tiger Woods rarely seem to get that excited. OK, so Nicklaus nearly decapitated Doug Sanders with his putter after his play-off win in the 1970 Open, but by and large all you ever get is a punch of the air, maybe a little hug for a nearby loved one. It's the unexpected, out-of-the-blue winners that are by far the most amusing. Some, like Sandy Lyle at the 1988 Masters and, more recently, Rich Beem at the 2002 PGA, make a first-class fool of themselves by breaking into an impromptu jig, the net result being that they look more like a drunken uncle at a wedding reception than a professional sportsman at the very peak of his powers. Others, like Ian Woosnam (1991 Masters), have the life squeezed out of them by their caddie. Some, like Jerry Pate at the 1982 Tournament Players Championship (TPC), take an unscheduled dip in the lake, and occasionally there are those like Nick Faldo who simply break down in tears and blubber like a child who has been sent to his room.

As celebrations go, Daly's was comparatively restrained. He simply raised his arms as if he was down the front at a Bon Jovi gig, put one hand over his head and dropped his putter on to the green. He looked battle weary. He looked beat. But in reality his victory was about as easy as they come. No late charges from any of his rivals, no need to eke out a birdie at the last. Just an assured performance that nobody else could live with.

Within moments, he was joined on the green by Bettye. The previous night the couple had spoken about how they would celebrate should Daly go on to win, and John had insisted that just like every other golfer who wins big, he wanted his girl to be there by his side. As the two embraced, tears welled in his eyes. The hick had won at Crooked Stick.

7. LIFE IN THE FAST LANE

'Watchin' the world go by,
Surprisin' it goes so fast,
Johnny looked around him and said,
"Well, I made the big time at last." '

'Shooting Star' by Bad Company

By his own admission, John Daly has watched the golf comedy *Caddyshack* over 50 times. He knows each lumbering one-liner, all the painful put-downs and every sordid gag about vomit and faeces. It is safe to say it is his favourite film. But amid the endless idiocy, there is one moment in Harold Ramis's film that could have been written with Daly in mind. The scene features Bushwood Country Club's daydreaming greenkeeper Carl Spackler (played by Bill Murray) as he engages in his favourite fantasy of winning the Masters. 'Cinderella story, outta nowhere,' he says to himself. 'Tears in his eyes, I guess, as he lines up this last shot. He's got about 195 yards left. Looks like he's got about an eight-iron.'

This was Daly's PGA victory all over, right down to the unfeasibly long eight-iron. But it wasn't really the 'Cinderella story' described in *Caddyshack*; it was more implausible than that. It was a ridiculous, almost incomprehensible tale of outrageous fortune and bizarre coincidence. Put simply, it defied belief. That it remains one of the greatest stories in modern-day sport is beyond doubt. It is up there with Buster Douglas dumping Mike Tyson on his backside, with England's unlikely Ashes triumph over Australia in 1981, and little David's shock win over the much-fancied Goliath.

According to the Sony Rankings, which grades the world's professional golfers, Daly's victory was the greatest upset in golf since the rankings system began in 1986. At the turn of the year Daly had been ranked 223 in the world, a position which had risen to 168 as he went into the PGA Championship. When he clinched victory on that Sunday, not only did he become the first Arkansan to win a major, he also became the lowest-ranked player ever to win one of the four titles. It was an inconceivable victory, and at times it seemed as though even Daly himself couldn't really believe it had happened. As he came back down to earth, the applause still ringing in his ears, he was met by CBS anchor Jim Nantz, who thrust a microphone into his face. 'I just want to say hi to my mom and dad, and I love them. Chickasaw, and these fans, I won it for y'all. And this beautiful woman here,' he said, squeezing Bettye. Cue rapturous applause.

Nantz continued. 'Your name is going to be engraved on a trophy that includes the names of Gene Sarazen, Walter Hagen, who won this trophy five times, and Jack Nicklaus. John Daly's name will be right there.'

'I tell you, I love Jack Nicklaus,' said the champion. 'He's been my idol ever since. I'm looking at his name right now. I love you, Jack.' More applause.

With the four-foot-high Wanamaker trophy at his side like a faithful dog along with a cheque for $230,000, by far the biggest of his career, Daly made his way to the press conference. As he sat down, someone handed him a beer which disappeared quicker than David Copperfield in a hurry. The questions came thick and fast.

What does it feel like to be famous?

'I love every minute of it. It's the greatest thing that ever happened to me.'

What do you put your success down to?

'I came here with nothing to lose, and that had everything to do with winning it.'

Were you surprised you played so well all week?

'I can't remember when I've hit my driver this straight. All four days, I didn't think. I just hit it. Squeeky just said, "Kill!" and I killed it. I just hit it so good this week, I had no fear out there.'

How are you going to spend all that money?

'I don't know what your guys' favourite charity is here in Indianapolis, but I'm giving $30,000 to it,' he proclaimed. 'The fans won this tournament for me. This is a miracle. Things like this just don't happen.' Then, he said, he was going to take care of the finance on Bettye's new BMW; there was also the mortgage on the house, and whatever was left could sit next to him on the blackjack tables in Vegas after he and Bettye had got married. Stick it in your diary, he said, 'October eighth, in Las Vegas.'

After the media frenzy had died down, it would emerge that Daly did indeed donate that $30,000 – to the family of Thomas Weaver, the fan who was killed by lightning earlier in the week, so that they could set up a college fund for his children. It was an act of generosity for which the Golf Writers Association of America would later award Daly the rarely presented Charlie Bartlet Award for services to humanity. He also gave $20,000 to a junior golf charity.

In the background, some other press guys were grilling Bettye. Name, age, rank. 'Just write down Daly,' Bettye replied, smiling. 'It'll be that soon enough.' Come on, they asked, what is the real John Daly like? We've heard he's a good ol' boy who likes a drink or two. Sure, said Bettye, 'but he's really settled down in the last year'. Talk about lighting the blue touch paper. Before the ink had dried on the story of John Daly's famous PGA win, another story was already unfolding.

Two hours later, the photo call and press conference were over and Daly and his old buddy Donnie Crabtree walked back to the locker room and closed the door. As John guided Donnie around, pointing out the famous names on the lockers, they looked at each other and cried. 'Man, can you believe this?' asked the champ. 'We're just kids from Dardanelle.'

Jim Daly's arms were aching. He had been picking that phone up for hours, fielding calls from friends, family and well-wishers, all eager to say just how well their boy had done. Folks they hadn't spoken to for years were calling up to say they had just seen their John on the TV and wasn't it all wonderful. Even potential sponsors were calling, asking Jim whether John would be interested in cutting a deal with them.

Bizarrely, Daly's parents had been on a week-long vacation in California and hadn't even known he was playing in the tournament until Friday night when they returned home and found several telephone messages telling them of their son's progress. After watching John extend his lead on Saturday they had considered flying to Indiana to cheer him on, but decided to watch it all on TV instead. It was better that way. The last thing John needed was his folks hanging around telling him to tidy his hair up or run an iron over his shirt just as he was lining up a birdie putt. So, when John crossed the finishing line on Sunday, the Dalys were holed up at home in Dardanelle, raising a glass and then the roof with John's Uncle Ben and Aunt Ann, and cousins Deward and Wanda Ferguson, who had dropped by to share in the celebrations. Jim Daly was tickled pink. 'Everybody doesn't have a son that does something like this,' he said proudly.

Around the South, those that knew Daly were still scratching their heads, trying to figure out if the John Daly they had seen on television winning the PGA Championship was the same John Daly they used to hang out with. Eventually, they had no option but to concede that, yes, it really was the same person. Helias principal Jim Rackers was staggered, calling it 'a great feeling', while his old ASGA sparring partner Jay Fox was beside himself. 'I was thrilled,' he said. 'I remember sitting in my living room watching it, and it was like goose bumps. John Daly has always been an Arkansas kid, even though he didn't really come here from Missouri until he was a senior in high school. But we sort of adopted him. He became our kid. And when he started winning that was pretty special, and something quite unique for us to hang our hats on.'

Remarkably, only his old University of Arkansas coach Bill Woodley was 'unsurprised' at Daly's triumph. Indeed, after Daly's third round he had received a call late in the evening from Gary McCord and a good friend of Woodley's, the Australian professional Steve Elkington. The pair were out drinking and wanted to know all about Daly. 'McCord said, "Bill, I just want to ask you, what about this guy?" and I said he's going to win. McCord giggled and said, "Do you think he's going to hang on?" I said, "F***, I *know* he's going to hang on." I mean, the guy is just so fearless.'

Back in Carmel, John Daly was already enjoying the trappings of becoming the biggest name in golf. With the champion's dinner over, Daly and his buddies set about some proper celebrating, Arkansas style. Donnie Crabtree and some of the boys hired a limo and filled the back with beer. Rick Ross was part of the convoy following Daly's car. He had driven up from Arkansas to be there on his star pupil's big day and now found himself in the surreal position of following a stretch limousine into a drive-thru McDonald's, the newly crowned PGA champion with his head and shoulders stuck through the roof ordering scores of burgers for anybody who wanted one. 'He was still hungry,' Ross said with a laugh.

Daly woke at 5.00 a.m. on the Monday with a thick head. The champion's party had gone on long into the night and he had managed only one hour's sleep. He wandered into the bathroom, splashed some water on his face and stared in the mirror. Then he remembered he was the new PGA champion.

But there was no time to kick back and savour the moment, or to plan how he was going to spend the couple of hundred grand burning a hole in his pocket. The phone was ringing. Daly was due on the CBS breakfast programme *This Morning*, and knowing his burgeoning reputation for being the hellraiser-in-chief of the PGA Tour the producers had called him at 5.30 a.m. to make sure that (a) he was still coming on the show, and (b) he wasn't holed up in some bar, dancing on the tables and waving his winner's cheque in the air. An hour later, Daly made his way to the makeshift studio on the 18th green at Crooked Stick and sank into a director's chair, the Wanamaker trophy gleaming next to him. As a cameraman fixed his collar and wired him up with a microphone, Daly turned to him. 'Pretty heady stuff, isn't it? It's still hard to believe all of this.' The interview was brief but, for a player who had barely appeared on television before, let alone been interviewed on one of the biggest shows in the country (with the mother of all hangovers), it was successful. 'I'm proud of the way I handled the pressure, especially over the weekend rounds,' he told the nation. 'I hung in there. I hope I can stay the same. I'll try to keep playing golf and go about my business. I'll just have to make a few adjustments, I guess.'

This Morning wasn't the only interested party. Johnny Carson's and Larry King's people had been in touch too, and there were a bundle of papers and magazines waiting in the wings: the *Washington Post*, *Sports Illustrated*, *Time*, *People*; even the *Rocky Mountain News* wanted to put John Daly on their cover. But there was one offer that had lodged itself in Daly's head and had steadfastly refused to budge, a proposal that was infinitely better than any amount of sponsor's lucre or all the media mumbo jumbo that was banging down his door.

Through the haze of a hangover, Daly recalled the conversation he had had on Saturday evening with Ron Meyer, the coach of the Indianapolis Colts football team. As the two chatted about gridiron, Daly happened to mention that before he dedicated himself to golf he had been no mean kicker with the Helias High School team. Meyer's mind had started to work overtime. His Colts had been having a miserable time of it on the field of late and the fans were starting to get on his back. They needed something to cheer about, and the way Meyer saw it, John Daly was the man to bring the good times back to the Hoosier Dome. Coach Meyer cornered Daly again at his victory party on Sunday evening. He had a proposal. The Colts had a game the following Saturday, and if he was up for it there was a kicker's shirt with the name JOHN DALY waiting for him. It made perfect sense. Meyer had seen at first hand the kind of wild, almost frenzied reception Daly got from the galleries and it was unlike anything he'd ever seen at a golf course before. If he could transfer that raw emotion, that genuine feel-good factor to the Hoosier Dome, then think of the reaction and the coverage they would get.

Daly drooled as Meyer continued. It would be for just one game, and he would come on only towards the end to kick an extra point. But there was an industrial-sized pin waiting to burst Daly's balloon. He was playing in the International tournament in Colorado the following week, and unless he missed the cut (unlikely for a guy at the top of his game) he wouldn't be able to make it. Meyer shrugged. OK, he figured, if you miss the cut you're in, if you don't, hey, it was a nice idea while it lasted. 'I'm dead serious,' Meyer added. Daly mulled it over with his agent and mentioned it to a few pals. Everybody was in agreement: he would be mad to pass up a chance to play in the NFL. There were a few concerns, though. As the newest inductee in golf's big time, John Daly was now a precious commodity, worth a bundle of bucks to far too many people. What if the worst-case scenario transpired? What if John's kick was charged down and he found himself buried under the bodies of three twenty-stone hulks with necks like giant redwoods and all the manners of a warthog in season? What if the career of golf's newest superstar was cut short by an injury he could so easily have avoided?

Perhaps it was too big a risk. Maybe it was just a nice idea they hadn't really thought through. Who cares? There was no way

John Daly, the new PGA champion and self-crowned king of the world, was saying no. The pair shook hands. It had been a hell of a week. Winning a major, and now kicking for the Colts. It was as if Lady Luck had ridden into Daly's life carrying a crate of Jack Daniels, his own McDonald's concession and a big blank cheque. Surely life couldn't get any better than this?

Later that night, as Daly toasted his success with anyone and everyone, he learned that Governor Bill Clinton had declared Monday to be 'John Daly Day' in Arkansas. 'Daly's emergence as an instant hero by winning one of golf's four major championships has brought fame and recognition to himself and to the state of Arkansas,' said Clinton, and nobody in the Natural State disagreed.

For the next week, the sports pages of the world's newspapers were dominated by Daly and the miracle at Crooked Stick. The media had gone mad for the Wild Thing and it was showing no sign of abating. The *New York Times* argued that Daly was golf's 'first folk hero in years', while over the Atlantic the *Guardian* was calling him 'the rookie of the century'. Predictably, most of the coverage centred on Daly's whirlybird swing and the mesmeric distance he could propel a golf ball. The tabloids revelled in the news that Daly's Cobra Ultramid driver had a head made from Kevlar, the same thermoplastic substance used in bulletproof vests, and that ordinary wooden-headed drivers caved in under the pressure of his immense swing. They laughed when he told them that he had to use a new ball on virtually every hole because the old one took such a battering. Most of all, though, they loved that swing, that extraordinary, awesome, killer swing. It was a swing that defied not only belief but virtually every coaching manual ever published, and, for that matter, most of the principles of physics too.

It has also been said that when the Daly swing is in full flow even slow-mo technology struggles to keep up with it. That's nonsense, of course. Nobody swings a club that fast. That said, Daly's swing is unique, and it's only made possible by Daly's super-flexible shoulders, or torque. He has a remarkable ability to rotate his shoulders at more than 90 degrees on both his backswing and his follow-through while managing not to lose balance. With high hands and a huge, elongated arc – he has the longest club-head travel time in the modern game – it is an amalgam of immense strength and no small amount of finesse.

While most coaches advocate the 'classic' neutral position of the club being parallel to the ground and pointing towards the target, the defining moment, the *pièce de résistance* of Daly's swing arrives at the very top. Take a look, by all means, but don't try it at home – unless, of course, you're keen to spend the rest of your days paying for the services of an osteopath. It is unorthodox, idiosyncratic and brutally effective, and comes complete with a ringing endorsement from the man himself. 'Don't worry if you go beyond the parallel position,' insisted Daly in *The Killer Swing*, a coaching manual he collaborated on with author John Andrisani. 'Just tell your teacher John Daly said it was all right.'

John and Bettye flew to Colorado for the International, leaving the BMW behind in Indianapolis. It was a 900-mile drive from Carmel, and not even the superhuman PGA champion could stomach that, especially after the week he had just had. Moreover, Bettye had tripped over a table while running to reach the phone and had put her shoulder out. Her arm was in a sling and there was no way she could share the driving.

Back in Dardanelle, Don Tyson, the man behind the Tyson chicken empire, had given Daly's parents his private jet so that they could fly over to Colorado to see their son play. Tyson had also paid for a condo for them to stay in. Jim and Lou hadn't seen John play in a PGA event since the St Jude Classic in Memphis in late June, and when they got to the Castle Pines Golf Club in Castle Rock they soon realised the full, bewildering impact of their boy's win at Crooked Stick. Walking around with Bettye, they found John pursued by the kind of galleries that followed the game's superstars around. 'This is unreal,' said Bettye, struggling for a view of her fiancé. 'I used to be able to watch every shot.'

On the course, Daly had teamed up again with his regular caddie, Dave Beighle, as Squeeky had returned to work with Nick Price. It was the first time they had seen each other since Daly had won at Crooked Stick. 'He [Daly] came out of the locker room and said, "I don't know what to say," ' Beighle recalled, 'so I just told him he had played great and we carried on.' Having missed out on the chaos of the PGA Championship (and his $20,000-plus cut of the winner's cheque), Beighle could not believe the transformation in the crowd's reaction to his boss. 'It was night and day. This kid had gone from just another good young player on tour to the number one draw in golf. Every now and then he would have that deer-in-the-headlights look on his face, but he handled it pretty well.' Remarkably, Beighle can now look back on the week when he missed out on the biggest day of his caddying career and laugh. 'It was the ultimate caddie nightmare: watching the guy that you're working for win when you're not working for him. But it was just one of those things that if you hang around caddying long enough it will happen to you. You hate missing out on a major but things work out for a reason, and the magical things that happened that week with Squeek, well, they're part of golf history now.'

Unlike regular PGA Tour events, the International employed a scoring system that gave two points for each birdie but docked one for any bogey a player made. It also had a cut after three rounds. Although Daly played well on Thursday and Friday, impressing everyone with his mammoth drives, by Saturday it was clear that the whirlwind of his new life was catching up with him, and he missed the cut. But if Daly thought his premature exit would now mean he would get his chance to kick for the Indianapolis Colts in their pre-season game against New Orleans, he was wrong. Jim Irsay, general manager of the Colts, had rejected Ron Meyer's idea in the interests of Daly's safety. 'I would have loved to do it,' the PGA champ reacted to the news. 'I would have signed any waiver they wanted.'

Still, there were plenty of other opportunities for Daly to explore, and while Bud Martin and John Mascatello fielded calls from would-be backers, Daly hooked up with CBS, who were keen for him to take part in a quirky news item. Knowing Daly's reputation as the longest hitter in the game, the TV channel took him to an airport in Denver and set him up at one end of the runway with his driver and some balls. The object of the exercise was simple: just hit the ball as far as you can. Much to everyone's amusement, Daly obliged: he struck one that travelled 330 yards through the air, bounced on the concrete runway and eventually stopped rolling some 808 yards away. Almost half a mile. There was more fun to be had that day. After the disappointment of the rejection from the Indianapolis Colts, the Denver Broncos had stepped in and invited Daly along to their training session that morning to take some kicks at goal. He had five attempts and made every one of them.

Estimates of what the Crooked Stick win could do to Daly's bank balance were startling. Some said it was worth ten million dollars, others twenty million. Suffice to say that with sound financial advice and a sensible attitude to his new-found wealth, John Daly would never have to worry about money for the rest of his days. There was just one problem, though. This was John Daly they were talking about.

Reebok, one of the companies to ring Jim Daly at his home in Dardanelle in the wake of John's win, was first to score, bagging a $400,000-a-year plus bonuses clothing deal, but there were other offers in the pipeline including instructional videos, a Wild Thing video game, a book, and endorsements for cars and long-distance telephone companies. All the clubs that had had neither the nerve nor the foresight to back Daly in his time of need were now falling over themselves to court him. Chickasaw Country Club weighed in with an honorary membership, as did Russellville, while the board at Chenal Country Club in Little Rock voted to offer Daly a course-side lot, club membership and tour supplies from the pro shop. Everybody wanted a bit of John Daly and, as Bettye was discovering, there wasn't enough to go round. Soon she would grow tired of the constant demands on her man's time, of the way in which she was always being brushed off like a fly on the cheek. Worst of all, though, was the shameless manner in which all these golf groupies had suddenly emerged. According to Rick Ross, however, this was nothing new. 'I've been caddying for John when women have removed their panties and sat in his eye-line while he's reading a putt. There were women ready, willing and available. Other guys have their opportunities, but they didn't have first pick. From time to time they got our attention and we had to run away so we could refocus and play golf.'

Financial considerations aside, it was the many exemptions that winning the PGA Championship brought that really appealed to Daly. By winning the title he had now guaranteed a place in the PGA Championship for the rest of his life, as well as earning a starting place in the other three majors for the next five years. Moreover, the victory came with a ten-year exemption to the PGA Tour itself, a fact which obviated any need to go back to Q-School – and you couldn't put a price on that.

But if Daly imagined that his life would now be one long, easy ride punctuated by offers of riches you can only ever win playing lotteries, he was wrong. If anything, it was the start of a whole new barn full of problems. Wherever he went, people would recognise him and yell 'Wild Thing!' across the street; every newspaper and magazine wanted an interview; and when he actually played some golf he found fans getting upset when he refused to use his bulletproof driver. Amid the hullabaloo, Daly's form suffered. After a brief appearance at a pro-am event in Oklahoma, he laboured to a tie for 40th at the NEC World Series of Golf in Akron, Ohio, at the end of August, and it was clear that the demands on golf's newest sensation were having an adverse effect on his game. Still, it was another seven grand in the bank, and a nice PGA official had even driven their BMW over from Carmel, which at least meant he and Bettye could drive back to Dardanelle with some time to themselves. 'We'll be driving the car to everything, if we can,' explained Daly prior to leaving Akron. 'No airplanes for this boy if he can help it. I'll fly if I have to, but if I don't, I won't. Two things are wrong with airplanes: one is that if that thing goes down, you can just kiss your ass goodbye, and two is that there is no McDonald's in the sky.'

Friday, 30 August 1991. Another 'John Daly Day', this time in Dardanelle. After his exploits in Carmel, the town had turned out at the Bay Ridge Boat and Golf Club to welcome home their most famous resident. A whole bunch of bigwigs were there too, basking in the reflected glory of Daly's stardom. There was Doc Bryan, the speaker of the state House of Representatives, Dardanelle mayor Dana Merritt, state representative Lloyd George and state senator Lu Hardin. Bill Clinton wasn't there, but he sent an aide, Field Wasson, who presented Daly with a state flag and said that the governor couldn't make it because he was busy studying his family tree for any possible link to the guest of honour. Daly was introduced to the 300-strong crowd by Kevin Ryals, a family friend and one of John's old drinking buddies. He had even written a country song for the occasion called 'Long John Daly':

Oh, he played the best, and he beat 'em all,
The blond-haired boy from Arkansas.
Hog at heart, a golfer by dream,
Just a baby-faced boy, but a monster on the green.
It was Crooked Stick where his dream came true,
Now nobody's askin', 'Well, John who?'
Long John Daly, Big John,

Everybody in Dardanelle's
Yellin', 'Give 'em hell!'
When ol' Squeeky hollered, 'Kill!'
John said, 'I think I will!'

As Daly addressed the crowd, he was visibly moved by the show of affection. 'Dardanelle is in this big heart of mine for as long as I will ever live. Here I am, twenty-five years old, and it's just the greatest feeling in the world to know I've got friends and family like you. I just want to keep Dardanelle on the map for ever and ever.'

But while John enjoyed his Dardanelle deification, Bettye's mind was elsewhere. Bibb County, Georgia, to be precise. It was there that her lawyer had filed papers seeking the annulment of her marriage to a man by the name of Michael D. Blackshear. Amid the rush of their flourishing romance and Daly's heady elevation to the PGA Tour, it had apparently slipped Bettye's mind that she had been married on 19 May 1986; even though she had been separated since April 1989, she had yet to get a divorce. It wouldn't be the first surprise she would spring on her fiancé.

When Bettye had engulfed John on the 18th green at Crooked Stick, her floral print dress billowing in the gentle breeze, the world had warmed to the happy couple enjoying their day in the sun. What she had singularly failed to realise, however, was that the PGA Championship wasn't some nondescript stop on the Hogan Tour, it was one of the four biggest events in golf and there were 5.5 million people watching it on televisions around the country and countless other millions around the world. Somebody, somewhere, was bound to recognise her.

Sure enough, the whispers began. Back in Arkansas, Rick Ross was already fielding calls from across the South from people who knew Bettye. They had seen Ross's name mentioned in press reports of Daly's success and had called him to set the record straight on a few matters. The questions came thick and fast. Did John know that Bettye was still married? To her second husband? What about her thirteen-year-old son from her first marriage who lived in Georgia? And why were all the papers saying she was 31? As far as anyone knew, Bettye Fulford, Blackshear, or whatever she was called, was 39. Ross was stunned, and called around to check if anybody else had heard anything. Sure enough, the rumours had spread. Even the PGA had been notified. If these stories were true, and there was no reason to think otherwise, John was about to marry a barefaced liar.

When Daly learned of the gossip, he dismissed it out of hand, putting it down to the idle chitchat of jealous folk with nothing better to do. Bettye did the same, laughing off the stories, although she would concede that she was technically still married. Besides, argued Bettye, why would she lie to him? She had quit her $40,000-a-year job to be with him on the Hogan Tour and had been there with him when he barely had a cent to his name, so it wasn't as if she was after his money, was it?

After a weekend spent resting (although he still managed to squeeze in an on-pitch appearance at the Razorbacks game against Miami on Saturday night), Daly drove to Hot Springs Village for an exhibition at the opening of the new Ponce De Leon course. Though tired, he was as courteous as ever, engaging the crowd with his cheerful demeanour and belting balls into the woods at the end of the driving range. Eventually, when the display was over and every last autograph hunter had been satisfied, Daly, his planet spinning ever faster, confided to a local journalist, Kelley Bass, 'All I want to do is sleep.'

Indeed, his fatigue was all too evident when he missed the cut at his next PGA Tour event, the Hardees Classic at Coal Valley, Illinois. While seeking to maximise his opportunities in the wake of his PGA victory, Daly was letting slip the one thing that had put him in the spotlight – his golf. He didn't even have time to dine with George Bush at the White House. Later, he would claim that he had not in fact turned down the offer to meet the president, 'We just haven't been able to give him an answer.' The story was typical for a man whose life had changed beyond all recognition, and not always for the better. While the financial rewards were more than welcome, there were other, less agreeable aspects to being the man in the spotlight. Increasingly, Daly found himself surrounded by do-gooders and sycophants, and it didn't sit well with him. 'I really appreciate how happy everyone is, but it's just that some people you can really read through. They come up all buddy-buddy, and I'm going, "Right. Where were you when I needed you?" Those are the ones I just can't get along with.' Unsurprisingly, there was little sympathy from Daly's agent, John Mascatello, who felt his client really needed to ride this wave of goodwill for as long as he possibly could. 'The hardest thing for John has been learning to say no,' he said. 'He loves people, but this is a time when he can't let himself get exhausted.'

Returning to see the people he genuinely cared about, however, was never a problem, as Ray Hentges discovered. Earlier in the year, Hentges had asked Daly if he would like to play an exhibition match to raise funds for his school's Helias Foundation. Keen to do anything he could to help, Daly had agreed and had pencilled the date in his diary. 'Between the time he said that and the time of the tournament in September he won the PGA at Crooked Stick and we thought, "Oh my God, is he going to come back and honour us?" ' Hentges recalled. 'But he did. He even turned down another invitation to play with Jack Nicklaus in Ohio, and they would have given him $50,000. We didn't give him a dime, and he still came back.' In a trademark act of generosity, Daly also handed his old coach a thousand-dollar bill towards the appeal and helped raise an additional $50,000 when the school auctioned off a foursome to play nine holes with him.

The hearsay about Bettye continued well into September, so John repaired home with her to Memphis for a short break away from the circus his life had become. Not knowing who or what to believe, Daly announced soon afterwards that he and his fiancée were postponing their October wedding in Las Vegas, the official reason being that there would be just too much publicity for their liking. 'Now we're going to go get married and come back and say, "Hey, we're married," ' he said. Anybody who had a handle on their situation, however, knew the real reason.

As Daly adjusted to his overnight fame, he also found that his whistle-stop dash around the country had taken its toll on his figure. Within two months, he had put on thirteen pounds. Racing around with barely enough time to sit down and enjoy a proper meal, he was existing on a diet of fast food; he admitted that he made an average of five visits to McDonald's every week, and when he wasn't enjoying a Big Mac or three it would be Taco Bell that got his business. 'I could eat that ten-pack of tacos in a heartbeat,' he said, laughing. With Daly promoting McDonald's in virtually every interview he gave, his agent Bud Martin became convinced that the burger chain would soon be knocking on John's door waving a big cheque under his nose. 'If McDonald's doesn't do that deal, I'm selling my stock,' he said. 'He's already done a million dollars of free advertising for them.'

But it wasn't like Daly desperately needed the money. Having secured another $138,000 for a third-place finish at the final PGA Tour event of the season, the Tour Championship, Daly could sit back and reflect on an astounding first year on tour. Incredibly, he had won almost ten times what he had taken on the Hogan Tour the previous year, his final earnings of $574,783 leaving him seventeenth on the PGA Tour money list ahead of such stellar names as Tom Watson, Tom Kite and Hale Irwin. Furthermore, Daly had also claimed the number one spot in the PGA Tour's statistics for driving distance, his average drive measuring 288.9 yards, comfortably ahead of Greg Norman and Fred Couples in second and third respectively. It came as no surprise when he was named the PGA's 1991 Rookie of the Year.

But this being major league golf meant there was always another money-making event just around the corner, and though he was tired and needed a break, Daly was in no mood to pass up the chance of a few dollars more. His first port of call was the US Skins Game in California, a made-for-TV event in which just four players play off over eighteen holes and line their pockets with cash whenever they win a hole.

Prior to the competition, Daly filmed a trailer for ABC television promoting the event. Originally, the idea for the promo was for Daly to smash a golf ball out of Anaheim Stadium before the Rams played the San Francisco 49ers, but the stunt didn't quite go to plan. Having teed his ball up in the corner of the stadium in front of the Rams' tunnel, Daly took an uncharacteristic half-swing, clearly concerned that he was going to damage either the vehicles or the people in the parking lot. The ball screamed across the field, over the heads of the half-time entertainers who were rehearsing, and landed in the opposite corner, narrowly missing the windows of the executive boxes. Realising that that wasn't really the kind of typical Wild Thing bazooka blast ABC wanted, Daly put down another ball and this time gave it the full treatment. The ball was still rising as it left the stadium, heading toward the 57 Freeway. Sadly, the ABC cameras failed to keep track of it and they were forced instead to show a barefooted Daly kicking a field goal from 44 yards.

When the $540,000 Skins Game began, Daly, the first rookie to be invited to the event, was determined to put on a good show, especially as he had flown his friend Donnie Crabtree over to California to watch. Playing against Curtis Strange, Payne Stewart and Jack Nicklaus, he helped himself to $120,000 and a couple of new cars over the first nine holes alone. He also bagged an additional $50,000 from Reebok for deliberately toying with his new shoes in full view of the TV cameras. Even Nicklaus had to concede that Daly had 'stolen the show', and he took the opportunity to invite John up to his place in North Palm Beach, Florida, for a cosy weekend together. Hamstrung by a chronic sense of unworthiness, it was an offer Daly would never accept.

Curtis Strange's caddie that day was Greg Rita. Hailing from Jacksonville, Florida, he had been at Strange's side when he had won back-to-back US Opens in 1988 and 1989 – the first man to achieve the feat since Ben Hogan in 1951 – but now their working relationship was coming to an end. Rita had also been impressed by Daly and the manner in which this kid from the sticks had stirred up this most genteel of games. As the cash was being counted, Rita approached Daly and told him that as he didn't have a bag for 1992 he would be more than interested in working with him if the opportunity arose. Daly made a mental note and headed home.

After the unexpected financial boost of the Tour Championship and the US Skins Game, Daly flew to South Africa, personally invited by Sun City resort owner Sol Kerzner, to take part in the richest golf tournament in the world, the Sun City Million Dollar Challenge. That week, the 1985 Masters champion Bernhard Langer ran away with the competition with a five-stroke victory over Mark Calcavecchia. Daly, meanwhile, showed none of the form that had got him the invitation in the first place, finishing some 22 shots behind Langer and blaming his eighth place on jet lag. But while Daly's golf was nothing to write home about, his antics off the field certainly gave cause for concern. On the Saturday night, the competition organisers had arranged an informal function for the players and hired a live band to entertain them. At around midnight, Daly, who was just getting started, was hauled on to the stage and the band started playing 'Wild Thing', the Chip Taylor song made famous by The Troggs. Grabbing fellow competitors Ian Woosnam and Steve Elkington as support, Daly stripped his shirt off – as did his backing singers – and began to sing (although many of the guests had another name for it):

Wild Thing!
You make my heart sing!
You make everything groovy.
Wild Thing!

Little did Daly know that the pictures of his impromptu turn would appear in countless newspapers around the world that week. The sight of the reigning PGA champion, the current Masters champion and supposedly one of the most elegant golfers in the game standing on a stage, semi-naked, screaming down a microphone with all the vocal ability of alleycats in agony was enough to put many millions of good people off their breakfasts. And Daly hadn't stopped there. With a belly full of beer, he'd headed off to the casino and promptly lost a reported $150,000 on the blackjack table, before returning to his hotel room and rearranging it in his own inimitable fashion, just as he did in 1990. Despite a cheque for $110,000 for his eighth-place finish, Daly left South Africa and headed home more than $40,000 worse off.

Back in Memphis, Daly decided to confront Bettye. While he was out of the country some of his friends had been amassing a wealth of evidence about the extent of Bettye's deception. Daly, astounded by the sheer volume of what they had presented, sat down to talk it through with her.

It was a heated discussion, Daly levelling accusation after accusation at his fiancée and Bettye blaming anything and everything on John's duplicitous friends. Again she rejected the charges, even though Daly produced her high school yearbook which showed that she had graduated in 1970. Daly was confused. Here was a woman he had spent eighteen months of his life with, who had helped him through difficult times on the Hogan Tour and had been there to pick up the pieces on those occasions when his temper, or the Jack Daniels, had got the better of him. And now, when the two of them should have been living the life they had worked so hard for, he didn't know what to think.

Then he had to go to Montego Bay in Jamaica. He had been invited to take part in the Johnnie Walker World Championship of Golf – which although sounding like the most significant tournament in the game was anything but – but the last thing he needed was Bettye there with him. He asked her to stay at home, but stubborn as ever, Bettye refused, insisting they go together and show a united front to anyone who dared doubt their love for each other. Too tired to argue, Daly relented.

The championship boasted a 26-man field with a guaranteed minimum of $50,000 for anybody who made the trip. Ordinarily it would have been one of those end-of-the-year events that Daly enjoyed, especially as it came with a sizeable gift-wrapped cheque, but this time, with his brain aching from the constant warring with Bettye, it would merely prove to be a miserable conclusion to his breakthrough year. In gale-force winds and with a 77 hanging over his head from the opening round, Daly set about his second round and, remarkably, managed to turn in a performance ten shots worse. It was a stinker of a round, and when he four-putted on the 12th green he exploded, snapping his putter over his knee and finishing his round putting with an iron. Later he marked his card with a five for the 18th when in fact he'd taken a six, and was disqualified for signing an incorrect scorecard. Speaking to reporters after the round, Daly admitted that he 'had had enough golf at the 11th hole' and had 'only finished to mark for [playing partner] Rodger Davis'.

Soon after that, the *Golfweek* columnist Dick Taylor published an open letter to Daly which noted that 'carrying the title of PGA Champion is an honor and a responsibility. You have a constituency. Don't lose it.' If the experiences in South Africa and now Jamaica proved anything, it was that while Daly was gradually mastering the art of playing professional golf, he was still an awfully long way from learning how to act like a professional golfer.

8. I FOUGHT THE LAW

'I don't know much about medicine or brain damage, and I'm not saying he's got it, but there's a switch in there that violently flies off. It's frightening and it's pitiful.'

Carl Perkins on Jerry Lee Lewis

It might have been Christmas, but the spirit of goodwill bypassed John Daly. When he arrived back from Jamaica, he decided it was high time that Bettye collect her things and move out of their Cordova house. All of this interminable squabbling was getting them nowhere, and Daly had made plans to head home to Dardanelle and spend the holiday with people who wanted nothing more than his company. He told Bettye it would be best for all concerned if she wasn't there when he returned.

Faced with an eviction from the place she called home, Bettye played her trump card. Out of the blue, she informed John that she was four months pregnant and that there was no question that the child was his. After everything she had concealed from him over the past one and a half years, this was the best yet. Daly didn't believe her. Why should he? As she wasn't showing yet, he demanded medical confirmation. He then packed a bag and headed back to Arkansas. By the time he returned to the suburbs of Memphis, Bettye would be gone.

By his own reckoning, Daly had spent over $110,000 on Bettye. He had bought her the BMW, jewellery, clothes, virtually anything she had wanted, and she had taken everything with her when she left Cordova. Not that Daly minded. To him, it was a small price to pay to be rid of her and her pernicious ways. But if he thought a shiny new car and a few fancy trinkets would mean the end of Bettye Fulford, he was sadly mistaken.

After leaving the house, Bettye had flown to Los Angeles to meet with the attorney Marvin Mitchelson. He was an acclaimed specialist in divorce and palimony cases and was the man celebrities went to when their love lives turned sour. Despite everything she had kept hidden from Daly over the course of their relationship, Mitchelson was certain she had a cast-iron case, especially now that she was pregnant with the PGA champion's baby. Their strategy was straightforward: they would decide on a settlement figure and suggest it to Daly and see if he was ready to cough up, the theory being that as a public figure with an image and reputation to maintain he would rather put his hand in his pocket than face an awkward and very public court case. And if he didn't, which given Daly's increasingly intransigent mood was always possible, then fine, they would hit him with a palimony and paternity suit and see him in court.

When Bettye's divorce from Michael Blackshear was finalised in the Superior Court in Bibb County, Georgia, on 6 January 1992, Daly was meeting with representatives from Wilson Sporting Goods and putting pen to paper on a five-year, five-million-dollar agreement. Daly had agreed to use their new range of Ultra irons and to carry the company's Staff bag, starting at the first PGA Tour event of the new year, the Infiniti Tournament of Champions in Carlsbad, California, in mid-January. For Daly, the Wilson deal was long overdue. It had been nearly five months since his victory at Crooked Stick and aside from the agreement with Reebok there had been no significant activity on the endorsement front. Now, the large fries were on John.

Founded in 1914 as a subsidiary of a meat-packing firm, Wilson had been languishing in the doldrums for decades. A golf and tennis specialist, the company had grown rapidly in the first half of the twentieth century thanks largely to the sales of their tennis rackets, and by the end of the Second World War they had become the largest sports manufacturer in the US. The post-war period had been less successful, however. As the likes of Karsten Manufacturing's Ping range of clubs and Prince's oversized tennis rackets soared in popularity, Wilson stood by and watched as their position as market leader was gradually usurped. The comparatively recent success of new and more fashionable players in the market such as Nike and Reebok had also dented their profitability. The downturn in Wilson's fortunes could be traced back to 1970, when the company was acquired by PepsiCo. It was a poor fit from the start. Pepsi sold cheap drinks and snacks in their millions every day, while Wilson's expertise lay in the more expensive, durable goods consumers bought very rarely. Sure, there were some talented people driving the company, but when you had golf ball product managers who knew everything there was to know about diet sodas and money-off coupons but had never swung a golf club in their life, what use was that?

For Wilson, seemingly unconcerned by press reports of his recent misdemeanours overseas, the Daly deal was the first step in rebuilding an image that had also been tarnished by a recent decentralisation programme that had seen widespread redundancies across the company. Although twenty players on the PGA Tour already used their clubs, Wilson still ran a distant second to Ping and were languishing third in the golf ball market. In Daly, they saw an instant fix to their ongoing image problems. He was the average Joe with the seismic swing and the redneck haircut, perceived by many as that blue-collar boy (even though he had enjoyed a relatively comfortable middle-class upbringing) who hit the ball eight million miles. He was the chubby, cheerful, unpretentious man in the street. He was Everyman.

When Daly and the Wilson people shook hands on their big-money deal, both parties pronounced themselves delighted. Unfortunately, so did Bettye Fulford and Marvin Mitchelson.

Daly arrived at the Tournament of Champions with a hardened resolve and a new caddie, Dave Beighle having been replaced by Greg Rita. 'He [Daly] needed a lot more than I could give him at that point,' admitted Beighle. It would prove to be an encouraging start to their working relationship. Despite a couple of 75s, Daly took his tie for 21st as a sign that with the experienced Rita by his side he could move on to the next level and start to accumulate some consistently high finishes.

While his golf was satisfactory, his interview with ABC-TV's Brent Musburger was quite the opposite. Typically, golfers, and for that matter broadcasters, are used to interviews with about as much bite as a blancmange. Tacitly, it is agreed that the questions will be no tougher than a lazy full toss the players can just bat away to the boundary. But now, much to his surprise and his chagrin, Daly found himself being cross-examined by Musburger as if he were standing in the dock, accused of everything from alcoholism to gross stupidity. First topic for discussion was the disqualification at the World Championship of Golf in Jamaica and the speculation as to whether he intentionally signed an incorrect scorecard just so he could collect his $50,000 and leave as early as possible. Daly denied the claims, then rounded on Jamaica itself. 'The food was horrible,' he moaned. 'I'll never go back there ... It's a pitiful place to play golf.' As the interview continued, Daly was clearly irritated. There were questions about his alleged drinking on the final nine holes of the PGA Championship ('It's illegal to drink while you play; I was drinking a Diet Coke at the PGA and somebody might have thought it was a beer'); about his predilection for redesigning hotel rooms ('I tore up a hotel room,' he replied with a shrug); and his volatile relationship with Bettye (they were 'no longer together right now').

Daly was rattled. He was annoyed that some of the guys on tour had been gossiping about him, and laid down a challenge. 'A lot of players are starting some stuff, and I think they ought to come to me and say it,' he fumed. 'But they're too scared to do that. If somebody has got something to say, say it to my face. I might hit 'em, I might not.' Nobody took Daly up on his offer – maybe he could punch as hard as he hit his driver – but it wouldn't be long before his fellow professionals began to take exception to the Dardanelle Destroyer.

The following week, Daly went to Palm Springs for the Bob Hope Chrysler Classic, a five-round pro-am competition which meant that John had to share his rounds with the stars of stage and screen. By and large, these events are a bugbear for the professionals, the problem being that they take so long. Imagine John Daly, the hit it, find it, hit it again king, waiting around for five or six hours as a bunch of C-list celebrities zigzag their way down the fairway laughing at how funny it is that they can't actually hit the ball. That said, it was a bona fide PGA Tour event with a $1.1 million purse, and ever since Bob Hope gave his name to the tournament back in 1965 it had managed to attract a better class of celebrity. Take one of Daly's four-balls that week. There he was, the new PGA champion, grouped with not just Bob Hope, but former president Gerald Ford and the then vice-president Dan Quayle. It was a week when Hope got to tell all his old gags again. It also presented him with an opportunity to surround himself with his showbiz buddies and, as men of a certain age, fame and wealth are wont to do, beautiful young women.

Every year, three 'Classic Girls' are selected to add some glamour to the occasion, each one wearing a top with either CHRYSLER, HOPE or CLASSIC emblazoned across their chests. When Daly arrived at the Bermuda Dunes course, his eye was taken by the girl proudly wearing the CLASSIC shirt. Her name was Paulette Dean and she was a model from Palm Desert. She said she was twenty years old, and this time, as Daly assessed her long legs, her pretty face and her lithe figure, he was sure she was telling the truth. What most appealed to Daly, however, was that Paulette knew as much about golf as he did about *haute cuisine*. 'I didn't know who Arnold Palmer was or who John Daly was; I didn't even know which end to hold a golf club,' she said. 'But the other girls were excitedly saying that Daly was playing, so I went to see what he looked like [and] he asked me out to dinner.' That week, the two partied the nights away in the bars and clubs of Palm Springs, their privacy invaded by scores of drinkers wanting an autograph or a picture.

Perhaps it was the partying with Paulette, or the elevated company he found himself in, but Daly missed the cut that week by a single shot. That said, it was more likely to be the increasing number of statements emanating from Marvin Mitchelson's office. On the opening day of the Classic, Mitchelson had issued a press release saying that he would be representing Bettye Fulford in her claim for palimony and had followed that with an announcement that as Fulford was pregnant, Daly and his advisers had until Friday, 24 January to reach a settlement or face a lawsuit. (John and Bettye would even meet up that week in Palm Springs. 'We talked,' Daly said. 'I wanted to hear it from her face to face. I'm just really upset that it didn't take her long to go to Mitchelson.')

With the media clamouring for the inside track on the demise of his relationship, Daly took the unusual step of setting the record straight on his former fiancée, maintaining that ever since the PGA win Fulford had become a markedly different person to the one with whom he had once shared the misery of schlepping around on the Hogan Tour. 'It's sad. It's hard to believe that someone could be that crooked, that mean,' he said. 'It makes me look stupid. Here I go with this girl for one and a half years and I don't know how old she is or that she has a kid . . . It's pretty obvious she was out for my money.' He also added that if Fulford's child was his, he would fight her for custody because 'I don't feel Bettye is capable of caring for it'. When Mitchelson learned of Daly's outburst, he was taken aback. He was used to clients on either side of such contests keeping their opinions to themselves, unburdening only if it got to court. Yet here was John Daly mouthing off like he didn't care if the whole world was listening. 'We'll just have to accommodate him with a lawsuit,' Mitchelson said. 'He's obviously out of control.'

The Friday deadline passed without any agreement being reached. After being granted an extra few days to consider their position, Daly and his Memphis-based lawyer Charles Hill decided to reject the settlement offer and await Mitchelson's next move. With no sign of any offer being made by Hill on Daly's behalf, Bettye Fulford's lawsuit was duly filed on 29 January in Shelby County Court, Tennessee. The action sought a million dollars in damages, in addition to child support and the recovery of her legal fees, and it came as no great shock to the defendant. Indeed, a greater surprise to Daly was the decision that week to honour him with the Tennessee Sports Hall of Fame's Professional Athlete of the Year award – this despite a wholesale lack of professionalism in his game over recent weeks and an absence of any passing resemblance to what could realistically be termed an 'athlete'. Still, it was another gong to show the folks back in Dardanelle and further proof that he was really going places.

Promoters, too, were still keen on selling their events with Daly as the main box-office draw. Whatever anyone thought of his boorish behaviour and his reputation for hell-raising, he still sold tickets. Australia was a case in point. Daly had accepted a gilt-edged opportunity to play in two events there. It was a win–win situation. All his expenses would be taken care of and he would also be paid to play. Appearance fees are outlawed on the US PGA Tour, but if a player accepts an invitation to go and play an event on a different tour then he is free to bank whatever fee the promoters choose to offer them.

At the first event, the Australian Skins Game at Port Douglas, Daly led the way, bagging $69,000 in a strong showing. The following week, at the Australian Masters on Melbourne's Huntingdale course, he was less successful. Groggy after a night on the tiles and irked by the snail-like pace of the players ahead, Daly played out a round littered with mistakes and when his ball disappeared up a tree at the par-five 14th and failed to come back down, he gave up trying. Two holes later, he would even ask his manager to call the airport and see if he could book some seats on the next flight back to the States. With an eight-over-par 81, Daly trudged wearily back to the scorer's hut, checked his scorecard and then left without signing it. The penalty, again, was disqualification. As usual, he was unrepentant. 'I just haven't played well anywhere overseas,' he explained later, apparently forgetting the success he'd enjoyed on the Sunshine Tour. 'You always want to play well in different countries, and the fans here have been supporting me even when I've been playing bad. I'm just ready to get home and get back into rhythm.' Through their spokesman Frank Williams, the organisers of the event, International Management Group, later confirmed that despite his disqualification Daly would still receive his $35,000 appearance fee.

When Daly got back to the States, he received some news he had not been expecting: Bettye had dropped her legal action. It had transpired that state law in Tennessee did not recognise the notion of palimony. Keen to pursue the case, however, Fulford had moved back to Georgia and established residency there instead. The fight would continue.

Though they were noted, Daly's abrupt exits from the competitions in Jamaica and Australia were not really the concern of the PGA. Their view was that as long as it wasn't done on their doorstep, it was fine. Increasingly, though, there were several warning signs that the new PGA champion, who had already complained of 'burnout' in Jamaica, was beginning to feel the claustrophobia of celebrity. Some commentators had even started to call him 'Long Gone Daly', implying that his game and his brain were in danger of meltdown.

Sure enough, Daly soon found that whatever he said would always be heard by someone somewhere. During a live TV interview with Gary McCord, Daly claimed he 'couldn't give a shit' what people thought about him. It was an innocent aside from a man who used the word like others use 'please' and 'thank you', but at the office of the PGA Tour commissioner, Deane Beman, it went down like a lead balloon encased in a deep-sea diver's outfit. Indeed, after receiving a handful of letters of complaint about his on-air obscenity, Beman cautioned Daly as to his future conduct.

There was further evidence of the strain Daly was feeling at the Players' Championship at the PGA's HQ course in Ponte Vedra, Florida. For three days he battled a mysterious body rash, a problem that was compounded when he forgot to bring his prescription pills with him for the first round. According to Daly, there was only one reason why he was suffering – stress. 'My dermatologist said he'd never seen a 25-year-old so stressed out,' said Daly, who added that the rash 'is driving me nuts. I shouldn't scratch it, but man, I have to. It feels good.' (As a variety of reporters noted, it gave an entirely new meaning to the term 'scratch golfer'.) By the final round Daly and his rash had played themselves out of the reckoning. Having started with a first-round 68, he had followed up with rounds of 75 and 78; when Sunday arrived, he found himself in the first pairing of the day with Mark Calcavecchia.

Daly and Calcavecchia were cast from the same mould. They were both straight-talking, no-nonsense guys, bullshit-free zones who hated to be kept waiting. With nobody in front of them and with nothing to play for, the pair decided to make things interesting by playing the fastest round they possibly could. Two hours and three minutes later, they were back in the locker room, Daly's 80 shading it by a shot. It had been a riot of a round and was, arguably, the best exercise Daly had taken since Steve Loy had had him running bleachers. Trouble was, the middle-aged lady marker who'd accompanied them hadn't been able to keep up. Breathlessly, she lodged a complaint, and again Deane Beman wasn't impressed. Golf, after all, was a serious business, and as he had already given him a warning that week he decreed that Daly and Calcavecchia would be fined for their shenanigans and 'put on notice' for 'failure to exert their best effort'.

9. HAIL TO THE CHIEF

'I don't have a drink problem – except when I can't get one.'

Tom Waits

The first major of the year is the Masters. Held in the majestic surroundings of the Augusta National Golf Club, Georgia, it is arguably the most prestigious event in the golfing calendar during which players do battle to earn the right to wear the coveted green jacket. Now, there are fancy clubs, there are exclusive clubs, and then there is the Augusta National. You could say that at the old plant nursery brought to life by the imagination of Bobby Jones they have certain standards. Spectators, for instance, are not called fans; they are 'patrons'. There is no tournament sponsor, nor is there any advertising on or around the course. And you will never, officially, know the size of the winner's cheque. The organisers of the Masters would never think of revealing anything quite so vulgar. In fact, nothing is left to chance. The organisers control everything from the TV commercials (just four minutes of adverts during each hour of coverage) to who will and won't be able to work there. Take the case of Gary McCord. The PGA Senior pro was removed from his job as CBS analyst at the Masters when the powers that be at Augusta took a distinctly dim view of his on-air remark that the greens there were so fast they looked like they had been 'bikini-waxed'. Another comment, about there being 'body bags' over the back of

101

the notoriously difficult 17th, also failed to raise a chuckle in the National's committee rooms.

Tradition is a huge part of the Masters experience, and the weekly schedule of events never changes. Tuesday, for instance, is the day on which the reigning champion is invited back to host the champion's dinner. It is his right, and his alone, to choose the menu (a fact which prompted Daly to suggest that if he ever won it, 'it'd be no suits, no ties and it would be McDonald's'). Wednesday plays host to the par-three tournament, Thursday sees the ceremonial tee-off, and it's dinner time again on Sunday evening as the new champion gets to meet the members.

For as long as he could remember, John Daly had wanted to wear the green jacket, and now here he was, in the spring of 1992, on the verge of his first appearance at the Masters. Dressed in chocolate-brown shirt, beige slacks and white shoes, and with a cigarette dangling from his lips, Daly made his way to the practice ground in front of the famous colonial-style clubhouse. When he arrived, there was a star-studded line-up already warming up. There was Nick Faldo and Freddie Couples, Davis Love and Gary Player, all of them tinkering away as a hushed crowd of a couple of hundred fans watched on from the grandstand. As he took his place a spontaneous round of applause broke out; Daly, surprised that the normally reverential Masters crowd could behave in such a way, waved back in appreciation.

The driving range at Augusta is 270 yards long and players hit their balls towards the perpetually busy Washington Road, a thoroughfare which is protected only by a 50-foot-high fence and some tall trees beyond it. This had never before presented a problem for the organisers; nobody had ever cleared the fence. But with John Daly about to take his bow in the event, the Men of the Masters had tagged an extra fifteen feet on to the fence, just in case. Although Augusta officials would later insist that the raising of the fence had nothing to do with Daly's impending visit, the fans and the man himself took it as a challenge. Instead of taking out the wedge and limbering up with a few gentle pitch shots, as most professionals do, Daly whipped his new Killer Whale driver out of his bag like a gunslinger on the draw and proceeded to batter a ball straight over the fence; it clattered into the branches of the trees guarding the traffic on Washington Road. It was a carry of over 290 yards, and the only thing that prevented a potential pile-up was the giant pines at the end of the range. With tumultuous applause ringing in his ears, Daly left the range to begin his practice round with Fuzzy Zoeller, claiming, 'I did it for the fans.'

As usual, Daly and Zoeller were on good form, their constant wisecracking and good-natured ribbing keeping the large galleries entertained. But as they turned for home at the 10th tee, a small man brandishing some papers slipped under the ropes and asked Daly if he was John Daly of Cordova, Memphis. Daly nodded, and the man – 'a little weasel', according to Daly – handed the papers over. It was a paternity suit from Bettye Fulford. Like women members, littering is forbidden at the Augusta National, so rather than lose his cool Daly simply handed the papers to Rita and told him to stick them in his golf bag. 'For all I knew,' he said later, 'it was a love letter.'

The suit, filed the previous day in Bibb County Superior Court, requested punitive damages 'in amount sufficient to deter the defendant from similar conduct', and sought monthly support money for their soon-to-be-born child, recovery of medical and 'lying in' expenses incurred as a result of the pregnancy, and recovery of all damages caused by the 'defendant's breach of his promise to marry' and the 'defendant's negligence'. Bizarrely, it also alleged that Daly's sudden success in his golf career was largely due to the encouragement and motivation Fulford had provided.

Unfazed, Daly finished his round and later told reporters that try as she might there was little Bettye could now do to wreck his first trip to Augusta. 'It's no big thing,' he insisted. 'This is Masters week, and I'm not going to worry about that.' After a strange day even by his extraordinary standards, Daly thought about what his first competitive round at the Masters would hold and prepared for it in time-honoured tradition: he disappeared downtown to Broad Street and to the Discotheque Lounge, Augusta's premier strip club.

By the end of the week, after a final round of 68 had secured him nineteenth place in his Masters debut, it had occurred to Daly that as Bettye was now back living in Georgia it would be foolish not to hook up and try to have a civil conversation without any lawyers at hand twisting things this way and that. When they eventually met, all the old feelings Daly had held for Bettye came flooding back. He knew he still loved her, even though she had lied repeatedly, and came to accept her explanation that the only reason she had kept so many things from him was because she didn't want to lose him. By the end of their meeting the couple were laughing and joking, recalling those long days on the road with the Hogan Tour when they would squabble about what tape to put on the stereo. It was as if nothing had happened.

Daly hatched a plan. He had been invited to go to Italy to play in the Lancia Martini Italian Open in Monticello and he wanted Bettye to go with him. Perhaps they could take in Venice beforehand, he suggested. The relationship with Paulette, fun though it was, had foundered, and Daly had been thinking more and more about Bettye and the baby. Before they left, Bettye told Daly she was dropping her legal action. If they were going to make a go of this relationship they needed to start with a clean slate, and that meant no more lies and no more lawyers.

When they arrived in Monticello, the couple had already enjoyed a 'wonderful, romantic vacation' in Venice complete with obligatory gondola ride through the canals. After a first-round 72, a cheery Daly spoke to reporters eager to get his reaction to his first appearance on the European Tour. But Daly had other, more important matters he wanted to talk about. He wanted to go on record saying that after all the deception, the endless fighting and the litigation, he and Bettye, now eight months pregnant, were very much an item again. Cue double takes all round the press room. 'We would love to marry, but I have been on the road for several weeks and I have a busy schedule throughout May,' explained Daly, who also claimed that their recent differences were merely the result of communication problems between their respective legal teams. 'We have not set any date for the marriage, but we want to marry.' For someone who had cancelled his wedding just six months earlier for fear of the publicity it would attract, it was, perhaps, not the wisest move Daly had ever made. But he was happy, and he wanted the whole wide world to know about it.

From palimony to matrimony in four short months. Only in the soap opera of Daly's life could such a preposterous plot line exist. Not even the *Dallas* scriptwriters, who famously brought Bobby Ewing back to life in 1986 and explained it away by insisting that an entire series had actually been a dream sequence, could have conjured up something quite so ridiculous.

Having begun in the most unlikely of circumstances, John and Bettye's Italian adventure concluded on an equally surreal note. In an interview with his local newspaper, the *Orlando Sentinel Tribune*, Daly's fellow PGA Tour pro Mark O'Meara recalled returning to the players' hotel after his final round at the Italian Open to find Daly with some unexpected company. 'I got back from the course on Sunday,' said O'Meara, 'and he's sitting in the lobby of the hotel having a beer with Sylvester Stallone.' A year earlier John Daly was the rookie pro trying to keep afloat in the choppy waters of the PGA Tour; now it was instant recognition wherever he ventured. His life had become one implausible merry-go-round of pro-ams with presidents and beers with Rocky Balboa. Sooner or later, he would want to get off.

Friday, 8 May 1992 was the day Bettye Fulford finally became Bettye Daly. It had been a long, rocky road to marriage but they'd finally made it. Rather than a roll-on, roll-off ceremony in Las Vegas, Daly had opted for the home comforts of his parents' house in Dardanelle. They had the minister come over, Lou put some food on, and everyone had a good drink – except Bettye of course. With the birth of their child imminent and Daly becoming increasingly anxious at the prospect of becoming a father ('I'm scared to death of being a father; I don't know much about being one; I know my dad wanted to hit me about a hundred thousand times'), the newlyweds were also considering a move away from Memphis. As part of their new life together, the Dalys had agreed that they needed to get away from Cordova and Chickasaw and find some seclusion. Bettye asked John where he would like to live, and John, recalling how taken he'd been with Colorado when he'd played there in the International, suggested Castle Rock.

Daly didn't have to wait long to become a dad. On 10 June Bettye gave birth to a six-pound baby girl, Shynah (pronounced 'Shine-uh', as in black eye), at the Baptist Memorial Hospital East, Memphis. The couple had arrived at the name when they were driving back from a tournament out west one night and Daly had spotted a shooting star, a shiner. Hours after the birth, as Bettye rested in her hospital room, Daly strode into his living room and lobbed a two-inch-thick wad of hundred-dollar bills on to the table. Liar's poker was the game, $100 a hand the stakes. Joining Daly at the table were Fuzzy Zoeller and two of his buddies, while Daly invited two of his closest friends along: cigarettes and alcohol. According to Don Cline, a spectator that night, it was a good night for the new father. 'Best I remember.

John won a lot of money. He's got a pretty good poker face. Other than mine, maybe the best I've seen.'

With his paternity leave over, Daly returned to action at a charity event, coincidentally in Castle Rock, which pitted him against another big-hitter, the in-form Davis Love III. The exhibition, billed as 'Thunder in the Pines', saw Daly in relaxed mood. It had been ten months since he had first appeared at Castle Pines, and he had returned to find that the Colorado fans loved him more than ever. On the practice tee, a small boy asked him about his titanium-shafted driver, and Daly ushered the kid forward. 'Come on out here and hit it,' he said. On his second attempt, eleven-year-old Tim Liley unleashed a 200-yard drive that bounded down the fairway. Daly was impressed. 'Take the driver,' he said, handing the club to the boy, 'it's yours.' The kid left with a new club in his hand and a huge smile on his face.

During the day, Daly spotted a house he really liked. It was situated up in the woods and it overlooked the 15th green, five bedrooms and half a million dollars of proper luxury, the kind of pad a successful person like him should be living in. Within weeks, it would become the Dalys' family home.

As Daly and Greg Rita left Denver the Monday night after the charity event, they stopped off for a few beers as they waited for their overnight flight to Newark to leave Stapleton Airport. It was the Continental Airlines 12.50 a.m. flight, and they were heading for Rye, New York, for the Buick Classic at Westchester Country Club. Daly was nervous, but then he always was when he had to fly somewhere. A few Miller Lites would sort him out. When their flight was finally called and Daly and Rita boarded the aircraft, they found that their first-class seats had been taken. Daly asked one of the flight attendants for two adjacent seats, but got no joy. Then, when Rita asked the same attendant for some assistance in storing a carry-on bag, the stewardess said she couldn't lift it because she had a bad back. As the flight prepared to leave, the attendant lifted the lever and closed the weighty cabin door. It was too much of a temptation for Daly. 'If you've got a bad back,' he shouted, 'you shouldn't be closing that door.' Irritated, the attendant hit back. 'That's when she said to me, "Would you like to get off this airplane?" ' Daly explained. 'Rather than cause a scene, I said, "Yes, we would." '

The following day, Daly withdrew from the Buick Classic explaining that he couldn't now get to the Westchester Country

Club in time to fulfil his commitments. He also said that as he had played six straight weeks on tour he desperately needed some time with his wife and daughter. Trouble was, an official at the Buick Classic had been telling the press that the real reason Daly had been thrown off the plane was because he was drunk and unruly, and the papers had gone with it. Amid the claims and counter-claims, Continental Airlines also issued a statement through their spokesman, Dave Messing: 'The crew on Mr Daly's flight determined it would be in the best interest of the other customers as well as flight safety if Mr Daly and his travelling partner disembarked before takeoff.' When Daly read the statement and the papers' reports of the disturbance, he was furious. Sure, he had had 'a few beers', but he was certainly not drunk. 'That was just not what happened,' he insisted. 'We weren't being treated right by the stewardess so we just left the plane so as not to cause a scene. Hell, half the time I really was drunk on a plane nobody said a thing.'

Back at PGA HQ in Ponte Vedra, Deane Beman read the reports of Daly's latest brush with authority and made another note in his diary.

But the combination of Daly's much-publicised aviophobia and his new-found unpopularity among the nation's airlines wasn't a huge problem because on his return from Australia earlier in the year Daly had dropped by a car dealer in San Diego and splashed out $140,000 on a state-of-the-art American Eagle motor home, the idea being that, whenever possible, he and his brother Jamie would drive from one event to another and then sleep in it when he was done playing golf. It was a beast of a vehicle. Forty feet long, with two televisions, a satellite dish, telephone, washing machine and luxury kitchen, it was in effect a mobile hotel, but with the added bonus that if Daly happened to flip his lid one night he could tear it up safe in the knowledge that he wouldn't have to offer any apologies to anyone. Now he could just kick off his shoes at the end of the day, slump in his dime-store lounge chair and crack open a cold one without ever having to worry about what time he had to be downstairs for breakfast. 'I relax back there on the bus. I don't have to worry,' he said with a beaming smile. 'The bus pulls over in campgrounds and we cook our own meals. I can drink beer. We just sit there. It's private.' Private, that is, until someone recognised the GRIP IT AND RIP IT slogan splashed on the side.

It was better that Jamie did the driving. In the weeks since the birth of Shynah, Daly's form had been shocking (four successive cuts missed, including one at the US Open at Pebble Beach) and he was feeling down. To the casual observer it must have appeared that all the sleepless nights of fatherhood were catching up with him, but according to Bettye it was a by-product of a greater and altogether more sinister malaise. One afternoon, for example, Daly was out driving with Bettye and Shynah. It was quiet in the car, suspiciously quiet, and, as usual, John was driving like a man possessed. There was a red light ahead at a busy intersection. Bettye looked across at John and pointed it out, suggesting he might want to go easy. He ignored her, then put his foot to the floor. Bettye was petrified. She screamed at John to stop, but he didn't. Luckily, they made it through to the other side. Later, Bettye would recount the story to Rick Reilly from *Sports Illustrated*, suggesting, 'If that's not depressed, what is?'

It might have been the biggest, baddest motor home on the PGA Tour, but even Daly's beloved American Eagle couldn't drive to the United Kingdom. Daly flew to Scotland in July for his debut in the Open Championship, hosted at Muirfield by the Honourable Company of Edinburgh Golfers, a body with the same kind of attitude to women's rights as the Men of the Masters.

It was Daly's first visit to Britain, and it was also the first taste the British media had enjoyed of Daly. Predictably, the tabloids went into overdrive. Chief culprit was the *Sun*. On the Tuesday prior to the beginning of the tournament, they carried a double-page interview with Daly topped off with the headline I'M NO WILD MAN BUT IF I WIN I'LL GET SLOBBERING DRUNK. Imagine Tiger Woods or Ernie Els saying that today? Daly's story was perfect for a newspaper obsessed with celebrity excess, and in his interview with John Roberts Daly gave them everything they wanted, from tales of adolescent drinking to the perils of living in the limelight. 'Maybe winning the US PGA happened too fast,' he reflected. 'I wasn't ready for it – my life has become a soap opera. If I'm seen in a bar, the next day people say, "Hey, John Daly was drunk again last night." It hurts me that you can't do anything about the criticism. If I have one beer, ten beers or just a Diet Coke, people still have a go at me.'

In high winds, Daly laboured in his first links experience. It was hardly surprising. For one, links golf is an entirely different game to the one he was used to. Played on coastal courses invariably in gale-force conditions, and with undulating greens unlike anything else in the world, it requires a certain finesse and a good deal more imagination than the target golf of the American PGA Tour. For someone like Daly, who admitted that he wasn't really prepared for the event in the first place, it was a totally new and unpleasant experience. He made the cut – an achievement in itself – but carded an 80 and a 75 in his final rounds to finish last. Afterwards he concluded that it was touch and go whether he would ever return to contest the Open. 'These conditions definitely do not suit my game. We play in some wind, but you have to change to keep the ball real low over here,' he said. 'I really don't know about playing over here next year . . . But it would be nice to come back and conquer this one day. Andre Agassi didn't like Wimbledon when he first came over, but now he loves it.'

In mid-August, on the eve of defending his PGA crown at the Bellerive Country Club in St Louis, Missouri, the press again found Daly in reflective mood. 'All the stuff I've gone through this last year makes it seem like I've been out here for ten years,' he said. 'But when I actually think about the golf tournament, it seems like it happened yesterday.' And in combative mood, too. 'Some reporters or newspapers haven't written the facts about some of the things I've said. Some of the things I've said in a positive way have been turned around and made me look bad. That's been the hardest thing to deal with.' When asked to elaborate, all Daly would say was, 'I don't want to get into it. I'd be here for a while.' If the idea was to persuade the press pack to lay off, it was a curious strategy.

Clearly there were many issues Daly needed to get off his chest, and when Jim Nantz of CBS taped an interview with him on the Friday of the tournament, it was surprising just how many grudges he was harbouring. The piece, which aired on Saturday, was as far removed from the cosy chitchats that usually pass for golf interviews as they come, Daly denouncing ABC's Brent Musburger as 'one of the worst announcers I've ever seen in golf', asking golf writers to examine their own lifestyles before commenting on his, and then insisting that as the whole Continental Airlines story had been stirred up by an official at the Buick Classic he would never be buying a Buick car again. Concerned that Daly's remarks could be interpreted as those of his employer, Nantz signed off the feature by saying that Daly was merely expressing his own opinions and that they were 'not necessarily shared by us at CBS Sports'. It was an understandable caveat, designed to placate not just the PGA but Buick, who happened to be the title sponsor of four tour events and one of their biggest network advertisers too.

Nantz might have managed to extricate CBS from a potentially uncomfortable situation, but Daly was treading on dangerous ground. There had been ample time for him to learn the basics of media management, but then John Daly never was one for learning. There was at least one person willing to vouch for him: Bettye insisted that since the birth of his daughter John was a new man, even if a wealth of evidence suggested otherwise. 'Fatherhood has made a difference in him,' she argued, holding Shynah in a child seat. 'I think he's a lot more settled. I guess it's made him realise there are other things in life. He's very good with her. He wakes up at night and gives her bottles. He hasn't changed any diapers yet. I'm still working on that.'

Bettye should have helped him work on his golf game, too. Daly's defence of his title was an embarrassment. He finished at twenty over par, which left him ahead of just three players in the final standings (ironically, his title was taken from him by the man whose caddie he had used at Crooked Stick, Nick Price). Moreover, his inability to mount anything like a respectable challenge at Bellerive, not to mention the two months of dreadful form that had preceded it, gave further credence to the doubters who felt that Daly's fifteen minutes of fame had come and gone a year ago in Carmel. Nobody would come right out and say it, of course, but there was a growing feeling that Daly's PGA win had been an outrageous fluke, a one-off week during which every aspect of his game had come together and nobody else's had. It was understandable. Players had simply looked at the ludicrously large galleries that followed him, his multi-million-dollar endorsement deals and the amount of column inches the papers gave him and asked what, apart from winning one tournament, he had ever done to deserve such fame and fortune.

The thought must have crossed Daly's mind, too. Having all that money in the bank was great, but it couldn't buy the respect of his peers on the PGA Tour. He could only do that by winning golf tournaments. It was high time he began to justify the faith the likes of Wilson, Reebok and, perhaps most importantly, the fans had placed in him. So that autumn he practised with a rare diligence, taking full advantage of his proximity to Castle Pines GC and working on anything that could turn his fortunes around. Gradually, he began to see some results. He took fifth at the International on his new home course, then a twelfth place at the Canadian Open, and at the B.C. Open at Em Joie in late September, despite being seen sinking three six-packs of beer in town the night before the tournament (and walking away as if he had been drinking water), Daly's golf was a revelation. Making judicious use of his driver, he made just one bogey over the 72 holes and none in his last 56. In the last three rounds he hit 46 of 54 greens in regulation, and 31 of 39 fairways, returning rounds of 67–66–67–66 for a six-shot victory over joint runners-up Ken Green, Jay Haas, Joel Edwards and Nolan Henke. It was an irrepressible performance, best summed up by Green: 'John just whomped us.' In addition to a winner's cheque for $144,000, Daly also became the first player on the PGA Tour since Corey Pavin in 1985 to win tournaments in each of his first two years.

It was a vital victory, and one that provided a perfect riposte for those in the game who doubted his talent. 'I don't think anybody thought I could win one again,' he said. 'I guess this shuts some mouths up. I wanted to prove something. I don't care what anybody says. The first tournament is not the hardest to win. The second one is.' Some years later, Daly would reveal that prior to every round at En-Joie he had sat in the locker room and helped himself to a morning tipple, just to take the edge off. 'It was so cold that I never went to the driving range all week,' he recalled. 'I sat in the locker room with a nice buzz before I went out. Took out a couple of clubs, swung a little, and went out.'

Daly kicked back at his house in the Rockies. With his bank balance swollen by the bonuses from the win at the B.C. Open, he decided to pass on most of the end-of-year cash bonanzas and spend some time at home with his wife and baby. Deep down, though, he missed the wild nights with the Chickasaw guys. He was, after all, still only 26 years old, and here he was living the life of a recluse, stuck up in the mountains, with a baby crying and his wife giving him grief about getting some professional help for his drinking.

But it was nearly Christmas, and that meant parties. On 19 December, the Dalys threw a bash for a dozen friends. His brother Jamie showed up with his new date in tow, and one of John's new celebrity pals, Dan Hampton, the former lineman of the Chicago Bears, made it too with his girlfriend Julie. Everyone was having a great time. Daly was holding court on the pool table, Jamie was showing off his new girl, and the booze was flowing. This was more like it.

But Bettye was suspiciously quiet. She had taken an instant dislike to Hampton's girlfriend and had become convinced that she was flirting with her husband. She was used to women being friendly with John – he was a millionaire sportsman, after all – but this friendly? It was too much for Bettye. She exploded, telling Hampton to keep his girlfriend under control before turning her attention to Julie and screaming, 'This is my house!' Scared for her own safety, Julie ran upstairs with Hampton in pursuit. Then Daly, who had been drinking heavily as well, lost it. 'Slow down there!' he screamed. 'We're all havin' a good time!' Not surprisingly, Bettye disagreed. It wasn't what Daly wanted to hear. With the age-old rage taking over, Daly flipped out, obliterating his house like it was a hotel room in South Africa. He smashed windows, pictures, and the trophy case housing his clubs from Crooked Stick. He even took out the 57-inch television set. (The following year, Daly would recount the story in *Sports Illustrated*. 'Remember when Richard Pryor said he killed his car?' he said. 'Well, I killed my house.') Bettye grabbed Shynah and hid in a closet. When Daly was done, he jumped in his car and drove back to Arkansas, his hands still bleeding (Denver to Dardanelle, incidentally, is a journey of over a thousand miles).

Later that night the police turned up at Daly's house. Somebody had heard the commotion and called 911. Bettye refused to press any charges, but under Colorado state law police are required to do so at virtually every scene of domestic violence. Daly was a wanted man, and back in Arkansas he knew he had to go home, regardless of the consequences. He had spoken to Bettye and she still wanted him to come back and celebrate their first Christmas together as a family; the police, too, wanted him back, advising him that if he did not return to Colorado to be arrested and charged voluntarily then a warrant would be issued in due course. After one last drink with his old buddie Blake Allison at Hooters in Little Rock, Daly drove back to face the music.

The Colorado police were pinning their case on the fact that in the arrest affidavit Bettye had told officers that she had been thrown against the wall and had had her hair pulled during the fracas, even though it was an accusation Daly vehemently denied. 'I know I did a lot of things wrong, I destroyed my house, but I never hit my wife,' he maintained. 'I knew it, Donnie [Crabtree] knew it, and everybody at the party in Colorado knew it as well.' Daly pleaded not guilty to the misdemeanour charges of battery and harassment and posted a $1,000 bond. Then, in a statement issued through her lawyer, W. Carl Reynolds, and John's lawyer, Steven Frei, Bettye claimed 'I was not struck or physically injured in the incident. I neither reported the incident nor requested the sheriff's department to intervene.' In turn, Daly went on record saying that the couple had every intention of staying together and working through this problem. But Bettye's statement failed to head off the action. The Douglas County district attorney's office, which was responsible for the prosecution, confirmed that it was not in the habit of dropping charges in domestic violence cases, even if the victims refused to co-operate. A pre-trial conference was scheduled for 11 January 1993.

Deane Beman had had a gutful of John Daly. If he wasn't swearing on TV or trashing the sponsors he was giving the media the finger and larking around on the course. Now, just as Beman thought he could slip away from the circus of the tour and enjoy a quiet Christmas, the kid from the sticks had been and gone and done it again. Daly's liberty was in the hands of the judiciary, but his golfing future was very much in the hands of the commissioner.

Despite an enviable record as an amateur golfer and four tour wins as a professional, Beman's real talent lay in administration, and it wasn't until he assumed the role of PGA Tour commissioner in 1974 that he finally began to make a real impact on the modern game. In the eighteen years since he'd taken over, Beman had presided over unprecedented growth in the tour. Having courted corporate sponsors and the world's media, he had helped mould it into one of the most successful sporting enterprises in the world. He had even managed to make the tour a non-tax-paying organisation. Moreover, he had fostered a strong sense of community and sportsmanship among the players; problems were dealt with in-house, and everybody pulled for one another. Make no mistake, the PGA Tour was Beman's baby, and there was no way he was going to let some drunk from Arkansas blacken its name.

With Daly, he had two options. He could fine and suspend him, then leave him to rot, or he could deal with him in a manner that not only got Daly off his back for a while but made the PGA look like the compassionate body he liked to think it was. As the son of a public relations guru, not to mention the head of an organisation with revenues running into the hundreds of millions, it was an easy decision to make. Beman called Daly and told him how things were going to be.

On 29 December, Daly issued a statement through the PGA: 'I deeply regret the incident at my home over the holidays. I realise the importance of seeking professional help and therefore I will pursue counselling immediately for an alcohol-related problem. I will check into an alcohol rehabilitation facility and will return to tournament play only when I am comfortable my life is in order.' The statement concluded with a quote from Beman himself: 'We wish John all the best in solving what is clearly a difficult situation for him and his family, and we hope that a successful rehabilitation will lead to a return to the Tour.' The wording made it appear as though it was Daly's decision; the fact that it had been issued through the PGA Tour made the subtext all too clear. Get yourself help, John, or you're finished.

10. I SEE GOD COMING DOWN THE ROAD

'It's like being in a public shithouse, and everybody's writing on the wall.'

Kris Kristofferson on the problems of fame

Generally speaking, the Christmas holiday period is a quiet time for the world's news gatherers. Television channels curtail their bulletins and allow their star presenters some time off, cancelling the leave of unfamiliar understudies and dragging them in front of the cameras instead. Newspapers, meanwhile, shrink to a fraction of their normal size, their hands tied by a wholesale absence of any story worth printing. Even serial killers stay at home at Christmas, it seems. But when the Daly story fell into their laps it was as if all their Christmases had come at once. Yet again the *Sun* led the way with their article entitled WILD JOHN'S BATTLE TO BEAT THE BOOZE, a piece by John Roberts that argued 'Big John Daly's wild fling as golf's Wild Thing is over.' Elsewhere, *People* magazine ran with IN THE ROUGH, suggesting that golf's longest hitter was already on the way to becoming its biggest problem, while Tom Callahan in the *Washington Post* suggested that Daly was 'temporarily off the circuit that laughed so easily at the sight of him, that didn't care enough to cry'.

As news of Daly's decision reverberated around the golf world, the reaction, by and large, was one of approval. It had been one of the worst-kept secrets in golf that he had a problem with alcohol but his resolve to make amends, regardless of whether it was prompted by the PGA or not, was admirable. Fuzzy Zoeller, Daly's closest ally on tour, was shocked by the developments but hardly surprised. After showing Daly how to play the PGA game in his first years on the circuit, he had watched as his young charge had been buried by an avalanche of money and publicity. 'I'm glad to see he's admitted he has a problem,' he said. 'If there's anything I can do for him, I will. We need John out here. He's a breath of fresh air.' Even Jack Nicklaus conceded it was a prudent move for Daly. 'It is the best thing for him,' he said. 'He obviously must need help, and I'm glad he's taking that step.'

While the positive response from his PGA colleagues was welcome, it was the reaction of his corporate backers that most concerned Daly. If they decided his reputation for hell-raising represented too much of a threat to the good name of their businesses, they could pull the rug from under his feet in an instant. If that happened, and the likes of Wilson and Reebok were well within their rights to cancel his contract, it would spell yet further trouble for Daly. After all, no future backer would want to touch tarnished goods, would they? Crucially, though, none of his sponsors seemed unduly concerned by the turn of events. Of course they had seen what had happened, but Daly's desire to deal with his addiction in an upfront and responsible manner seemed to have dissuaded them from taking any action. A typical response came from Dick Lyons, vice president of Wilson Sporting Goods: 'We don't condone what happened but you don't cut somebody loose over something like this.'

Early in the new year of 1993, Daly gathered some things together and began the journey to the Sierra Tucson treatment centre in Arizona. It was a long, lonely journey. He didn't really want to go to rehab, but he'd been left with no other option. On the way he had the space and the time to think about what had become of a life that had seemed to be progressing so well. Despite the favourable reception to his statement, he was still angered by reports of what had happened at his house the previous month. It was bad enough having the media report that he was drunk when the incident on the Continental aeroplane took place, but now, not only was he a drinker, he was a wife-beater as well. What was the point in carrying on? he thought. He was off the tour and facing up to two years in jail for something he and his supposed victim, Bettye, had repeatedly claimed didn't happen. No matter what he said, people were always going to believe the TV or the papers before they believed him.

A few miles out of Denver, he picked up the car phone and called Donnie Crabtree, his friend from the first grade, and put his foot to the floor. As the speedometer climbed ever higher, Daly saw the edge of a cliff in the distance and pointed the car in the direction of the guard rail. He told Donnie that the accusation that he had attacked Bettye was the final straw and that he was going to drive over the edge. Crabtree begged him to pull over. 'You didn't do anything but get drunk and destroy your house,' he insisted. 'You never laid a hand on her, we've got witnesses to that, so whatever you're thinking of doing, don't do it.' A 30-minute conversation ensued during which Crabtree managed to talk Daly around by stressing all the things he had to live for, like Shynah and Bettye, his mum and his dad. Later, Daly would recall the incident in an interview with Bill Blighton in the *Mail on Sunday*. 'I just wanted to float through the air and end everything in a fiery ball. I had had enough and I couldn't face living any more.'

Nestled in the foothills of the Santa Catalina Mountains near Tucson, the centre dedicated itself to the prevention and treatment of substance abuse and behavioural problems. According to their literature, it was a place where 'pain is met with compassion, fear is met with reassurance, and anger is met with understanding'. It was also a place, however, where Daly would receive a shock to his system unlike anything he had ever experienced.

When he walked through the door, all his preconceptions about rehab vanished. As he looked around him, instead of winos and wasters he found people from every socioeconomic background. Indeed, there was a saying in the recovery rooms: 'They come from Yale and they come from jail.' On entry, he was assigned to a detox ward for three days during which time staff plied him with vitamins, tranquillisers and fluids and helped drain every trace of alcohol from his system. It was about as much fun as a six-hour pro-am. He was then placed on a ten-day programme of activities which would help him deal with the cravings he would inevitably encounter. They would also teach him ways and means to counter that rage that all too often engulfed him. Whenever he felt down and the fury gripped him, the staff would give him a 'bataka', or giant foam club, and tell him to take it out on the foam furniture. It usually did the trick.

A key part of the programme was the presentation by Thomas 'Hollywood' Henderson, a former professional football player for the Dallas Cowboys who had frittered away his vast fortune on the kind of extracurricular activities that would have had Charlie Sheen hiding under the duvet. Henderson had acquired his nickname by virtue of this extravagant lifestyle, built on the foundations of the age-old A-list standards of cocaine, fast cars and faster women. Needless to say, his myriad addictions eventually ruined his career and his life, and having served 28 months for sexual battery and bribery charges Henderson emerged from his incarceration and dedicated his life to counselling addicts.

Though Daly was never really interested in drugs – he was purely a drinker – he listened intently to what Henderson had to say. He had read his autobiography *Out of Control* when he was a student at the University of Arkansas and it had stayed with him throughout his dramatic rise through the golfing ranks. 'It was the first book I picked up since I was a junior in high school,' he said. 'It really hit me.' Henderson, who would become John's personal rehabilitation sponsor, would tell Daly that recovery was not some one-off event that was completed as soon as they left the clinic, but the start of a lifetime journey.

With Daly doing as he was told, for once, and making real progress, he was surprised by a visit from his parents as he neared the end of his programme. They had some news for their baby: on the orders of his wife, Jim Daly had quit drinking too. During John's time in the clinic, Jim and Lou had sat down and worked through the whole blame and guilt thing. Was it their fault John was the way he was? Had they done enough to help him? And just what was it about the Dalys' genetic make-up that drew them all to drink? Jim's conclusion was sad, but true. 'I know I didn't set a very good example for my children,' he suggested. Later, John would pronounce himself 'proud as hell' of his old man's decision.

Daly emerged from Sierra Tucson looking like a man who needed a stiff drink. After three and a half weeks of in-patient care, he was clearly thinner and had managed as well to lose the excuse for a moustache he had been wearing. Within days, Daly received a call from Deane Beman's people. The commissioner wanted to see John as soon as possible and discuss a possible return to the

PGA Tour. They even sent a plane for him and flew him to HQ at Ponte Vedra, just so Beman could give Daly the once-over in person. It was agreed that if he felt up to it, Daly could play in the Phoenix Open the following week.

It was the kind of welcome news the game's promoters had been longing for. When Daly was in rehab he was no good to anyone, apart from himself, of course. The truth was that he was a cash cow whose box-office appeal was such that it had been estimated that over the course of a tournament his presence was worth an extra $500,000 in revenue from additional ticket and merchandise sales. Corey Pavin and Davis Love were great players and terrific guys, but they never got the punters parting with the dollars like John.

So on Tuesday, 26 January 1993, Daly began his long journey back to what passed for normality. His first duty when he arrived at the Phoenix Open was a 25-minute session in the media room with a pack of reporters keener than ever to hear what he had to say. With his hair trimmed to collar length, Daly looked almost respectable and seemed in good humour. Although he declined to answer any questions on the incident at his home in December, he spoke at length about the benefits of his treatment at Sierra Tucson and admitted that he now considered himself a member of Alcoholics Anonymous, even though that contravened the bit about anonymity. Significantly, he also blamed his condition on 'dysfunctional families . . . It starts with the mom and dad and it's generation after generation after generation. I'm putting a stop to it in the Daly generation.' It's unlikely that anyone in the Daly family tree had ever heard, let alone used, the phrase 'dysfunctional families' before John had sought help at Sierra Tucson. Now here he was sat in front of the world's media sounding like a fully qualified counsellor. Indeed, it was clear from the way he spoke about himself in the third person, as addicts (and sports stars) are wont to do, that rehab had perhaps had more of an effect on him than he had imagined. 'I'm starting to care about John Daly instead of other people,' he continued. 'If somebody offers me a drink I'll just say, "I'm not going to drink while I'm sober." I'll leave the table and go and have a Diet Coke.'

Diet Coke Daly's return to the tour was inauspicious – he missed the cut – but he had at least made those first tentative steps back on the road to recovery and had been welcomed back into the fold with open arms, although Tim Finchem, the deputy PGA

Tour commissioner, was quick to warn that only time would tell whether one treatment programme was sufficient. And though he had admitted to being a member of AA, Daly was not in fact following the accepted aftercare route of attending, say, five or six meetings each week. Instead, he had devised his own schedule, 'a real slow programme' which entailed making a meeting every couple of weeks. He had his reasons. 'How long can you sit and listen to somebody else's problems?' he asked. 'Can you see me all pumped up to play golf the next day in a tournament, and then some guy starts talking about how he got drunk and killed his best friend? I'd be too depressed to pick up a club. I've got my own programme.'

Part of that programme was finding means to distract himself from the very thought of drinking. First, Daly's cigarette consumption rose to three, sometimes four packs a day; he swapped his sixteen cans of beer a day for an equivalent amount of Diet Coke, and then, as many recovering alcoholics do, he began to crave sugar. With a compulsive personality like his, it was only a matter of time before he was waylaid by another addiction. Sure enough, as well as keeping track of his score, Greg Rita also had to keep a tally of Daly's M&Ms intake, noting that he was now up to 'six bags in a hole and a half'. Even Daly was concerned by the amount he was putting away. 'If I don't stop eating these goddamn things, I'm going to look like the Goodyear blimp,' he joked.

Still, with Henderson's 'don't drink while you're sober' mantra lodged in his head, Daly's recovery seemed to be on track. He had successfully managed to avoid any contact with alcohol and had even admitted to feeling sick whenever he smelt liquor on someone's breath. Surprisingly, Daly's preferred method of attending only the occasional Alcoholics Anonymous meeting also seemed to be helping, primarily because he was using virtually every press interview he gave as a kind of catharsis. Strange though it seemed, it actually made some kind of sense. Over the course of an average week, Daly's media commitments were such that he had far more opportunities to discuss his problems with journalists than with AA members.

On the golf course, however, he continued to find it tough. In the few months since his emergence from treatment, out of nine events entered his highest finish was a tie for twentieth, at the Honda Classic. All of which made his tie for third at the Masters in early April all the more remarkable. If Crooked Stick had been the Cinderella Story, a Daly victory at Augusta would have been the even less likely sequel, where Cinderella marries Hans Christian Andersen and gives birth to the Brothers Grimm. Everyone agreed that he played beautifully; it was one of those weeks when everything just clicked. On the final day, Daly almost made history by becoming the first player to make an albatross at the 555-yard 2nd hole. After a monstrous 375-yard drive, Daly hit a six-iron approach that pitched just inches to the left of the hole, kicked into the air, and pulled back to around a foot away. As Daly tapped in for an eagle, he turned to the crowd and joked, 'I pulled it a little.' Bernhard Langer took the title, but it was Daly's display that staggered the gentlemen of the press. Jaime Diaz of the *New York Times* argued that Daly had 'established beyond doubt that his exceptional length and underrated short game are ideally suited to Augusta National', before appending the crucial caveat, 'With added maturity and focus, he could eventually own several green jackets.' With his confidence restored, a rejuvenated Daly turned up at the MCI Heritage Golf Classic, shot a 79–75 and missed the cut.

Living in Colorado hadn't worked out as planned. The cooler climate in the Rockies meant that for three months every year Daly couldn't even practise, so he would just sit around, every now and then rowing with Bettye. After toying with the idea of moving to the desert climate of Phoenix, John and Bettye opted instead for Orlando, Florida, and a monster of a house in the area of Isleworth, just down the block from where the basketball superstar Shaquille O'Neal lived. Though he didn't say as much, the move to Florida was a last-ditch attempt to save his marriage. John and Bettye's relationship had been built around the accommodation of John's drinking; it was one of the few constants in their time together. But while the drunken John had been a handful, the sober one was an entirely different proposition, and the couple struggled to come to terms with Daly's new-found sobriety. Publicly, John still professed his love for Bettye and the support she had given him, but sooner or later he would have to concede that it was only his driver, and not his marriage, that was Kevlar-coated.

The dual strain of coping with a failing marriage and being without his favourite panacea, alcohol, was evident when Daly teed it up for his first round in the Kemper Open in mid-May. It was a tiresome round for Daly, and when he came home with a 77 he refused to sign his scorecard and was immediately disqualified. For once, however, it was an act of petulance that was almost understandable, given that in five days' time he would be up in court to answer the charges resulting from that ill-fated Christmas party. 'I shouldn't have been playing,' he later suggested. 'My mind wasn't on the tournament. My mind was going 500 different ways.'

One of which was back to beer. As the hearing grew ever closer, Daly met with his old friend Blake Allison and told him that he badly needed a beer. Conscious that Daly was showing all the signs of a relapse, Allison, who had admitted that business at his liquor store had plummeted since Daly gave up drinking, went on the offensive. 'If you do it,' he warned, 'I'll kill you.'

'Good,' snapped Daly. 'Kill me. Go ahead and kill me. 'Cause in five years I'd be dead anyway.'

Mercifully, Allison's plan worked and Daly didn't take that drink. Quite how long he could hold out, though, was another matter.

On Tuesday, 25 May, Daly attended Douglas County Court for the hearing. The maximum penalty awaiting Daly was a two-year prison sentence, but it was always unlikely that it would come to that, especially as he had undergone a course of treatment at rehab and shown a willingness to confront his alcohol problem. On the day, Daly pleaded guilty to charges of misdemeanour harassment as part of a plea bargain, while the original charge of third-degree assault was dropped. In return, Daly was sentenced to two years' probation and ordered to complete a programme on domestic violence. If he managed to stay out of trouble for two years, all charges would be cleared from his record. It was the best result he could have hoped for.

Although it was a weight off his shoulders, there were more pressing matters threatening to derail Daly. Having confided in Rick Ross, Daly had finally decided that there was no point staying with Bettye. Every day, it seemed, they were at each other's throats, arguing about the most ridiculous things imaginable then sitting around sulking like schoolkids. For everyone's sake, but especially for Shynah, it was best that they parted. And with the court case behind him and a resolve to start afresh, Daly also began to try to remedy the other main problem in his troubled life – his golf.

His first port of call was the tournament he missed in 1992 because of his dispute with Continental Airlines, the Buick Classic. After the debacle of the previous year, Daly was determined to make amends for that last-minute withdrawal, and though his golf was dreadful he did at least give the fans something to remember as they disappeared into the warm Westchester evening. Before he completed his second-round 82 (ten over par), Daly managed to snap not just his driver but his three-wood, too. For a while it was touch and go whether he would have enough clubs left to finish his round.

The following week he arrived at the US Open at Baltusrol in New Jersey, his confidence shattered and his game in pieces. Daly certainly wasn't one of the favourites to take the title, but there was a great deal of talk that week about whether the longest hitter in the game could achieve something nobody in the 72-year history of Baltusrol's Lower Course had ever managed before – reach the 630-yard 17th in two shots. As Daly made his way around the course, he noticed how everyone from the marshals and the volunteer staff to the players and the fans was nudging him as he walked past, asking if he was going to try to conquer the longest hole in championship golf. Initially he laughed it off, suggesting it was some silly sideshow, but there was no doubting it, the idea appealed enormously to him.

Daly told Rick Ross and Greg Rita that if he did nothing else that week, he was going to hit that green in two. He failed on day one, much to the disappointment of the thousands of fans who had lined the fairway. The next day he pulled out his custom-made driver from his bag. It was a new club that Wilson had made for him and it featured just seven degrees of loft, which meant that his tee shots could not only travel lower but further, too. His drive was perfect: 325 yards down the fairway and in prime position for a crack at the green. Faced with an uphill shot of some 300 yards, Daly took his one-iron and swung it so hard that he nearly fell over. As the ball left the clubface, the crowd, as one, tracked its progress as it screamed through the air. It looked good. It looked very good. Landing just short, the ball then bounced up on to the green and rolled fifteen yards beyond the hole. The crowd erupted. Even his playing partners Ian Woosnam and Payne Stewart applauded. Daly finished tied 33rd, but it mattered not. The Wild Thing had tamed the Baltusrol Beast.

* * *

On 18 July, divorce proceedings were instituted. Daly had just returned from the Open at Royal St George's (he tied for fourteenth) and had told Bettye that he was going back to Memphis. Although he had asked Bettye to leave their Isleworth home, there was little point in arguing because (a) she still needed somewhere for her and Shynah to live, and (b) when the divorce went through, it was a racing certainty she would get the house anyway, not to mention a more than generous cash settlement.

When young men split from long-term partners, they have a tendency to dust down their old address books and call up their ex-girlfriends, even though they may not have exchanged a single civil word with them since the day they broke up. For the most part, it is a decision borne out of some misplaced desire to prove that they have still got what it takes to attract the opposite sex, and typically the couple will exchange small talk until that vital snippet of information, whether they have a new partner, is revealed. If they have, well, it was nice speaking to you and have a nice life. If they haven't, well, maybe we should meet up some time, just for old times' sake. With his lawyers handling the divorce proceedings, Daly called Paulette Dean. She was surprised to hear from him. He told her that after everything they had been through it was finally over with Bettye and that it would be great if she could come down to Memphis to see him. Delighted, said Paulette.

The contrast between Bettye and Paulette couldn't have been more pronounced. Bettye was edgy, querulous and, as John had found to his peril, deceitful. Paulette, meanwhile, was upfront, honest and uncomplicated. She was easy to talk to and never hassled him like Bettye did. Perhaps more importantly, she was younger than John and was not heading into middle age, weighed down with the baggage of failed marriages. Seeing Paulette again was a tonic Daly badly needed.

A tonic, but not a curative. As the golf season drew to a close, Daly began to show worrying signs that he was becoming less interested in re-establishing himself as a force in the game and more concerned with getting himself into hot water with the PGA. During the St Jude Classic in late July, he grew tired of waiting to play at the 9th tee and proceeded to hit his tee-shot straight over the heads of scores of fans who were crossing the fairway some 200 yards away. Then, on 22 August, when Daly was holding a golf clinic at the Fred Meyer Challenge at Oregon Golf Club,

Portland, he turned around on the tee and fired a shot over the heads of more than five thousand ashen-faced spectators sat in a grandstand behind the 18th green. It was an insanely dangerous thing to do. Nobody was impressed, as fellow professional Jay Delsing explained. 'That Portland thing, it was not received well by the guys on tour. But in John's mind, he is so confident that he didn't think what might happen if he failed to hit the ball solidly ... He could have killed someone. He could actually have killed a whole row of people.' The madness continued at the Southern Open in Pine Mountain, Georgia. Daly reached the turn in a wretched 43 shots, and rather than carry on he simply walked off the course, jumped into his car and drove away, leaving everyone wondering where the hell he had gone.

With a mind seemingly intent on destruction, Daly resurfaced in St Andrews, Scotland, in mid-October to take part in the Alfred Dunhill Cup, an international team tournament. Despite everything, his country still needed him. Teamed with Fred Couples and Payne Stewart, and with Paulette by his side, it was Daly's first visit to the spiritual home of golf, and he soon found the fabled Old Course to his liking. There were no trees to catch his drives, there was a handful of reachable par-fours (for him at least), and he could blaze away with his Killer Whale driver all day long in the knowledge that if the rough coastal winds caught his ball and carried it away he could simply play it off the adjacent fairway. OK, so he wound up a few players by driving the 354-yard par-four 18th while they were still putting out, but nobody's safety was compromised.

By the end of the week, Daly had proved, much to the watching world's amazement, that he had what it took to be a successful team player, winning four of his five matches and helping the USA team to a 2–1 win over England in the final. His performance, coming on the back of the antics in Memphis and Portland, was a finger in the eye for those who had expressed doubts about his suitability, insisting that he was too self-obsessed and too preoccupied to make a difference. As John Daly left Scotland with a cheque for $200,000, he, and now everyone else, knew different.

11. YOU WILL BE LOVED AGAIN

'John's had his critics, but hell, even Jesus Christ had his critics.'

Jim Daly

Surprising though his performance at St Andrews had been, there was a postscript to his trip to the United Kingdom, an incident that suggested that even with Paulette there to support him Daly was still a significant way away from achieving the inner peace he and the PGA craved. Having helped his country to victory in the Alfred Dunhill Cup, Daly, with the inducement of a $50,000 appearance fee, headed south to the World Match Play Championship at the exclusive Wentworth West course in Virginia Water. In his pre-tournament press conference, he talked about how much he was looking forward to the end of his first year free from alcohol. Describing the past twelve months as 'horrible', he told reporters that he had been having a tough time of late and that he was just trying to make it through to 1994. 'My body is going through changes. One day I wake up in a great mood, the next it's terrible. I have more headaches than when I had a drink. I used to never get a cold, never feel pain. It's weird ... Only two months to go to get through the first year, and they say that's the toughest. I knew the toughest thing was going to be my putting. When I had a good buzz from drink or whatever I could putt real well.' It was an observation borne out by the PGA's official end-of-year statistics. While Daly remained at number one in the longest driving category, he was languishing at 171st in the putting division. Indeed, the extent of his putting troubles was apparent at Wentworth from as early as the opening hole of his first-round match against the Australian Steve Elkington. Faced with a five-foot putt, Daly rolled it past and was so disgusted with his effort that he lifted his putter and hurled it across the green with all the rhythm of an Olympic hammer thrower. No one was injured.

It was another juvenile tantrum in a season increasingly defined by the kind of car-crash golf that made great headlines for the papers but merely served to raise eyebrows in Ponte Vedra. Whereas once fans had paid to see Daly smite balls into a neighbouring state, now they were turning up just to see if he would actually complete a round without doing something stupid. The promoters didn't mind, though. As long as the fans still wanted to pay to see Daly, irrespective of which one turned up, they were happy.

The real problem for Daly was the PGA. The putter incident at Wentworth was comparatively minor (and, as it happened on the European Tour, not strictly the PGA's concern), but it was another indication that sooner or later Daly was going to do something that would not only damage the reputation of the PGA Tour but possibly the health of an innocent spectator as well. Predictably, the outgoing commissioner Deane Beman didn't have to wait too long before he was forced into action.

In early November 1993, Daly made the trip to the Hawaiian island of Maui for the Kapalua International. As one of the more glamorous locations for a made-for-television event, the quality of the field at Kapalua tended to be extremely high. The fact that there was also a huge pot of cash on offer also helped guarantee a better than average turnout. But Daly's divorce from Bettye, which was virtually settled, had been held up at the last moment when news of the out-of-court settlement his fellow tour pro Fred Couples had reached with his wife Deborah became public knowledge. Initially, the flamboyant Mrs Couples had wanted a reported $168,000 per month in alimony, but she eventually settled for $52,000 per month, a figure that was then reduced by an appeals court to $27,000. During the protracted negotiations, Couples' form had nose-dived, but when things were eventually finalised in October he returned to his old, congenial self almost overnight, and in the final three months of the year won a staggering $981,125. While Couples set about rebuilding his life and career, eventually remarrying in 1998, Deborah was less fortunate. Afflicted by chronic depression, she took her own life on 26 May 2001 by leaping seven storeys from the roof of a chapel in Los Angeles. She was 43.

The timing of the settlement of the Couples case couldn't have been worse for Daly. Just as they had seemed set to shake hands on a deal, along came the most high-profile precedent imaginable for Bettye's lawyers to get their teeth into. If anything, Bettye was in a stronger position than Deborah Couples had been. Like Daly, Couples had won a major, the 1992 Masters, and was one of the biggest earners on the PGA Tour. If his wife could walk away from their childless marriage with such a generous deal, there was no reason why Bettye, who also had Shynah as a bargaining tool, shouldn't do the same.

When Daly learned of the hold-up in the proceedings, he became agitated. He had wanted a swift end to their brief marriage so that he could start afresh in the new year, but now matters seemed set to drag on well into 1994. Of course, all these delays and deferments did nothing for his golf game, let alone his mental wellbeing. In the second round at the Kapalua International, Daly was rolling along nicely when he picked up round-wrecking double bogeys at seven, eight and ten. Despite the kind of run guaranteed to leave most folk reaching for a cut-throat razor, Daly picked himself up and gave himself a real shot of a birdie at eleven. He missed, and this time it was too much to take. Without a word to his caddie or his playing partners, Daly picked up his ball, tossed his putter on his bag and walked. And kept on walking. The result was immediate disqualification. 'I went back to my hotel with the shakes,' he would later explain. 'I was sweating. I nearly opened that fridge door and had a drink.'

It says a lot about a player when the shots they get genuinely upset about are the missed birdie putts, not any of the six in four holes they've just squandered. But after a year when Daly's name appeared in the press for all the wrong reasons, it was one misdemeanour too many for Beman. On the final day of the tournament, he summoned Daly for a meeting, before he could hop on a plane back to Memphis. As the two talked about Daly's latest breach of PGA regulations, Beman told him that while he appreciated he had perhaps more issues than most to deal with, there was absolutely no excuse for him walking out of a tournament in the middle of a round, and that after a similar incident at the Southern Open and his reckless behaviour at the St Jude Classic (which cost Daly an additional $30,000 fine) he was left with no option but to suspend him indefinitely from the PGA Tour. In a statement to the press, Beman explained that the suspension would apply to any PGA-related events for the remainder of 1993 and would continue for an undetermined time the following year.

While the suspension came as no real surprise to Daly or anyone else on tour, the punishment was unusual in that traditionally the PGA tended to keep in-house any disciplinary measures it took against players. In Daly's case, however, Beman argued that it was only fair because Daly's name had been used to publicise forthcoming PGA events he would now no longer be eligible to play in. Though the commissioner had finally scratched an itch that had been bothering him for some time, he told the press that Daly would be welcomed back to the tour in due course, providing he continued with his counselling and made strides to keep a lid on his temper. 'I care about him, I like him, but some of the things he does are unacceptable,' Beman added. 'On the one hand we're not going to permit him to play, but on the other hand we are going to support him. He can be a very positive force for golf. It's a difficult time for him. In the final analysis, John has to be responsible for his own actions and I have to do what I have to do.'

Daly's suspension applied only to PGA events, so he was still free to play in other competitions. He certainly didn't feel like it, but he nevertheless fulfilled some prior commitments in a couple of events in Mexico. After an exhibition at the Club de Golf Chapultepec near Mexico City, Daly gave his first official response to the suspension laid down by Beman and took the opportunity to deny reports that he had only been disciplined because he had started drinking again. 'That's the thing I want to stress the most, that I am not drinking again,' he insisted. 'I'll go get tested . . . if people want me to do that.' He added that the suspension would give him more time to spend with Shynah and allow him the freedom, away from the prying eyes of tour officials and the media, to sit back and think about just what he needed to do with his life. 'This year, I haven't been able to worry about golf,' he said. 'It's been drinking, M&Ms, burgers, personal problems . . . It's almost behind me.'

On their return, John and Paulette ventured west to her home town, Palm Springs in California. Amid the publicity of his suspension and his divorce proceedings, it had occurred to Daly that what he really needed was a new base to get away from everything, and Palm Springs seemed perfect. It was warm all year round, there were golf courses everywhere you looked, and, most importantly, it was almost as far away from Bettye as he could get. Taken with the area around Mission Hills Country Club, Daly pulled out his chequebook and bought himself a new apartment, a mere par-four away from the historic golf club. It was his third home in just seven months.

Golf coaches the world over have long advocated the benefits of positive swing thoughts, those little kick-starts every player needs to get his game going. It's a process designed to mould the swing into a reliable, consistent action that won't crumble under pressure. In the mid-1980s, Nick Faldo, arguably the greatest swing meddler of the modern game, enlisted the help of David Leadbetter to help remodel his swing. It was a major rebuilding job; some even thought he would have to apply for planning permission before work commenced. Faldo was concerned that his career, which by most players' standards was already extremely successful, was being hindered by his swing. Above all, what he needed was consistency, and Leadbetter, a journeyman pro on the Sunshine Tour who'd given up touring in favour of coaching, was the man to help him find it.

To the average club golfer, Faldo's swing appeared neat enough. It was good-looking, rhythmic and free-flowing, but it contained several serious flaws that Faldo knew needed ironing out if he was ever to fulfil his massive potential. Leadbetter did the trick. Countless titles and, more importantly, six majors came his way as Faldo matured into the greatest British golfer of the modern era. When he was inducted into the World Golf Hall of Fame he credited Leadbetter for the crucial part he had played in his success.

Apart from his ad hoc sessions with Rick Ross, John Daly had never had a coach, let alone a 'swing doctor'. On the face of it, though, his approach to the golf swing was an eminently sensible one, reasoning that the longer you stand over the ball, switching your gaze from ball to target and back again, the more time there is for the more destructive notions to invade the subconscious.

And in the case of Daly, a man who has been tormented by more demons than most, it was a potentially disastrous scenario. But occasionally a golfer's problems go beyond mere swing mechanics, and if the Leadbetters of this world can't fix your swing then maybe, just maybe, it's all in the mind. Scores of professional players now use sports psychologists to help iron out those little lapses in concentration and confidence.

On the European Tour, the current flavour of the month is the Belgian Jos Vanstiphout. Having studied Edward De Bono's theory of lateral thinking, 'mind coach' Vanstiphout now boasts a plethora of top golfers as clients, including Ernie Els, Retief Goosen, Sergio Garcia and Darren Clarke, and takes a basic £400 a week from each player during a tournament and a cut of any prize money they win. At the 2002 Open Championship at Muirfield, for example, he had a dozen or so clients playing; he also secured seven per cent of Els's £700,000 winner's cheque and six per cent of second-placed Thomas Levet's £285,000. What would Vanstiphout make of Daly? Or, more interestingly, what would a simple country boy like Daly make of Vanstiphout? Perhaps you would expect him to laugh in his face, tell him to take a hike, but the truth is that even John Daly has had occasion to seek the assistance of a sports psychologist. Hardly surprising, really, given that his swing thoughts usually lurched between where the next cold one was coming from to the heart-rending choice between cheeseburger and taco.

With time on his hands, John and Paulette repaired to the University of Virginia in Charlottesville to see noted sports psychologist Bob Rotella. As the author of bestsellers such as *Putting Out of Your Mind* and *Golf Is Not a Game of Perfect*, Rotella was the man to see if you needed your head sorted out. You could tell that by all those letters after his name. Scores of professional athletes, including several tour players, had already sought his help, and his name came highly recommended.

Over the course of a day with Rotella, Daly went through what was bothering him, why he felt his game was disintegrating and why he had the attention span of a three-year-old. Rotella listened intently. 'It's good to talk to somebody who deals with the mind,' Daly said. Rotella knew all about Daly already, but then who didn't? You would have had to have been living on the moon not to have known about the Wild Thing. Forget it, Rotella told him. Whatever has happened has happened. All those times you've screwed up or got drunk or lashed out, they're history. What Daly had to do now was look to the future and accept that mistakes and misfortune were inevitably going to present themselves over the months and years to come. The secret was in learning how to deal with them.

It was pointless working on the mechanics of Daly's golf swing. Besides, if there was anything Daly needed to tinker with, he could just pick up the phone and ask Rick Ross for some advice, and he was cheaper as well. Instead, Rotella taught Daly the importance of focus, why he should never overthink on the golf course and how he should learn to say no occasionally when people wanted a slice of his time. For one with an apparent aversion to learning, Daly took Rotella's advice on board and went on his way.

That winter, Daly began the long haul of trying to cope without the two things he thought he could always rely on, alcohol and golf. Occasionally, whenever he felt like he was wavering, he would call up Thomas Henderson and talk things through, but for the most part he simply threw himself into practising instead. Morning, noon and night he hit the range, working on his game the way he used to when he was a kid at Bay Ridge. Just him, his clubs and buckets of balls. 'Back to basics, like I'm ten years old,' he said. For a player who hadn't practised solidly for one week, let alone two months, it was hard work, but it was soon paying dividends.

Perhaps the greatest challenge for Daly, however, was learning how to have fun without drinking. It was a huge obstacle to overcome, especially since from an early age he had come to associate good times with alcohol. But with the support of Paulette and the guidance of Henderson, Daly soon realised that a good time didn't have to end up in hospital, and for the first time since Crooked Stick he actually started to relax. He bought himself a Fender Stratocaster and started to teach himself to play the guitar; Eddie Van Halen even gave him a few tips ('It's really helped me; I sit there all night and make the dogs bark'). He played basketball with a local league side (he made a great centre, apparently), and he squeezed in a few visits to see Shynah, too. Without beer to distract him and with the exercise from all-day golf and basketball, Daly managed to lose 25lb in weight, too. He was soon looking and feeling great.

By February 1994 Daly was, according to Fuzzy Zoeller, 'chomping at the bit' to return to the tour. In one of his last acts as commissioner, Beman called Daly and arranged a meeting in Palm Springs in mid-February to assess his progress and discuss a possible return to the fray. When the two met, Daly impressed Beman with his humility and his determination to rectify the mistakes he had made. He told him that though it had taken a long time he had now realised that he needed the PGA Tour more than it needed John Daly. It was precisely what Beman wanted to hear, and though he didn't say as much, he knew, deep down, that the PGA needed Daly just as much as Daly needed the tour.

After three months on the sidelines, Daly returned to the tour on 8 March at the Honda Classic in Fort Lauderdale, Florida, where he told the waiting press pack that he had now been sober for fourteen months and what they were about to see was a new, improved John Daly, a John Daly free from booze and dedicated to playing golf. 'I'm starting a whole new career right here. I've got a lot of personal things off my mind,' he boasted. 'I'm just going to forget about the past and concentrate on golf.' It was a mantra straight from the pages of a Bob Rotella self-improvement manual. That said, it worked: a tied-fourth finish in his first tournament in four months suggested that maybe Daly's mind coach had succeeded in setting him on the path if not to righteousness, then at least to a happier, healthier existence. 'If I was wearing a hat right now,' Daly said later, 'I'd take it off to myself. I'm real proud.'

'He's a lot more mellow now,' Paulette confirmed. 'He doesn't get angry any more, and I think he has a lot better sense of humour.' It was a sentiment that would have been applauded by Daly's biggest ally on tour, Fuzzy Zoeller. On the Tuesday before the Memorial Tournament in June 1993, Daly had been riding with Zoeller in his car, moaning about how stressful his life had become. Suddenly, Zoeller had pulled up next to the entrance of a cemetery.

'What are you doing, Fuz?' Daly had asked.

'Take a look in there,' Zoeller had replied, pointing at the gravestones. 'You think you've got it bad? There's some folks in there who'd like to have your trouble. And if you're not careful, you'll wind up alongside them a lot sooner than you're supposed to.'

It was a straight-talking lesson Daly would never forget.

If proof were needed of Daly's new nice-guy status, it came at the Masters in early April. Daly finished in a disappointing tie for

48th place after completing his final round with a triple-bogey seven at the 18th. In days gone by, such a catastrophic finale would have seen him leaving the course in a speeding car, the stench of burning rubber filling the Georgia evening air. This time, however, he decided to stop and chat, and rather than lambast the organisers or the course or the state of the greens, he reflected on his week with Woosnam, with whom, as the luck of the draw had it, he had played all four rounds. 'Me and Woosie are talking about getting married,' he told them. 'He told me this was the longest relationship he'd ever had.'

Daly's wisecracking gave way to a more visual kind of humour at the Greater Greensboro Open, and not simply because the standard of his golf was laughable. In his first round, things started badly and descended into farce. At the 1st, he hit his tee-shot out of bounds before putting out for a triple-bogey seven. Then, when another of his shots ended up somewhere it shouldn't have, he turned to the crowd and muttered, 'I swear to God I played better when I was drunk.' When Daly appeared at the course the following afternoon, people couldn't believe what they were seeing. Overnight he had shaved off every single hair on his head as punishment for his awful opening round of 78; he took to the tee looking like Yul Brynner's tubby brother. You could hear the cameras clicking in California. 'I'd done my chin,' he mused, 'and I just decided to carry on.' Later, Daly would explain that as he didn't drink any more he was fast 'running out of things to do', adding that 'I'm scared to do something crazy on the golf course because the last thing I want to do is pay more fines'. The new aerodynamic Daly fared no better in his second round. He shot an 84 and missed the cut by the small matter of eighteen shots.

At the Shell Houston Open the following week, Daly soon discovered that news of his sudden shearing had spread quicker than an epidemic of the flu. Everywhere he looked there were young men behind the ropes wearing latex skullcaps in honour of their idol. It was as if a Telly Savalas convention had come to town. Amused by the response of his army of onion-headed fans, Daly responded with some of the best golf he had played in months. Imagine the uproar, then, when at the 16th in his final round Daly dunked a 180-yard six-iron straight into the cup for a hole in one. That ace would add over $40,000 to his year's earnings, but in a press conference afterwards he admitted that, much as he was enjoying his new sense of purpose, the PGA Tour, with its scores of hospitality tents and its endless schedule of drinks parties, wasn't the ideal place for a recovering alcoholic to make a living. 'That's the hardest part. Just about everybody out here drinks. You smell it. You see it. The temptation is everywhere. Hey, I'm not going to lie. I want to drink every day. That stuff tastes pretty good. But I know I'm not going to live if I do.'

The tour trundled on into Georgia for the BellSouth Classic, but as Daly was fine-tuning his game word reached him that the hearing regarding visitation rights for Shynah was due to be heard the following day. In Orlando. Rather than fly, Daly leaped into his car and drove the 450 miles to the Sunshine State. Nearly a year after proceedings had been instigated, the divorce from Bettye had still not been settled, and the negotiations over just how often Daly could see his daughter was just one of many sticking points. With his bald head now giving way to a few blond bristles, Daly turned up at the hearing looking like a nightclub doorman; having made his case with his lawyers, he simply turned the car around and drove it straight back to Atlanta, arriving in the small hours of the morning.

When he took his place in the line-up at the Atlanta Country Club on Thursday, he looked beat. For once, though, it wasn't the result of some ill-conceived drinking contest or a lock-in at Hooter's, merely the inevitable outcome of driving nearly a thousand miles in 24 hours. Had he hopped on a flight instead, it would have taken him a little over an hour each way, but there was no way he was doing that, especially when he couldn't have a beer to settle the nerves. 'Flying is the hardest part of not drinking,' he would later claim. 'Halfway over the ocean, you're panicking and dying for a drink.'

On the course, Daly was trying to instil some much-needed consistency into his game. It was a new, some called it sensible approach to the game that he had never really considered before. He had dispensed with his fairway woods (there was no point, the holes weren't long enough) and had taken to carrying four wedges in his bag, one of which was so flat you could flip pancakes on it. Now he was trying to think his way around a golf course, minimising the mistakes and only using his driver on holes where he knew there was little danger. So what if some of the fans called him 'chicken shit' when he opted for the one-iron over the Killer Whale, they weren't the ones with one ex-wife, another on the way and a load of contracts to satisfy.

And it was working. After three days and rounds of 69–64–69, he stood on the 1st tee on Sunday as the tournament leader. Despite two victories on tour to his credit, this was unfamiliar territory for Daly. For the first time in his career he was faced with the prospect of winning a competition without any alcohol to take the edge off his nerves. At Crooked Stick in August 1991 he had dazzled everyone by fearlessly taking the course and the field apart, but back then he'd had Dutch courage flowing through his veins. Now, all he could do was trust his instincts and hope he had enough of what the American military call 'intestinal fortitude' to see him home.

Soon he'd amassed a four-stroke lead and seemed set for a comfortable victory, but then the reality of what he was about to achieve hit him like a legal bill and he began to drop a shot here, a shot there. When he reached the 18th tee he found himself in a tie for the lead with Brian Henniger and defending champion Nolan Henke; a par five would put him in a play-off, a birdie four would win him the title. After playing percentage golf all week (and clearly benefiting from it), he was left with a choice: play it safe and take his chances in a play-off or go for broke. He did what came naturally. He let the big dog eat. Some 320 yards up the middle of the fairway, Daly found his ball doubled up in agony. Faced with 172 yards to the green, he picked out his eight-iron but didn't hit it quite the way he'd intended, and his ball caught the bunker by the side of the green. Splashing out to four feet, a visibly twitchy Daly was left with one putt to claim victory. With his heart pounding, he stepped up, took two swift practice putts, then dropped it for his third PGA Tour title.

Everyone was impressed with Daly and the manner of his victory, not least the press, who commented on his new-found maturity and marvelled at his 'remarkable rehabilitation'. Daly, meanwhile, was as shocked as anyone. 'I wasn't this nervous playing golf when I was drinking,' he said with a smile, a cheque for $216,000 burning a hole in his pocket. 'It's the first tournament I've won on the PGA Tour in a sober manner, so it's a great feeling knowing I can do it sober. I don't think two years ago I could have pulled this off. I'm still shaking. This is great. I dedicate this tournament to my little two-year-old daughter.'

12. BE CAREFUL OF THE STONES YOU THROW

'The more you get, the more you get.'

Tom Petty

A month later, on the eve of the 1994 US Open at Oakmont Country Club, Pennsylvania, Daly sat side by side in a press conference with Wilson's young president John Riccitiello. Delighted with the new sense of purpose in Daly's game, not to mention his recent win at the BellSouth Classic, Riccitiello had torn up Daly's existing contract and presented him with a new ten-year agreement with his company. Although no figure was mentioned, the new deal was rumoured to be worth up to $30 million and came with all manner of performance-related bonuses. Daly was, understandably, exultant. When asked why he had signed the new deal, he dutifully towed the corporate line, but then who wouldn't for the money they were offering? 'Wilson has been with me during a lot of ups and downs,' he said. 'It's just a big family. I'm happy to be associated with them.'

The new deal was imperative for Wilson. In December 1993 they had lost their prized asset, the charismatic 1991 US Open champion Payne Stewart, when he defected to Spalding; with Daly back in the winning habit again, the last thing they needed was for one of their rivals to come in and lure the biggest star in golf away with a bigger and better deal. In Daly, Riccitiello recognised that they possessed a ready-made response to the widespread accusation that their brand was staid and uninspired. When people watched Daly play, they saw a player they longed to be, an up-and-at-'em, heart-on-the-sleeve guy to whom the concept of the lay-up was anathema. He was the player every Joe Schmoe who ever dug up a public course wanted to be. Nobody really wanted to be Nick Faldo or Paul Azinger. They just wanted to stick that ball down, grab the driver, grip it and rip it.

Later, when a reporter asked what the actual cash value of the deal was worth to him, Daly was unusually reticent. Perhaps he was embarrassed by the size of the figure, or maybe he thought that Bettye Fulford's legal team were eavesdropping. 'The whole contract is a big incentive for me to play my butt off,' he explained. 'The way we have done it, I can make a lot of money on performances. The figures, I don't even know.'

Lifted by the faith Riccitiello had shown in him, Daly took to the Oakmont course that week and set about showing the watching world just what Wilson were getting for their millions. He shot 81–73 and missed the cut.

Ireland is well known for being a wet and verdant land, but a true storm was about to break over Daly's head when at the end of June he flew to his ancestral homeland for the Murphy's Irish Open at Mount Juliet, County Kilkenny. During the event, at which he would finish tied for second, Daly sat down for a face-to-face interview with Ben Bacon, the golf reporter for the *Sun*, the UK's biggest-selling daily newspaper. As the two talked and the tape recorder whirred, the conversation turned to the subject of soccer and to the story of the Argentinian captain Diego Maradona's positive drugs test at the World Cup in the USA. Bacon asked Daly whether something similar could ever happen in golf. Much to his surprise, Daly suddenly launched into a lengthy diatribe on the problem of drug-taking in golf. It was like winding up a clockwork toy and letting it go. Alleging that 'plenty of guys on the PGA Tour do drugs and all sorts of crazy things', Daly insisted that he was not the only one who had experienced substance abuse problems and added that he would welcome the introduction of random drug testing on the tour because 'I know I'm one of the people who would test clean'. And there was more.

'There are certain people on the tour who do the crazy stuff,' he continued. 'They're never going to get exposed unless they are found out by the police and put in jail . . . People said I was the crazy one on the tour, but others were getting up to much crazier things than me.'

Bacon could scarcely believe it. Here was one of the most famous sportsmen on the planet openly accusing his fellow players of drug-taking. It was a major story. 'John obviously felt aggrieved after the treatment he had been given by some of his fellow professionals because of his colourful past,' Bacon explained. 'I'm sure there was a bit of jealousy there from the other pros because the fans loved him . . . and I just think he wanted to get a few things off his chest.' When the interview was over, Bacon called his editor and told him that he had just landed something very special. They agreed to sit tight until Daly made his way to Turnberry for the Open in a fortnight's time. The following week, Daly arrived oblivious at Gleneagles for the Bell's Scottish Open with his agents in tow. Ever since he had arrived in Europe he had been besieged by the media, and Bacon was becoming increasingly concerned that sooner or later he would give a similar interview to another newspaper. So he decided to air his scoop a week early.

Late on Thursday night, 7 July, John Mascatello was relaxing at the Gleneagles Hotel when he took a call from a journalist at the *Daily Express*. The reporter had seen the early edition of the following day's *Sun* and, having missed out on the original story, was eager to get the first reaction to Daly's drug accusations. Mascatello was flustered. This was the first he had heard of any such story. He asked the journalist who had written the story and then set about tracking down Ben Bacon.

At midnight, Bacon's hotel-room phone rang. It was Mascatello, and he was seething. Daly, he maintained, was denying everything he was reported to have said in the piece. It was bullshit, he said. Calmly, Bacon told him that he couldn't deny it because it was all on tape. That changed everything. With the interview on tape, there was no way he could claim that Daly had been misquoted or that his words had been taken out of context. Mascatello paused, then changed tack. He suggested Bacon might want to meet him and his partner, Bud Martin, for breakfast to discuss the interview and give them the opportunity to listen to exactly what John had said.

At 7.30 a.m. on Friday, Bacon arrived at the Gleneagles Hotel, tape in hand, and sat down with Mascatello and Martin. In front of them was a copy of the *Sun*, and on the back page was the headline DOPE TEST ALL OF US with the following subhead: 'It's the Only Way to Catch Stars Who Snort, Says Daly'. They wanted to hear the tape. Bacon pressed the play button. Just 45 seconds in, Mascatello turned to Bacon and told him he had heard enough. Now that they had listened to the tape themselves there was little point in any repudiation, especially when Bacon told them that if they continued to deny what Daly had said he would call his editor and arrange for the tape to be played down a premium-rate phone line so that the *Sun*'s readers could listen to it themselves. 'I'm sure it must have been uncomfortable for John, and I do have some sympathy for that because he is a nice guy,' Bacon added, 'but he said it, and it was one of the biggest stories of that year.'

As a lesson in how to lose friends and alienate people, Daly's outburst was inspired. It wasn't long before the new PGA commissioner, Tim Finchem, got wind of the story. He was livid. For someone like Daly, a player for whom they had cut a lot of slack over the years, to come out and publicly call into question the reputation of the tour was like a kick in the teeth. He sent word out that he wanted to meet Daly as soon as he arrived at Turnberry for the Open the following week.

The players, too, were less than enchanted by Daly's remarks. Tour veteran Curtis Strange led the backlash. 'I've talked to a lot of the guys about this and I think they all feel the same way I do, which is that they wish John Daly would crawl back under that rock he came out from,' he fumed. 'What's really disturbing about this is that by making comments like this John is capable of tearing down in a few minutes what Jack Nicklaus and Arnold Palmer have worked thirty-five years to build, and that's the image people have of the PGA Tour. I don't think that's fair.'

Amid the furore, the Scottish Open witnessed a spectacular third round of 61 by the eventual winner Carl Mason. Later, when the venerable English professional sat down at the press conference, the first question he fielded was simply: 'What are you on, coke?' With a smile on his face, Mason nodded and raised a can of the cola variety.

By the time the players assembled in Turnberry for the 123rd Open Championship, Daly found that he was about as welcome as a fire-eater in a gas station. On the Monday afternoon, Greg

Norman, the defending champion, approached Daly on the practice green demanding an explanation. He had had a week to calm down since Daly first went public but clearly it hadn't been enough. 'How could you say something like that, how could you make a blanket accusation like that?' he snorted. 'What in the world were you thinking?' Daly was unrepentant. 'Look,' he responded. 'I'm sick and tired of everyone making me the bad guy on tour. I'm tired of people acting as if I'm the only one who has ever done anything wrong. So don't give me a hard time. I don't want to hear it.' And with that he was gone. He didn't want a fight with Norman. It was the last thing he needed. That said, the thought had crossed Norman's mind. 'It wasn't worth wasting my time,' decided the Australian. 'I was livid with the guy, absolutely livid. How dare he say that any of us are on drugs. I'm not the one who beat up my wife; I'm not the one who is an alcoholic; I'm not the one who tears up rooms. It was just inexcusable. If I had done the things he's done, I'd have been ostracised so fast it would have been ridiculous. Almost anyone would have been. Then he goes around acting like people are picking on him.'

Unlike Beman, 47-year-old Finchem was not an ex-professional with a talent for administration. He came from a legal background, and had worked for Jimmy Carter during his presidency in the late 1970s. Now, as the game's new chief executive, he was determined to do things his way, and the Daly drugs story represented his first real test. When he finally met with Daly, he acknowledged John's huge public appeal and what he had done for a game that was increasingly seen as irrelevant and inaccessible, but told him that there was a very definite line when it came to what he could and couldn't say, and now he had crossed it. Moreover, if Daly was harbouring concerns about substance abuse on tour he should have spoken to him first, not blabbed to one of the world's biggest-selling newspapers. In his defence, Daly said he had made a public apology and that he was tired of being singled out as the black sheep of the PGA family. Finchem's options were limited. He could suspend him (again), but that wouldn't do Daly, the tour or the tournament sponsors any favours; or he could warn him as to his future behaviour and hand down another fine. As Finchem was keen to re-establish the tour policy of keeping disciplinary action under wraps, full details of the measures he opted for were never made public, but as Daly left the meeting with his playing privileges intact it was clear which route Finchem had chosen.

A deleterious double of a troublesome back and a plummeting popularity rating among his fellow players did for Daly at Turnberry. He made the cut, but a final-round 80 left him in last position, the second time in three appearances he had achieved that dubious honour. On his return to the States, Daly sought medical advice for the pain he was experiencing in his back; the diagnosis suggested swollen muscles and tissue, and he was given a programme of physiotherapy to help him recover. 'Yeah, they gave me some exercises,' he said, 'but I don't do them.'

'I've never been the type of guy to stand over a ball and think about what I'm supposed to do. I just see that little white ball and try to hit it as hard as I can . . . my best advice is, never hold back. Grip it and rip it.'

'Grip it and rip it' – five simple words from his golf manual *Killer Swing* that speak volumes about John Daly's approach to the game. That said, Daly has a back-up plan for those off-days: 'If you're playing bad, sip it, grip it and rip it.' Next time you have an opportunity to watch a tour event, be it in person or on television, take time to contrast the marked difference between Daly and, say, Sergio Garcia. While undeniably gifted, Garcia is one of the most infuriating players to watch on tour, waggling, twitching and regripping for an eternity before finally playing his shot. (During the Canadian Skins competition in July 2001, when Garcia and Daly played together, the Spaniard teed it up at the 1st and as he set about his tiresome ritual he was greeted by the sound of Daly counting aloud each regrip.) He's the kind of player who can, on the one hand, produce the miraculous (witness that shot from behind the tree at the 1999 US PGA at Medinah), and on the other leave spectators, caddies and coaches alike tearing their hair out and pleading with him just to hit the damn thing. During the first round of the 2001 Nedbank Golf Challenge in Sun City, faced with a second shot across water to the green, Garcia racked up 60 – that's 60 – regrips before backing away from the shot, screaming 'Hit the f***ing ball!' and throwing his two-iron back in the bag. Moments later, he whipped out a wedge and laid up instead. Clearly, here was a player whose brain was getting in the way of executing the shot he wanted, and it was no surprise that in the wake of Sergio's all too public implosion his father, former European Tour pro Victor Garcia, took him straight off to the range and made him practise with his hands taped to the club. His old man did the trick: Sergio won the event and pocketed $2 million (or about $500 for every regrip that week).

Of course, Garcia isn't the first pro to suffer from an almost compulsive and potentially career-threatening pre-shot ritual, and he certainly won't be the last. Former US Open and PGA champion Hubert Green might have won nineteen times on the tour between 1971 and 1985, but he ducked and bobbed and weaved over the ball so much that *Los Angeles Times* columnist Jim Murray once remarked that he looked like a drunk trying to find a keyhole in the dark. Irish professional Fred Daly (no relation) won the 1947 Open Championship despite a style that involved placing and replacing his putter dozens of times before finally striking the ball. Even Daly's boyhood hero Jack Nicklaus wasn't immune from criticism. There was a time when the Golden Bear stood over his putts for so long that the greens resembled the first cut of rough when he finally got round to taking the shot.

In a sport where tinkering and tailoring are as much a part of the game as planting the little white ball in the hole, Daly's set-up, address and swing is as brief as they come. Give him the yardage, give him the club and let him get on with it. Trouble is, there are precious few other players that play at the same breakneck pace. Former tour pro David Feherty once said he 'had to call a cab to keep up with him'. And it's not just his playing partners that have trouble with Daly's pace of play, it can also make the caddie's job a nightmare. In 1993, *Golf* magazine measured the time it took players to hit drives, irons and putts, and Daly was found to be the quickest overall. With a driver in his hand, Daly averaged just 18.7 seconds, while his iron shots took him only 15.6 seconds. Each putt, meanwhile, took him just 21.1 seconds, almost half the tour average. 'He's actually getting better,' explained Greg Rita. 'I used to be in the middle of getting his yardage when he'd hit. Now at least he waits to hear how far he's got.'

In late August 1994, at the World Series of Golf at the Firestone Country Club in Akron, Ohio, Daly's lightning speed finally caught up with him. It was clear from the outset that he was in an impatient mood, and the trouble started when Daly, who was growing tired of waiting around at each and every tee, fired a shot across the bows of Greg Norman, the player he had so incensed with the much-publicised drug story. Norman bit his lip, but his caddie, Tony Navarro, stormed back down the fairway to find out just why Daly seemed so intent on decapitating his employer. Daly let fly. 'If you guys would get going,' he shouted, 'maybe we could play some f***ing golf out here.' Navarro's riposte did little to ease the tension. 'Are you in such a hurry to shoot 80?' he quipped.

Daly simmered. The following day it was Andrew McGee's turn in the firing line, Daly bombing drives in his direction before he was out of range. Another day, another altercation. Strangely, Saturday passed without incident, but on the final day matters reached a head. Daly was fifteen over par and out of the reckoning. He was playing like a dog and on his way to a hideous 83. He wanted out of there, and fast. At the 14th, a dogleg par-four, he unloaded one off the tee which cut the corner and landed close to little-known Michigan club pro Jeff Roth. Roth, who had won his place in the starting line-up by virtue of his triumph at the National Club Pro Championship, let it go, figuring that as it was a blind tee-shot this kind of thing was bound to happen from time to time. But at the very next hole as well? Someone, somewhere, it seemed, was out to get him.

The 15th at Firestone is a reachable par-four, and if there are three words guaranteed to get Daly's blood pumping it is 'reachable par-four'. It's like a red rag to a bull that's had a really bad day at the office. As Roth stood on the green ahead, Daly grabbed his driver and shaped to shoot, much to playing partner Neal Lancaster's surprise. 'Maybe you ought to wait?' he offered. The suggestion fell on deaf ears, just as it had done when Jay Fox had suggested the same thing back at Morrilton in 1987. Whack. The ball fizzed through the air like an Exocet and landed pin-high at the side of the green, just three feet away from Roth. When Daly arrived on the green, Roth's parents, who had come along to see their son's week in the big time, were waiting for him, eager to point out some of the finer details of golfing etiquette. As Roth's mother, Dolores, berated Daly, he waited for her to finish before trawling out one of his stock responses. 'You know something,' he said. 'You remind me of my ex-wife.'

If Daly thought that his wisecrack would put an end to the spat he was mistaken. After the round, Roth and Daly clashed again in the car park. As the row subsided, Roth's 62-year-old father Bob butted in to let Daly know exactly what he thought of him.

Courteous as ever, Daly told him where to go. And when Dolores offered a few choice words of her own, why, John just gave her the same directions. It was one insult too many for Roth senior. Displaying all the agility of a man half his age, he leaped on to Daly's (bad) back and wrestled him to the asphalt. With an ever-increasing and incredulous crowd taking up ringside seats, the pair grappled until they were separated. The judges scored it a draw. For Daly, it was an embarrassing end to another miserable tournament. As he trudged wearily out of Firestone that evening, he was heard to say, 'F*** the PGA Tour. I'm sick of it. I'm outta here.'

Though they didn't say as much, the PGA were sick of him too, and in September Daly 'volunteered' to sit out the rest of the year rather than face another suspension, citing persistent back trouble as the reason. Tim Finchem revealed that Daly would be returning to the tour at the season-opening Mercedes Championship in the first week of January 1995, stating that in the interim John would 'prepare himself mentally and physically to come back. He [Daly] has a history of having some difficulties. We view John Daly as a strong potential asset to the tour. He has some back problems, but he clearly has some things beyond physical problems he has to deal with.'

Reebok and Wilson also viewed Daly as a strong potential asset, but not when he wasn't playing. Concerned that they would now be paying Daly to sit at home and watch cable, both companies temporarily suspended their deals with him soon after Finchem's announcement, saying that they would reconsider when he eventually returned to the tour.

13. BET YOUR BOTTOM DOLLAR

'The third marriage is the charm.'

Willie Nelson

While the media continued to doubt the legitimacy of Daly's claim that it was he, not the PGA, who had suggested the idea of a voluntary suspension, John left them to their ruminations and turned his attention to matters at home. In the early summer of 1994 he had indulged himself once more in the property market, snapping up a house on a new development on the Tournament Players Club complex at Southwind. And while there wasn't much change from a million, it was worth it just for the pool and its large Razorback logo on the bottom. Over the course of the year, John and Paulette had been dividing their time between the condo in Palm Springs and a rented house in Memphis, and with a lengthy vacation ahead of him Daly now felt it was better that they settled there and enjoy their new home while they had the chance. And how they enjoyed it. By September, Paulette was pregnant.

That autumn, Daly used his downtime to hook up with some old friends. After his induction into the Razorbacks Hall of Honor, he took time out to meet up with Bill Woodley, his old coach at the University of Arkansas. Woodley had kept tabs on Daly's roller-coaster career and, like anybody with an interest in the game, knew all about his decision to sit out the rest of the

Right Draining a putt at the eighteenth during the second round of the US PGA at Crooked Stick, August 1991.
(© The Phil Sheldon Golf Picture Library)

Below Makc mine a Marlboro – savouring a cigarette with Ian Woosnam at the US Open at Baltusrol, June 1993.
(© The Phil Sheldon Golf Picture Library)

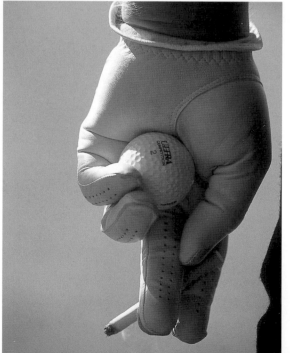

Above Fast food for thought – Daly chews the fat with caddie Greg Rita and then girlfriend Paulette Dean at the Alfred Dunhill Cup, St. Andrews, October 1993. (© The Phil Sheldon Golf Picture Library)

Left Glove story – smoking his way to victory at the British Open, July 1995. (© The Phil Sheldon Golf Picture Library)

Right Sitting pretty –
holding the Claret Jug on
the Swilcan Bridge at St.
Andrews, July 1995.
(© The Phil Sheldon Golf
Picture Library)

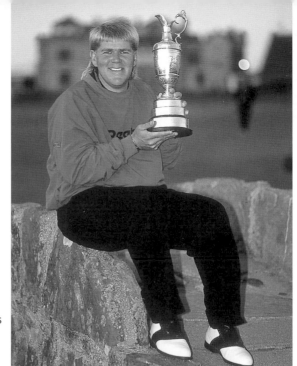

Below A close shave –
another late night takes its
toll on the Wild Thing.
(© The Phil Sheldon Golf
Picture Library)

Above Attempting to break the long driving distance world record at Santa Monica airport, July 1995. (© The Phil Sheldon Golf Picture Library)

Left Grip it and rip it – five little words that speak volumes. (© The Phil Sheldon Golf Picture Library)

Right Singin' the blues – relaxing at the Johnnie Walker World Championship, Jamaica, December 1995. Daly would finish that week in last place with a score of 40-over-par. (© The Phil Sheldon Golf Picture Library)

Below If the cap fits – Daly sports his new Callaway hat, complete with largely ignored slogan. (© Getty Images)

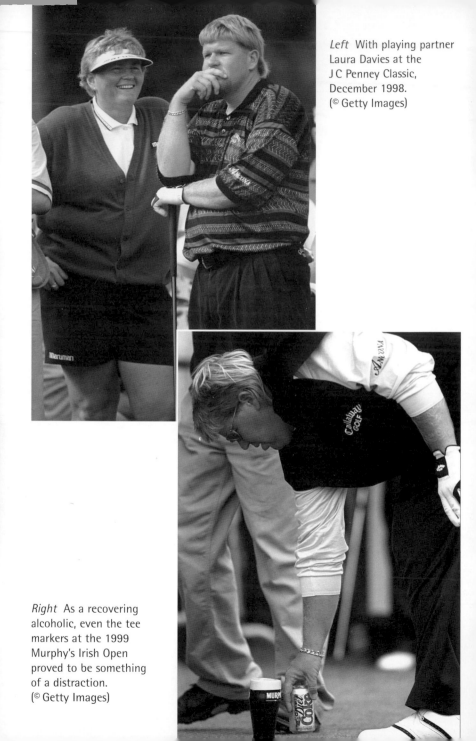

Left With playing partner Laura Davies at the J C Penney Classic, December 1998. (© Getty Images)

Right As a recovering alcoholic, even the tee markers at the 1999 Murphy's Irish Open proved to be something of a distraction. (© Getty Images)

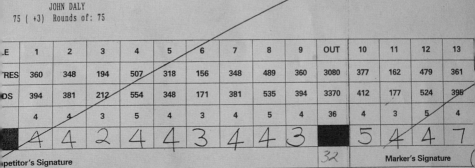

Right At the Alfred Dunhill Cup in October 2000, with trademark Marlboro welded to his lips. (© Getty Images)

Below At the 2002 Australian PGA, Daly carded a 78 in his second round, despite a four-under-par front nine. He was later disqualified for failing to sign his scorecard. (© Getty Images)

AUSTRALIAN PGA CHAMPIONSHIP
Round: 2   Date: 29-11-02
Match: 41   Start Time: 12:10
Ref. :122   Tee : 1
              JOHN DALY
75 (+3) Rounds of: 75

LE	1	2	3	4	5	6	7	8	9	OUT	10	11	12	13
RES	360	348	194	507	318	156	348	489	360	3080	377	162	479	361
DS	394	381	212	554	348	171	381	535	394	3370	412	177	524	395
	4	4	3	5	4	3	4	5	4	36	4	3	5	4
	4	4	2	4	4	3	4	4	3		5	4	4	7

Competitor's Signature   32   Marker's Signature

Above King of the Road – Daly's $1.4 million motor home rolls into the US Open at Farmingdale, New York, June 2002. (© Getty Images)

Left Like a five-star hotel, only better – inside Daly's luxurious mobile home. (© Getty Images)

year. The two talked about Daly's plans for the months until he returned to the PGA Tour and, sensing an opportunity too good to pass up, Woodley suggested that if Daly wanted to help out with coaching the Razorbacks golf team, he would be more than welcome.

Daly liked the idea. Throughout his education, he had never really appreciated the invasive manner in which coaches had tinkered with his game, preferring instead to rely on what he had gleaned from the John Daly School of Golf Tuition. Now, though, he had an opportunity to show some kids with the same hopes and aspirations he'd once harboured just what they could achieve if they put their minds to it. When Daly showed up at that first session, the students couldn't believe what they were seeing. This wasn't some failed minor tour player or embittered ex-club pro showing them the ropes, this was the undisputed heavyweight champion of the golfing world.

Despite a major title and millions in the bank, however, Daly soon discovered that his superstar status counted for little when it came to teaching ('If anyone says coaching is easy,' he sighed, 'they're crazy'). That said, Woodley was impressed with Daly's ability as a coach, not to mention the rapport he quickly established with the students. 'He loved it, and the students, they just loved it. He was great with them. He's just a sweet guy. When you see him on TV you see this kind of big guy who can hit it 400 yards, but what you don't see is that he's just a big old teddy bear.'

When he wasn't with the Razorbacks golf team, Daly caught up with some other friends he hadn't seen in a while. One Monday, for instance, he rented for $600 the entire nine-hole Rock Creek golf course for some buddies and then turned up with a full beard, looking like a hobo, and took part in a knockabout ten-some. He supplied the food and the beer (and Diet Coke), too. And he won. Seven under, for the record, and he was playing the other nine's better ball. He also spent some time with his old Dardanelle buddy Donnie Crabtree, and the two of them made regular excursions to the new riverboat casinos at Tunica, Mississippi, so that John could waste some of the Wilson money on high-stake slots and blackjack. Indeed, Crabtree recalled one weekend when Daly just couldn't lose. 'He won like three days in a row, like maybe $80,000. It seemed like that was the point that he was hooked.' In the years to come, when Crabtree couldn't make it,

Daly would simply grab his mother and take her to Tunica instead, and while she sat with a bunch of chips her son had dropped in her lap, Daly would wander off and take his seat at the big boys' machines.

Virtually the only issue that threatened an otherwise enjoyable few months off was the ongoing delay in the divorce case. Some sixteen months after filing for divorce, Bettye still wasn't Daly's ex-wife, but there was, according to *Golf World*, some progress: the magazine reported that a settlement had been agreed in principle and that a deal would be signed and sealed in December. It happened in January 1995, actually, virtually coinciding with Daly's return to the tour at the Mercedes Championship in Carlsbad, California. Daly stood with Paulette on the veranda of the La Costa Resort and Spa's imposing clubhouse and told Malcolm Folley of the *Mail on Sunday* that he was looking forward to the competition and that Paulette was expecting. On the eve of the tournament, John and Paulette had kept an appointment at the hospital, their curiosity clearly getting the better of them. 'We went to find out the baby's sex,' Paulette explained. 'It's a girl. We will call her Sierra Lynn.' Only John Daly could name his unborn child after a rehab centre.

Daly seemed at ease. Paulette's pregnancy, coupled with the fact that he had been granted generous access to Shynah as part of his divorce settlement, had left him in a positive frame of mind. Considering it was his first competition since that unscheduled wrestling bout at the World Series of Golf, he played reasonably well. His scores improved as the week progressed, his back held out, and his total of 290 left him in a tie for twentieth. But the early promise of the new year soon gave way to the kind of form that most commentators would label a slump. Daly didn't really care; he had other things on his mind. When he missed the cut at the Phoenix Open, he decided that as Las Vegas was just 300 miles away – a short hop for a driving junkie – he might as well take Paulette down the Strip and make an honest woman of her.

On Saturday, 28 January 1995, Paulette Dean became Paulette Daly. It was John's kind of wedding. Held at the celebrity chapel the Little Church of the West, it was done and dusted in fifteen minutes. John wore jeans and cowboy boots; Paulette didn't. There was no time for a honeymoon, and after a night celebrating on the Strip Daly flew to Australia for three events. Three years earlier he'd made the same trip and annoyed fans and promoters alike by scooting through his appearances with one eye on his $35,000 fee and the other on the long flight home. This time, though, there were 375,000 good reasons why he should make the trip.

Sponsored by the famous Dutch brewery, the Heineken Classic was played in Perth in the wild west of Australia. It was the height of the Australian summer and the temperatures were nudging a hundred. Everywhere Daly looked there were huge signs promoting Heineken or fans nursing an ice-cold bottle of the stuff. Even the tee markers had Heineken plastered all over them. For a recovering alcoholic baking in the midday sun, it was hell. But fanned by a $125,000 appearance fee, Daly persevered.

Despite his insipid form on the PGA Tour, Daly had told journalists that he was determined to make amends for the poor showing of 1992, accepting that perhaps he hadn't really given it his all on his last venture down under. This time, he maintained, the Aussie fans were going to see a different Daly, more prudent on the course and wary of any dangers the course presented. No more reckless driving off the tee, just sensible long irons and a resolve to cut out those daft mistakes that had been costing him dearly of late. It wasn't what the promoters wanted to hear. They wanted the other Daly, the one that clubbed balls until they lost their shape, that threw a fit whenever he hit a duff one. They had paid for the Wild Thing, not the Mild Thing.

Daly persisted with his safety-first policy, and it went down about as well as an alcohol-free beer. In his first round he hit two-iron after two-iron off the tee, despite grumblings of discontent in the galleries. It was like going to see Sinatra and have him turn down requests for 'My Way', or buying an under-the-counter porn flick only to get it home and find that everyone kept their clothes on. The natives were restless, a fact which did not go unnoticed by the tournament director Tony Roosenberg. 'If he doesn't pull the driver out soon,' he observed, 'he's liable to have a riot on his hands.'

Daly's plan to leave the driver wrapped snugly in its Razorback head cover worked like a dream that day – a really bad dream. During his round of 80, Daly recorded six bogeys and two double bogeys, leaving him fourteen shots off the lead. So much for the new cautious approach to the game. 'I think I was put on this earth to use a driver,' he concluded. He fared only marginally better in the second round, shooting a 76 and missing the cut by nine shots.

After appearances at the Australian Skins game at Laguna Quays (where he banked another $24,000) and the Australian Masters in Melbourne (tied for 33rd), Daly returned to the States. While he hadn't pulled up any trees on his latest visit, everyone conceded that he had at least tried this time around, and he returned home knowing he had gone some way to erasing the memory of his ill-tempered trip in 1992.

Daly arrived at the Masters on the back of some terrifically average play on the PGA Tour. That week at Augusta he found himself inundated with visits from familiar faces: first, Ray Hentges and Jim Rackers from Helias High School arrived on practice day; then Bill Woodley came down from Fayetteville to lend his support and offer a few impartial pointers as to where he thought Daly's game was failing. Unusually, Daly listened.

Ever since Daly had started working with Woodley and his team, the bond between him and his old coach had developed into a genuine friendship. Now, as Daly awaited his tee-off time in the first round, the two sat in Daly's American Eagle, chatting – or 'bullshitting', as Woodley calls it – about everything from the progress of their Razorbacks golf team to just how surreal the entire Masters experience was. As Daly got dressed and prepared to make his way to the range, Woodley looked at his shirt.

'Man, that's a good-looking shirt, John,' he remarked.

Daly looked up. 'You want it?'

'Hell, no,' replied Woodley.

But Daly was having none of it and immediately took his shirt off and handed it to Woodley. 'Here, take it!' he insisted.

Laughing, Woodley accepted the shirt. 'He literally gave me the shirt off his back,' he recalled. According to Woodley, it was just another typical gesture of generosity. 'He's f***ed up a million times, but he'll literally do anything for you. If I was to ring him up and say, "John, I just ran into this guy, a golf pro, and he's lost everything and he needs some money," he would say, "Well how much does he need?" Honestly, he really would do that. He's just the most charitable guy you could ever meet.' Indeed, later that month Daly would host his own charity day at Bay Ridge, raising $25,000 for the Dardanelle Boys and Girls Club. He helped roast the hogs, he played his guitar, and before the auction commenced he placed five $100 bills in the hands of two young boys from a single-parent family. They would leave with a full set of clubs and a bag each, too.

Sadly, though, the Augusta National wasn't anywhere near as giving, and Daly laboured to another inconsequential finish, tied for 45th. And so on to Texas, where Daly's generosity showed no sign of abating. In the pro-am event at the Shell Houston Open, Daly was paired with Rex Doyle, one of the tournament sponsors, and his caddie, the Houston Oilers' six-foot-five-inch, 315lb man-mountain Kevin Donnalley. Daly was still a huge fan of football and liked to collect players' jerseys whenever he met them, so when Donnalley offered him his, he was bowled over. As the two sat in his RV after their round, Daly warmed to the giant right guard and explained how living in the motorhome had given him so much more time to himself. On the morning of the pro-am, for example, he told Donnalley that he had woken up at 7.00 a.m., arrived at McDonald's at 7.15 for breakfast, reached the putting green at 7.29, taken two quick practice putts, then made his way to the first tee and rattled one right down the middle. When the Oilers star left the trailer he was laden down with all manner of Daly memorabilia including golf balls, gloves and, amazingly, Daly's autographed driver.

Indeed, the pair hit it off so well that they dined together that day, along with Paulette and Rex Doyle, at Marco's Mexican restaurant in town. In keeping with Daly's compulsive nature, it was, according to Paulette, the eighth straight day they had eaten there. Over lunch, Daly told his new best friend that he had enjoyed their round together and that they should try to keep in touch. Donnalley agreed. Then, Daly handed over his unique business card. 'He wrote his phone number and address on a $5 bill and gave it to me,' recalled Donnalley. 'He told me to call him any time.'

Though Daly and his bellyful of fajitas missed the cut at the Woodlands, his form improved significantly when he teed it up a week later in Atlanta. As the reigning BellSouth champion, Daly had something to prove that week, to himself and to everyone else. In the two tour titles he had defended so far he had put up about as much fight as a worm trying to fend off a crow. If he wanted to be a truly great player, he needed to do much, much better.

His defence started well, his first-round 67 equalling his lowest round of the year. Afterwards, a cheerful Daly met up with Daron Norwood, a local country and western singer whose song 'Bad Dog, No Biscuit' had been receiving a lot of airplay. Norwood had been hanging out with Daly and helping him with his guitar lessons; he'd also been giving his eager student some grief over the straggly mess that passed for his hair. Daly's response was typically frank: 'He [Norwood] said he cuts his family's hair now and then, so I said, "Hell, just cut mine." I think he did pretty good.' On Friday, Daly arrived at the Atlanta Country Club looking like an extra from *Deliverance*. As much as he approved of his new hairstyle, there were plenty of people (especially those with a sense of style) who didn't. With its shaved sides, flat top and bushy back, it was truly heinous; some reporters even likened it to a French Foreign Legionnaire's hat. Yet it did Daly no harm whatsoever, and another 67 left him in the lead at the halfway stage. It was the best he had played all year. Would this be the week when Daly finally managed to put together four solid rounds? The answer, predictably, was no. Slipping away with rounds of 71 and 72, Daly finished tied for twelfth. Despite surrendering the lead and failing to claim a top-ten spot, Daly drew some consolation from his performance. Unlike the PGA Championship in 1992, he had at least made a decent fist of defending this title, and his placing was his highest of the year so far. He had also provided the abiding memory of the week when in the final round he drove the green at the 335-yard par-four 14th, coming within two inches of holing in one.

By the end of May, Daly's luck was changing. Trouble was, it wasn't on the golf course. Dismayed after another missed cut at the Colonial National Invitation in Fort Worth, Texas, he'd driven east to Mississippi, to the Horseshoe Casino in Tunica. Daly had always been a gambler, but now, with no alcohol to fall back on when he was feeling downhearted, he was spending increasing amounts of time at the slots or the blackjack tables. It gave him the rush alcohol used to give him. Sometimes he could gamble for 36 hours straight, no problem. Occasionally, when he was feeling lucky, he would commandeer five high-stake slot machines and feed them $1,000 each. He would take over a blackjack table and play all five hands for $15,000 a hand. If he doubled his bets or split the cards, he could be gambling $150,000 at a time. The Horseshoe Casino billed itself as a 'gambler's paradise' and boasted over 2,000 slot machines and 70 table games, all of which were equally willing to take Daly's money. That night, he plumped for the $100 slots. As he sat there working the machines, a crowd began to gather behind him, not simply because it was someone with the nerve and the wherewithal to tackle the big machines, but because it just happened to be John Daly, the most famous golfer on the planet. Imagine the commotion, then, when the machine exploded into life. With all manner of bells ringing and lights flashing, it was as though someone had set off the fire alarm. They hadn't; it was just that Daly had hit the $100,000 jackpot. After all his misfortune with women, the bottle and the PGA, a little slice of luck had finally come his way.

News of Daly's windfall spread quickly, not least because John foolishly allowed himself to be photographed being presented with a man-sized cheque by the casino manager, an image the Horseshoe then used for publicity purposes. It was a naive decision he would regret. Soon, the word on the street was that John Daly had a gambling problem, too. It was an obvious conclusion to draw. After all, everyone knew Daly had a wildly compulsive side to his personality, and the concern, understandable really, was that he had merely substituted gambling for alcohol. When confronted about his rumoured addiction, Daly said there was nothing for anyone to worry about. 'Yeah, I gamble,' he admitted in an interview with the *Commercial Appeal* newspaper in Memphis. 'I gamble for fun and pleasure. I do it because I can, and it's relaxing. It's the most relaxing thing I do besides playing guitar.'

When friends, family and the PGA Tour had asked Daly to quit drinking, he had done as they requested. When he was sober, they started asking questions about his cigarette consumption or the amount of candy he was putting away. Now they were pointing at his gambling and saying that if he wasn't careful the casinos would soon do for him. Maybe, said John, but it wasn't a problem for him. 'I'm not going to quit gambling,' was his definite reply.

On 1 June, Sierra Lynn Daly came into the world weighing in at almost ten pounds. A fortnight later, a bleary-eyed Daly returned to the tour just in time for the US Open. Back in 1986, he had arrived at Shinnecock Hills as the prodigious young talent taking his first tentative steps in the world of major championships. Now, nine years, three marriages and a million column inches later, John Daly had returned to the scene of his major debut for another crack at the title.

With his wife and their new baby at home and plans afoot to move house again (to Rogers, Arkansas), a preoccupied Daly soon found that Shinnecock Hills hadn't got any easier. He made the cut, despite a 75 in the second round, but his mind seemed to be elsewhere, and matters were not helped when he received a surprising invitation for Saturday night. One of Daly's favourite rock bands, the golf-obsessed Hootie and the Blowfish, were playing a concert nearby and had asked Daly to join them on stage. Despite the tips from Norwood and Van Halen, Daly's prowess on the guitar still hadn't progressed much beyond his favourite chords ('I'm a G, D, C guy; every now and then I throw in an A'), but he had always fancied himself as a rock star and the opportunity to live out another of his dreams was just too good to pass up. On the Saturday night, Daly walked on stage in front of 25,000 fans and gave it his all in a rendition of the rock standard 'Mustang Sally'. Norwood would have been proud of him. It was, he said, 'way more nerve-racking than teeing off in a major, cos I don't know what the hell I'm doing'.

Daly's golf that week was worse than his guitar playing, but thankfully not quite as ghastly as his showing in 1986. Recording four rounds in the seventies, he made little impression on the leaderboard and had to settle for a tie for 45th. In the fifteen PGA events Daly had played in 1995 he had just three top-twenty finishes and no top tens. Sooner or later he would have to realise that, first and foremost, he was a professional golfer, not just some celebrity who happened to play a bit of golf every now and then.

14. WALKING AWAY A WINNER

'I always find him a very nice man. He's always very grateful for anything you do for him. He was always very polite. He's quiet.'
Former Secretary of the Royal & Ancient, Sir Michael Bonallack

John Daly's Open Championship record sucked. Three times he had played in the event and twice he had finished last. The sole occasion when he had made any kind of an impression on the event was when he dumbfounded everyone at Royal St George's by driving the 421-yard par-four 5th during a practice round with Jack Nicklaus.

It had been a peculiar year for Daly. On the one hand, he had finally taken a firm grip on the chaos in his personal life and had continued to steer clear of alcohol; on the other, his golf was on a steady slide in the wrong direction. Going into the third major of the year at St Andrews, he had won just $102,582 from sixteen tournaments on the PGA Tour with a stroke average of 72.03 shots per round. In the cut-throat world of the tour, that simply wasn't good enough. It didn't augur well for the Open.

Earlier that year, Daly had contacted his old caddie Greg Rita and asked if he would like to team up again. The pair had split at the end of 1993 when Daly had been suspended from the PGA Tour, but now John, with his game on the wane, needed an experienced caddie by his side. Rita was intrigued. With Curtis Strange, he had already worked St Andrews at a couple of Dunhill

Cups, and at the last Open held there in 1990. Crucially, though, Rita had been on Daly's bag when he'd teamed up with Fred Couples and Payne Stewart to take the 1993 Dunhill Cup, and he had never forgotten just how well Daly had played during that event. 'He won four of his five matches and was a major factor in the US team's win,' he recalled. 'I felt St Andrews suited his game, so I snapped up the chance of working for him again.' After his joyless showing at the US Open, Daly had gone to the Greater Hartford Open and missed another cut. His game was in a rut. Between them, Daly and Rita agreed that given that nothing was going John's way, the best plan of action was to take a month off and get everything in shape for an assault on the 124th Open Championship. 'He'd said all along that if he was going to win a British Open it was going to be at St Andrews,' Rita added. 'I've been to nearly all the Open venues, and I definitely agreed with him.'

In the lead-up to the championship, Rita became increasingly excited about his employer's chances, even if the bookies thought he was no more than a 66–1 shot. 'He had stopped drinking, and a sober Daly was an entirely different prospect to the other character,' he explained. 'His actual playing form was not that stunning in May and June since I took over the bag. What was good, though, was his attitude and temperament – and his health. He proclaimed to me, "I'm really going for it this week. I'm going to win this thing."' Rita's hunch was shared by Michael Bonallack, then Secretary of the Royal & Ancient Golf Club, the St Andrews-based administrative body that governs the game outside the USA: 'He's got a magnificent short game and he's a long hitter who likes to draw the ball. If you're a long drawer of the ball and you've got a good short game at St Andrews, it suits your game perfectly.'

When they arrived in St Andrews, Daly and Rita went their separate ways. Being the pro with the fat wallet, Daly headed to the grandeur of the 'big house', otherwise known as the Old Course Hotel; Rita, meanwhile, made his way to some shared lodgings a bunch of fellow caddies had turned into a frat house for the week. It was a 'fantastic house', he said, 'turrets and all'. When Daly showed up for his practice round on Wednesday, still sporting the haircut from Hades and with a Marlboro seemingly welded to his lips, he and practice partner Phil Mickelson chided each other over their chances, staking $100 bets on each hole.

Ordinarily, Daly would have taken Fuzzy Zoeller out with him and the stakes would have been much, much higher, but Uncle Fuzzy was back home suffering from a bad back. Still, Daly reacquainted himself with links golf and mapped out his strategy. 'You can miss it left all day here,' he told the waiting press pack. 'That's where I intend to miss it.'

As usual, Daly would also rely on his length off the tee. Wilson had given him a new driver, the Invex, which he had already used at the US Open. It had just eight degrees of loft and was designed to lower the flight of the ball, making it ideal for the blustery conditions that often batter the Fife coast. His game plan was to do to the Old Course what he had done to Crooked Stick: hit it hard and hit it long. He earmarked those par-fours he felt capable of driving (there were five, maybe six), and the par-fives were there for the taking. And as for St Andrews' notorious bunkers, well, there were so many of them littered all over those ancient fairways that you were going to find them whatever club you took off the tee, so why not try to go over as many of them as you can? 'He had to go for it,' explained Rita. 'Anything else was so out of character, he would not have got the best out of a great opportunity.'

When Daly saw his draw, he smiled. For the first two rounds he would be paired with the 1987 Masters winner Larry Mize and former St Andrews winner Seve Ballesteros. Like Daly, Ballesteros was often wild off the tee but was blessed with a delicacy of touch around the greens that could extricate him from the most evil of positions. Having won at the Old Course in 1984, Seve was still a huge crowd puller in this part of Scotland, and as he was announced to the galleries to the usual deafening reception, Daly turned to Rita and told him that one day he hoped these very same crowds would be getting behind him in the same way.

Ironically, Daly started his first round with a migraine. 'He's been off the drink for two years and he has a headache!' joked Rita. Once under way, though, he soon found the Old Course to his liking, with birdies at two, three and four. It was like he had never been away. Elsewhere on the course, Daly's idol, Jack Nicklaus, was having a major headache of his own. At fourteen he found Hell bunker, and it soon lived up to its devilish reputation. At times, as he thrashed his club around with ever-increasing irritation, you could have been forgiven for thinking that here was the Golden Bear engaging in a bit of vigorous gardening, or attempting to dig the foundations for the mother of all sand castles. When he eventually emerged from the bunker he had taken four shots to get out, and went on to record a ten. Hell indeed.

Daly's distance and accuracy plan was paying off. Apart from the par-threes, the only holes he hadn't taken a driver on were thirteen and fifteen, and even his plan to 'miss it left' came into its own on the 18th. The fairway, which adjoins the first, is wider than the M25 and the only real trouble, if you can call it that, is if you block your tee-shot right and out of bounds. Daly stuck to his game plan and blasted one way, way left. The ball bounded and skipped along until it rattled under the temporary stand that lined the first fairway and came to a halt. With a free drop, Daly threw a sand wedge at his ball, leaving it seven feet from the hole, and then made the putt for birdie. A first-round 67, five under par, left him with a share of the lead with his compatriots Ben Crenshaw and Tom Watson, and the Zimbabwean Mark McNulty.

Two days in and the Open was already throwing up some new stars for the watching world. The biggest of these, literally, was the giant Scottish amateur Gordon Sherry. At six feet eight inches, Sherry was in real danger of toppling over as the winds gradually picked up and took their toll on the players' hairstyles. A first-round 70 followed by a 71 had left his playing partners, some guys called Tom Watson and Greg Norman, trailing in his wake. Also making waves was another amateur, Tiger Woods, the kid Daly had beaten back in 1989. As the reigning US Amateur champion, the slender-looking nineteen-year-old from the States was making his debut in the Open and was looking every bit the phenomenon people were calling him. Some commentators even marked him down as a future winner. Little did they know that he would return to St Andrews in 2000 and leave as champion.

But there was one other name that was threatening to dominate proceedings at the Home of Golf, at least in the mind (and stomach) of John Daly. That man was the intriguingly named Otis Spunkmeyer. The first thing you should know about Otis, incidentally, is that he is a fictitious character. His is a name dreamed up in some marketeer's head to promote a brand of chocolate-chip muffin. Rich, stodgy and hugely calorific, it is difficult for a normal person with an average appetite to consume just one of Mr Spunkmeyer's muffins, but on the 8th tee alone Daly demolished four without so much as a pause for breath. That said, he had an excuse. 'I'd been awake since four a.m.,' he explained. 'My wife and I forgot to close the drapes and we didn't realise it got light up here around that time. I didn't feel like having any breakfast, so by the 8th tee I was starving.' Further muffins at ten, fourteen and eighteen gave Daly the energy to get around in a one-under-par 71. Even the Scottish, a race who by and large have taken to healthy eating like a duck to concrete, were taken aback by the Arkansan's insatiable appetite. For once, it seemed, Daly was marching on his stomach, not on his liver. 'Tracking down chocolate-chip muffins became a major task for me,' said Rita. 'I had to seek them out about every other hole. There was a big supply, particularly behind the 10th. John sure ate a whole lot of muffins that week.' Later, Daly would deflect media interest in his on-course overindulgence by saying, 'Listen, as long as my pants fit, I really don't care.'

As Daly ploughed through the confectionery, his golf was proving an ideal match for the demands of the Old Course. The new Wilson driver was working well, and as for his putter, well, that was on fire. 'His lag putting was just phenomenal all week,' Rita recalled. On St Andrews' trademark double greens, Daly was regularly faced with putts of over 50 feet; top of the pile, however, was the 180-foot monster he found himself up against on the 12th. He left it just four feet away. 'It was the hardest I swung all day,' he joked. 'We don't have any 180-foot greens in the States. I mean, hell, the 8th green is like a Canadian football field.'

As Daly left the 18th with a share of the lead with Brad Faxon and Katsuyoshi Tomori, his playing partner Ballesteros gave the press an idea of just how far Daly was hitting the ball. 'He play spectacular,' the Spaniard observed. 'There are no par-fives for him. Well, there are no par-fours for him either.' And a good day was about to get better. When Daly returned to his hotel he found a box of chocolate muffins waiting for him. One of the traders, grateful for the ringing celebrity endorsement he had given his stall, had arranged for a consignment to be left in his room.

Ben Crenshaw is one of those legendary golf names you automatically assume has a trunk-load of major titles stashed away in his double garage, but it was not without reason that 'Gentle' Ben was once described as 'the best damn second- and third-place finisher in the majors the world will ever know'. A marvel on the greens, Crenshaw eventually claimed the Masters title in 1984 after five runners-up places in majors, and had added another Masters to his record earlier that year. For Daly's third round, Crenshaw was the perfect foil. 'John considered him an all-time great sportsman and gentleman and looked up to him,' Rita explained. 'That's why he was pleased to be playing with Ben because I think that settled him down right away.'

A bogey at the 1st hinted otherwise. Nevertheless, Daly looked as relaxed and as focused as a man with a potentially crippling chocolate habit could be. He even took time out to autograph a TV camera lens on his way round. After bogeying the short 8th, Daly unleashed a rapier of a tee-shot at nine, driving the 356 yards to the green, much to the delight of the galleries, and clawing back one of the dropped shots. But all the good work of the round, and indeed the opening rounds, was in grave danger of being written off by a calamity at the Road Hole. But that's St Andrews for you. You can ease yourself along, picking up the odd birdie here and there, minding your own business, when whack!, something as pernicious, something as bloody irritating as the Road Hole rears up and slaps you back down again. Daly had paid an unscheduled visit to Scholars bunker, which like most other bunkers on the Old Course is about as welcoming as a Wild West saloon. It cost him a double bogey. 'It's just a tough golf hole,' he would say after his round. 'It's not a hole I'd want to have to make birdie on to win a major championship, I can tell you that. Making par there is almost like making a birdie.'

Daly checked the leaderboard. The name of New Zealander Michael Campbell stood at the top. On his way to a third-round 65 he had notched up eight birdies in his first fourteen holes and played what can only be described as a miracle shot out of the Road Hole bunker. It was unquestionably the round of the tournament. At nine under in the clubhouse, Campbell was five shots clear of Daly. If he was going to stay in the hunt, Daly would need a birdie at the last.

If Daly had suffered some cruel misfortune at seventeen, he would benefit from the biggest slice of luck imaginable at the final hole. Visibly irritated, he stepped up at eighteen and took all his frustration out on the ball. His drive was simply enormous, reminiscent of Nicklaus whipping off his sweater and driving the green there in the play-off in 1970. Low and hooking, it skipped straight through the Valley of Sin that surrounds the front of the green before scuttling up the little hill in front of the clubhouse, sending amazed R&A officials scurrying out of the way. Daly and Rita watched it, fearing that it was heading out of bounds, but as it reached the top of the hill, it slowed up and obligingly rolled back down again. Another foot and Daly would have been out of bounds and out of the reckoning. 'When you're talking about a golf ball going 360 yards, as John's ball had done, and less than a yard more and the ball's out of bounds, that's scary – scary for the caddie as well,' Rita commented. Daly made the most of his good fortune. He putted down the slope to eight feet and duly holed out for a much-needed birdie. His 73 left him tied for fourth at five under. Despite his worst round of the week, Daly was upbeat about his chances. 'On this golf course if you're seven or eight shots back you're still in it,' he reasoned. 'They say the wind's supposed to blow a lot harder tomorrow, so I'm kinda glad I'm not in the last group.' And, as a bona fide major winner, what, ventured a reporter, would Daly's advice be to the leader Campbell? 'Just go and make three or four double bogeys so I have a chance to win,' he replied.

Fail to prepare, they say, and you prepare to fail. Look at Tiger Woods. The guy is up with the larks and hitting balls before most of us have stuck our hands out from under the duvet and located the snooze button. Or Faldo. He'll be down on the range with Fanny hours after everyone has long since retired to bed or to the bar. Other players will have one-to-one sessions with swing gurus, 'mind coaches', with managers and agents. Some even talk to their wives.

You could say that John Daly's preparation for his final round in the 1995 Open Championship was a mite unorthodox. He was due to play with the South African Ernie Els in game 50 and he wasn't due out until just after 2.00 p.m. Nevertheless, he woke early (even though he and Paulette hadn't got to sleep until 3.30 a.m.), 'ate five or six chocolate croissant things' for breakfast, then slumped on his bed and watched some movies (*Mr Baseball* with Tom Selleck followed by Richard Dreyfuss in *Another Stakeout*, for the record). After that, 2.00 p.m. still seemed like an age away and there was no way Daly was hitting the range when the wind outside was blowing the slates off the roofs. So what does a good country boy do when he's got some time on his hands? Why, he rocks out, of course. Daly spent an hour working off the calorific damage of breakfast by dancing around his hotel room with Paulette to some Wilson Pickett CDs.

For once the Met Office had got it right, and the wind was now gusting at over 50mph. It would make spectating, let alone playing, extremely difficult, and Daly's suggestion that someone as far back as seven or eight shots could come through to win seemed eminently plausible. But with the weather taking a turn for the worse, there were several commentators who felt Daly's all-guns-blazing approach would prove to be his undoing. Sceptic-in-chief was none other than Jack Nicklaus. 'I don't think this is his day. Daly will have a tough time in this wind because, like me when I was his age, he hits the ball too high and too hard. He has trouble keeping it low.' According to Greg Rita, though, there was a far more pressing problem than the gales whipping the Old Course. Try as he might, the caddie couldn't find one chocolate-chip muffin in town. 'I think John must have had the last batch the night before!' he said with a smile.

There was no time to worry. It was high time to prove to everyone that John Daly could tackle this sea breeze head on, and beat it. He started magnificently, picking up three shots on the front nine, while the pressure of being the championship leader was clearly getting the better of Campbell. The New Zealander dropped shots at five and six, and when Daly sank an eighteen-footer at eight for birdie, the Wild Thing had a lead of one.But then Daly, too, found that having the label of 'tournament leader' hanging round your neck was a heavy burden to bear. The birdies dried up and, critically, the swirling wind was now making club selection virtually impossible. Only the portly Italian pro Costantino Rocca was hanging in there with Daly, but even he was three shots adrift when John took to the 16th tee.

Surely now the claret jug was his. Daly whipped his driver out of the bag when everyone, including Nicklaus in the commentary box, was advising a more conservative play. But, just as he'd thrown caution to the wind at the final hole at Crooked Stick, so he would again at St Andrews, and he produced an imperious drive that split the fairway. 'He was totally unafraid about using the driver all week,' remembered Rita. 'That was his strength, and he knew that he would live and die by the driver.' Sadly, his putting wasn't as hot, and he had to hole a five-footer just to avoid four-putting the hole. Daly's lead was down to two, and in front of him was arguably the hardest par-four in golf.

In the calmest of conditions the Road Hole is still unfeasibly hard. It is 461 yards of abject misery, with thick rough down the left and the tiniest of greens at the end. To have any chance of making the green, your tee-shot needs to flirt with the out of bounds along the right of the fairway to give you the best angle in. Overshoot on the second shot and you'll find yourself on the road over the back of the green. Short and left, and you'll be buried alive in the most famous bunker in the game.

As Daly stood on the tee, the wind blew in hard from the right. It brought tears to his eyes and made his hair look like a haystack in a hurricane. He was shaking. The bogey at sixteen had released a battalion of demons in his head and they were in danger of getting the better of him. Ahead of him stood the one hole that could render his entire week's work pointless. One hole between him and history.

So what does Daly do? He lets the big dog eat. Nicklaus was dumbfounded. 'Oh, my gosh. Oh, no,' he spluttered, in much the same way a motorist would if he collided with a cat. This time his fears were well founded. Daly's tee-shot started left and got blown even further left into the rough. His second shot was much the same.

'Is that all right?' Daly asked Rita as the ball flew through the air. Rita looked worried. 'No,' he said. 'It's left.'

'Left' meant the Road Hole bunker, and when Daly got there he found his ball up against the face. Some players call this situation an 'Arafat', i.e. ugly and in the sand. Fortunately, Els had deposited his ball in precisely the same place and it was the South African to play first. There aren't enough adjectives to describe just how horrendous, how thoroughly wicked this bunker is. Suffice to say that the TV companies now put a tiny camera in the face of it just so the viewers back home can have a live close-up of a man's career taking a traumatic turn for the worse. Somehow, though, Els managed to dig himself out from the mess he was in and by doing so gave Daly some hope. 'I don't know what I would have done if Ernie didn't hit first,' Daly would explain later. 'I figured, hey, if he can get it out then maybe I can, because I really didn't have any other way to go with it.' Chopping out to 40 feet, Daly missed his par putt but managed to walk off with a bogey. A lead of one going down eighteen.

There were now three players just one shot behind Daly. Little-known English pro Steven Bottomley had recorded the best round of the day, a 69, and was in the clubhouse at five under, but it was Rocca and Campbell in the final group behind Daly who were the real threats. Time for caution. For the first time that week, Daly took an iron at eighteen, just in case bravado or adrenalin got the better of him and he ended up putting the windows through on the clubhouse. It was Sunday after all, and have you ever tried getting a glazier on a Sunday?

Way left again. A par from here would be a result. Daly chipped up to twelve feet and left himself a birdie putt. Knock that in and surely that old jug would be his. But he didn't knock it in. Agonisingly, it missed by inches. Still, a round of 71 gave him a six-under total of 282. All he could do now was watch and wait.

Campbell and Rocca stood on the 18th tee knowing full well what they had to do. Campbell had toiled manfully but still needed an eagle two to force a play-off. He wouldn't get it. But Rocca, the former box maker from Bergamo, needed only a birdie and that was well within range. His drive was long and left and resulted in a 35-yard pitch in for his second shot. He was in with a real chance. Rocca stood over his ball and drew his wedge back. Then, much like your granddad trying his hand at crazy golf, he duffed it. The club caught the turf before the ball and spooned it just a few feet closer to the hole. Those in the game call such a shot a 'chilli dip'; Rocca doubtless had another, probably four-lettered, name for it. The crowd groaned. In an instant, Rocca had metamorphosed from championship challenger to 24-handicapper novice. He looked distraught.

The Dalys, meanwhile, had repaired to one of the TV vans to watch the final group finish on the monitors. When Rocca fluffed his chip, Paulette squeezed John, prematurely congratulating him on his second major win; Bud Martin started to jump around behind the 18th green like a baboon. Even Daly afforded himself a little smile. Rita was less confident. He had seen the American Jim Gallagher Jr hole a similar putt on the opening day and was telling himself, 'It's not over. Got to be ready for a play-off.'

Rocca's normally jovial demeanour had vanished into the fresh Fife air and been replaced by a worn-out, washed-out expression more befitting a man at a funeral. His caddie reached into the bag and pulled out the putter. Thankfully, he had forgotten to pack the revolver. Remarkably, Rocca held himself together with admirable fortitude and checked out his line. There in front of him was a putt of some 65 feet, through the infamous Valley of Sin.

It was three-, maybe four-putt territory. Get down in two and second place would be his.

The Italian crouched over the putt, made his stroke and immediately began walking after the ball. When a player moves so soon after a putt it can mean one of two things: either it's missed by a country mile or it's dead centre. As the ball meandered down towards its target, the crowd sensed that it was going to be very close. On and on it travelled, down, up and over the Valley of Sin, weaving its way towards the cup. When it eventually reached the hole it fairly rattled in. Bedlam. 'Absolute total amazement' according to Bonallack. Rocca couldn't believe his eyes. He dropped to his knees and began beating his fists on the ground like a teenage boy roughing up his little brother.

'I feel like I've been kicked in the stomach,' moaned Paulette.

'I feel like a jerk,' muttered Martin.

Now it was Daly's turn to look shattered. The 124th Open Championship had been in his grasp, but had been taken away from him by a plump Italian bloke who used to work in a box factory. 'It was just unreal. I could not believe it,' he would explain later. 'It was more of a shock than anything. But I shrugged and said to myself, "OK, let's go to the 1st tee." My state of mind going to the 1st was, "Let's play, see what happens." People often wonder why I didn't crumble after that putt, but remember, Costantino was emotionally drained too.'

As Daly composed himself, Corey Pavin, Bob Estes and Brad Faxon all passed by and offered words of advice and encouragement. Despite everything – the drug accusations, the boorish behaviour, the life-threatening tee-shots – it seemed the other players were still pulling for him. Mark Brooks even handed over his yardage book when Rita couldn't find his. Daly was touched. 'I've made some mistakes, and my big mistake in 1994 was talking to that guy [the *Sun*'s Ben Bacon]. But it was really nice of Mark and Bob and Corey to kind of rally behind me there. I needed it.'

And there was no doubting that the momentum had shifted in favour of Rocca. From wanting the 18th fairway to open up and swallow him whole, the 39-year-old Italian was now in pole position and it was Daly's turn to pick himself up and steel himself for another four holes. The pair would play the 1st, 2nd, 17th and 18th again until a winner emerged.

Those expecting an enthralling play-off with two of golf's genuine heavyweights slugging it out would be disappointed. It was effectively all over by the second hole. At the 1st, Rocca three-putted for bogey while Daly made a steady par; at the second Daly drained a huge 40-foot putt for a birdie. Two shots clear after two. But it was the 17th that not only cemented Daly's victory but proved beyond any doubt that here was a player who had so much more to his game than just 'grip it and rip it', a player who could think his way around a golf course and who could call upon an array of shots when the need arose.

Rocca had dumped his second in the Road Hole bunker in almost the same spot Daly had been in an hour or so earlier. It didn't look good. All Daly needed to do was find the green, which he duly did with one of the shots of the championship. With the wind still dominating, he conjured up a low, hooking punch with a nine-iron that curled from right to left and ran up on to the green, twenty feet from the cup. Par was a nailed-on certainty. Rocca took three shots to escape from the bunker, and it was game over.

Incredibly, Daly had a lead of five shots going into the 18th. The only way he could lose now was if the Royal & Ancient decided that he would have to play the last hole left-handed and wearing a blindfold. Fortunately, they didn't. Instead, Daly walked up the fairway as the Open champion, even if he still had to finish the hole. At just 29, he had become only the fourth player in the post-war era – after Jack Nicklaus, Tom Watson and Johnny Miller – to win a second major before the age of 30. As Paulette rushed on to the green, the crowd rose as one to applaud.

Earlier in the week, when Daly had breezed into this bleak Fife town looking like a trucker who had taken a wrong turning at Edinburgh and had stopped to ask directions, he was asked whether he would join the Royal & Ancient if he won the Open and the powers that be gave him the nod. For most professionals – players who know on which side their millionaire bread is buttered – such a question would elicit the kind of deferential, reverential response usually reserved for meetings with the Queen or Arnold Palmer. For Daly, though, it was no big deal. 'I ain't joinin' if there's rules and crap,' he answered. 'I hate them rules and crap.' Anyway, there were more serious things to consider. A few pals back home had promised to shave their heads if Daly won. 'Hell,' he added, 'I might do it too.'

As he stood among the assembled suits of the R&A in front of 30,000 fans and countless millions of television viewers around the world, the enormity of what he had just achieved began to kick in. Sir Michael Bonallack approached the microphone. 'The champion golfer of the year and the winner of the Gold Medal with a score of 282 – JOHN DALY!' More applause, then this tubby guy in a green sweatshirt with a haircut they hadn't seen in these parts since Kajagoogoo played at the university shook hands with the Secretary and took possession of the most famous trophy in golf. Bonallack ushered him towards the microphone.

'What the hell do you want me to say?' he joked, before getting as serious as John Daly ever gets. 'This is unbelievable. I . . . I . . . I'm just lost for words. But this goes to everybody, all my fans at home, but especially to all you people who rooted for me this week. God bless you, this is awesome.'

The hick had gone and done it again.

15. SWEET DREAMS

WILD THING – YOU MADE OUR HEARTS SING

Daily Mirror headline, 24 July 1995

Even in the world of John Daly, where black is often white and where night sometimes passes for day, it had been a preposterous year. There had been another suspension (albeit a voluntary one), a long-awaited divorce, a shotgun wedding, the birth of his daughter and now, to cap it all, the chain-smoking ex-drinker with the heavy-metal haircut and the hamburger habit had gone and won the greatest competition of them all. And it was still only July.

While the R&A colonels lurched between laughter and tears, Daly sat in the press conference surrounded by a multitude of microphones. Clearly bewildered, he looked at the claret jug and took a deep breath, followed by a long, satisfying pull on a Marlboro. 'I feel wonderful, on top of the mountain,' he said. 'Looking at the Open Championship trophy makes me just grateful I kicked the booze into touch. I've won a trophy that is littered with greats. My name is now up there. It's almost as good as beating booze – but not quite. That was my greatest battle.' It was time for some dedications: Greg Rita ('I owe a lot to him'); Mum, Dad, Rick Ross, the fans; there were so many folk he needed to thank. At the top of the list, though, was his wife Paulette. Describing her as his 'cornerstone', Daly explained that there had been some tough times over the years, times when he had seriously considered quitting the game. Throughout the darkest of his days, however, Paulette had always been there for him, and now, with an eight-week-old daughter as well, Daly was the happiest he had been in years. What's more, he had some very definite plans for the future. 'Paulette had better be ready to have more,' he announced, 'because I'm going to get a boy.'

When Daly had completed the formalities of the press interviews, the photo calls and the meetings with the Championship Committee, he went to locate his caddie. When he finally found him, they smiled at each other. John asked Greg whether he would like to have his picture taken with him; Greg said yes, and the two walked down the 18th fairway and sat on the famous Swilcan Bridge as the photographers clicked away. Then, as Rita made tracks to one of his old haunts, the Dunvegan Hotel, for 'a few lagers', Daly headed back to his hotel room with Paulette ('I guess he went looking for chocolate-chip muffins,' joked Rita) and managed to toast his success with nothing stronger than a Diet Coke.

Somewhere in the background, Bud Martin was desperately trying to locate a calculator. As one of Daly's representatives, he had watched his client's latest victory with a mile-wide smile on his face and was doubtless endeavouring to work out just what 15 per cent of a huge amount of money was. Before he set foot in Scotland, Daly had already held sizeable contracts with Wilson, Reebok, Hudson Foods and Oakley sunglasses reportedly worth up to $5 million to him every year. Now, in the wake of his Open triumph, even conservative estimates suggested that that figure could double. 'John is already a dollar millionaire. Now the sky is the limit,' Martin enthused. 'The next contracts are going to start out at really high levels. Everybody will be playing with John Daly clubs.' It was a view reinforced by Martin's partner, John Mascatello. 'People who don't even play golf know John Daly's name,' he argued. Such recognition, he added, would not come cheap, and soon the likes of Haagen-Dazs and Coca-Cola would come a-courting, not merely with offers of untold wealth but with an endless supply of free samples, too.

As a two-time major winner, though, Daly was being a tad more circumspect about what the prestigious title of Open champion would do for his stop–start career. After his spectacular victory at Crooked Stick, Daly had gone everywhere and done everything just to keep the people happy and it had very nearly cost him his place on tour, his marriage and his sanity. If he had learned anything from his first major, it was that big as he was, there still wasn't enough of John Daly to go around. 'When I won the US PGA, I told my agency to book me everything, to let me see the world, because I hadn't done so before,' he explained. 'Now I'll be more selective. I suppose you could say I have grown up. I won the PGA at 25 but, boy, I was a young 25. Now I'll try to be more patient.'

Back in Arkansas, Jim and Lou Daly were shaking. They had just witnessed their son claim the most famous trophy in golf at the most historic course in the world and were, understandably, ecstatic. But they had nearly missed it. As John had prepared to start the play-off, a violent thunderstorm in Dardanelle had knocked out the power at their home and they were forced to race to Wanda Ferguson's house some five miles away to watch the conclusion. They arrived just as John was tackling the 17th again. 'We had to get there in a hurry,' recalled Jim, who nearly made the trip to Scotland with John. 'John had tried to get me to get a passport and go with him, but I didn't, and now I'm kind of kicking myself. It would have been nice to be over there, but it was nice to watch, too.' Later, Daly found some space and time to call home. 'I've got to say he was pretty happy,' Jim added. 'We were kind of all screaming into the phone. And I guess we've probably had twenty or more calls from friends. It's been pretty exciting.' It was only when the phone was handed to his mother that John suddenly found himself unable to speak. It was OK, though; Mama Lou knew what he wanted to hear. 'Son,' she whispered, 'you did wonderful.'

Just as in 1991, it seemed as though everyone in the South had stopped whatever they were doing just to watch Daly's march towards golfing immortality. Daly even took another call from his old buddy Bill Clinton, only this time Bill had gotten himself a big promotion and a nice new oval-shaped office in Washington DC.

Like the Dalys, Don Cline was also waylaid by the storm in Dardanelle. 'It was one of the biggest moments in John's life. Then, poof, my television blew up. I went upstairs to what I call my John Daly Room. It's a room filled with all kinds of Daly memorabilia – and a small TV set.' To his relief, it had a clear picture. Jane Witherell, the teaching professional at Bay Ridge, meanwhile, grabbed her mother Shirley when the power went in the clubhouse and drove around the area until they found a house with a light on. 'We knocked on the door, but no one answered,' she recalled. 'I could hear the television and I had to see John win more than life itself.' Fortunately, the elderly couple inside invited them in rather than chase them off their land. 'No one round here knows much about golf,' added Witherell, 'but they can all tell you about the British Open.'

Elsewhere, the reaction to Daly's win was unanimous: 'It was so funny to hear Jack Nicklaus say John should do this or that. John has never fit the norm from the time he was a teenager. He's got his own way of playing golf courses. You have to give him credit. He won and is part of golf history' (Jay Fox, executive director, ASGA); 'Boy, I was sweating like a racehorse at that point [when Rocca holed his putt]. I didn't know whether to go to the bathroom or throw up. But I wasn't surprised, because he's been working his tail off on his short game. He's also one of the few guys who can hang in there and get the job done when he's in the hunt. He might hit a bad shot, but he won't choke' (Bill Woodley, University of Arkansas golf coach); 'We're the only school that's got an assistant coach that's won the British Open. This is publicity for the state of Arkansas that we couldn't buy for millions of dollars' (Frank Broyles, University of Arkansas athletic director); 'I actually fell out of my chair when that guy [Rocca] made that putt. I couldn't believe it' (Ken Garland, Daly's Southwind neighbour); 'He hasn't been around here in a little while, but we had to pull for him, and we're all real happy for him' (Dan Shineberger, professional at Chickasaw Country Club).

While friends and family were celebrating the latest of Daly's improbable victories, the world's media had cranked up the Daly press machine once more and slipped it into overdrive. Generally speaking, what had impressed most commentators was the manner of his victory. While his Crooked Stick win had been characterised by his obscene length off the tee and some super-slick putting, the conquest of St Andrews had been built on something previously unseen in Daly's golf game – patience. It was a sure sign that, finally, maturity was catching up with the 29-year-old.

What Daly would also discover, however, was that after his repeated clashes with the game's authorities and the shenanigans of his all-too-public private life, being the Open champion had now given him a new legitimacy in the game. Where once he was viewed as some faintly amusing sideshow to the main event of the PGA Tour, now it was like lifting the claret jug had magically wiped the slate clean. Everyone was slapping him on the back and telling him how well he had done. People were even talking of him in the same breath as proven winners like Nick Price and Nick Faldo, and these were players who had never come near to drinking themselves to death or destroying their houses.

For a press faced with an army of identikit players on tour and still hungry for a new star in the game, Daly's triumph-over-near-tragedy story was perfect. The London newspaper the *Evening Standard*, for instance, declared that Daly had written the script for a sure-fire hit, maintaining that his win 'included all the ingredients any Hollywood producer would be looking for in a blockbuster movie'. The *Los Angeles Times* decided it was the day 'golf needed smelling salts', adding that 'they [the R&A officials] were afraid he'd clap the Queen on the back, ask the Prime Minister if he'd heard the one about the two rabbis and the priest, and drink coffee with the spoon in'. The *Commercial Appeal* in Memphis, meanwhile, kept it short and to the point: 'Hail, Big John, king of Scotland.'

Two days after his victory, Daly was in Holland for the Heineken Dutch Open, politeness personified and endeavouring to fulfil all his prior commitments. For once, he was behaving like a genuine champion.

Daly had arrived at the Hilversum course near Amsterdam after his stablemates from the Cambridge Sports Agency. Alongside Daly there was a group of Mascatello and Martin's clients playing in the event, the idea being that if a promoter wanted Daly at his tournament he had to take a handful of the agency's other players too, the net result being that it looked like some kind of mass golfing package deal. One of these players was the American Mike Springer, whose caddie happened to be Daly's old bagman Dave Beighle. Before the tournament, Beighle and the guys gathered in Daly's hotel room. As Daly had been swamped by the media in the wake of his victory at St Andrews, this was the first opportunity any of them had had to congratulate him on his success. Opening the door, Daly smiled and ushered them inside; each of them filed past, slapped the champ on his back and ruffled his hair. When everyone was inside and the door was closed, Daly spoke. 'Hey, come over here, I wanna show you something,' he

said, pointing to a metal suitcase in the corner of the room.
Nobody knew what to expect. After all, this was John Daly, and
they were in Amsterdam. Calmly, Daly walked over to the case,
picked it up and placed it on the table. Then, with all the caution
of a bomb disposal expert choosing the right wire, he opened it.
There, inside, was the Open Championship trophy.

Beighle couldn't believe it. 'Is that really it?' he asked. 'Are you
telling me they're letting you take this?'

Daly nodded. Despite his reputation as one of the more
unpredictable players on tour, he had been carrying the most
illustrious trophy in the game around with him like it was an
overnight bag.

'There's no way they're letting you take this thing around and
you don't have like a guard outside your door,' Beighle continued,
shaking his head.

Daly sniggered, a mischievous look in his eye, and closed the
case.

That week, he would manage to drag himself away from the
claret jug long enough to claim a tie for 50th place. He would also
take the clippers to his head and shave himself bald. A bet was a
bet after all.

It was another sunny August morning in California. John Daly
stood on one of the runways at Santa Monica airport with a golf
ball at his feet and the new Wilson Invex driver in his hands. As
he shaped to hit the ball, a small aircraft stopped in his path some
way away. Daly looked up. 'Those guys got insurance?' he asked,
before spanking the ball nearly 600 yards down the runway.

It was Daly's first public appearance in the United States since
winning the Open, and Wilson had set up the stunt to publicise
the driver Daly had used at St Andrews. The company's ad men
had even thought up a catchy new slogan: 'Today the British
Open – Tomorrow the World'. Also on hand was the Wilson
president John Riccitiello, the man who had signed Daly to his
ten-year deal and had given him the tools to do the job in
Scotland. That said, he was also the man who had pulled the plug
when Daly had voluntarily taken a four-month break at the end
of 1994, but that was history now, wasn't it? 'We had no question
that we were going to stick with him,' maintained Riccitiello.
'We're big backers, and I personally am a big fan. It's incredible
what he's pulled off. We're proud of that.'

When Daly was done frightening pilots, he made his way to the studios of the *Tonight Show* with Jay Leno, part of a line-up of guests that included the comic Bill Maher and the supermodel Linda Evangelista. With his freshly shaved head and wearing a leopard-skin jacket, Daly received the kind of raucous welcome he was gradually getting used to. Asked why he had cut his hair again, he told the host that he was bored with the old style and had cut it off without telling the wife. Later, Leno dragged an audience member on stage and let Daly loose on his head with a pair of clippers. By the end of the show, he was bald.

The chief reason for Daly's trip to California, however, was not just to defrost after the Scandinavian Masters in Sweden or to rub shoulders with supermodels; he was there to take part in the PGA Championship. As the last major of the year, the competition at the Riviera Club in Pacific Palisades was also the final event in which Daly could win qualification points for the American Ryder Cup team. Before his victory in the Open, Daly's chances of making the team were remote, bordering on extinct. Now, after his triumph at St Andrews, a third-place finish or higher at the PGA would guarantee automatic selection for the match with Europe at Oak Hill in late September.

It is one of the great sporting anomalies that John Daly has never represented his country in golf's premier team competition. To date, he is the only player to have won two major championships never to have qualified or been picked to play. Scores of other players with far less talent, not to mention charisma, have played in the event and a great many, like Colin Montgomerie and Phil Mickelson, have never won a major. That Daly has been extremely unlucky is beyond question. In 1991, when he won the PGA Championship, the qualification rules for the American Ryder Cup team changed so that the PGA champion no longer received an automatic place; as he finished seventeenth on the money list he missed out again. He was invited to attend the event at Kiawah Island, South Carolina – the so-called 'War on the Shore' – as an unofficial team member, but he declined. Daly's dream of a place in the 1995 Ryder Cup team was as good as over by the twelfth hole of his first round when an ugly triple bogey buried any lingering chance he might have had. Still, it wasn't all bad. After holing out at twelve, Daly was walking to the next tee when a female spectator reached out over the ropes and gave him a doughnut 'right out of the box'. It made his day.

When the PGA was completed on Sunday and Daly's old friend Steve Elkington had captured the Wanamaker trophy, the American Ryder Cup captain Lanny Wadkins announced his two wild-card picks for the competition, his experienced chums Fred Couples and Curtis Strange. Daly, according to the powers that be, wasn't a team player. Nonsense, said Bill Woodley, who even wrote a letter to Wadkins demanding John's inclusion in the team. 'I wish he had been selected to a Ryder Cup team because there was no one more team-oriented than John Daly,' he insisted. 'We [the University of Arkansas golf team] lost the Conference by two shots one year and we were just devastated. John was just sobbing uncontrollably. I never saw him get that upset about a poor individual performance. He was a tremendous team player.'

Though Wadkins' decision rankled with Daly, he soon let it go. It would have been nice to play for his country, he reflected, but it wasn't the end of the world. Instead, he turned his thoughts to his new home, just behind the driving range at the Pinnacle Country Club in Rogers, Arkansas. Although he had kept the house at the Southwind, Daly had decided to move back to Arkansas to be closer to home – and to the Razorbacks, of course. 'I miss seeing Arkansas football and basketball games,' he said.

Daly's decision to head back to the Natural State and the bosom of his family was taken as proof that his second major title, and all the many fringe benefits that accompanied it, wasn't going to his newly shaven head. Indeed, as Jim Murray of the *Los Angeles Times* argued, 'it would take more than a British Open to change Our John', adding that he was still the kind of goofball who would 'spot Prince Charles in the gallery, sidle over and mutter: "Say, Bo, got a light?"'

16. THE SONG REMAINS THE SAME

'Without a drink, I'm like a tea bag without water.'

Jeffrey Bernard (1932–1997)

A s the first tournament of the new season, the Mercedes Championship is one of the few PGA events at which the majority of players look rested, healthy and cheerful. With a new campaign ahead of them, there is none of the anxiety, self-doubt or loss of form that will inevitably rear its head at some stage. It is a clean slate, a fresh start for everyone; hope springs eternal and golfing immortality is always just 72 holes away.

Except for John Daly, obviously. While most players had returned home for a peaceful Christmas with their families, Daly had spent his vacation trying manfully to avoid the sherry. Matters had reached a head on New Year's Eve when with the whole of Memphis partying Daly had grabbed his Uncle Ben and, in a bid to ease the almost overpowering urge to drink, flown to Las Vegas for a sober night at the slots. Then, when he was sure that the fun at home was well and truly over, he boarded a dawn flight and returned to Southwind.

His desire to drink was understandable. When he arrived in San Diego for the season's curtain-raiser he was already riddled with anxiety, crippled by self-doubt and suffering a loss of form that had seen him record a score of 36 over par for his last four rounds of competitive golf. That week he started shakily again, a four-over-par 76 doing little to convince anyone that the Open champion was ready to tackle the challenge of the new season head on. After his second round, a clumsy 75, Daly sat down and spoke to Bill Blighton of the *Mail on Sunday* and explained how his continuing woes on the course were the very least of his worries. 'The only thing in my life I am afraid of is that I might drink again. That's the one thing I have to stay away from. If I keep away from booze then I am not afraid of anything,' he declared. 'If you've got a problem you are going to want it all the time. It's like golf and food. I am a die-hard golfer, junk-food eater and Marlboro smoker.'

During the course of the interview, Daly informed Blighton that as part of his enduring struggle with alcohol he was still avoiding AA meetings like they were a gymnasium, preferring instead to speak with his friend and rehabilitation counsellor Thomas Henderson whenever he felt the need for support or guidance. In short, he was still trying to do things his way. 'He [Henderson] understands the problems of being in the spotlight all the time. Another athlete understands the problems you have better than someone who has never been in competition. The one thing he said that really sticks with me is: "I regret I will never know how good I could have been." I've got time on my side and I hope, I sure hope, that I will never have the same regret.'

While the diminution of his powers was all too evident, Daly was nevertheless still enjoying huge support from the galleries and, crucially, sponsors. In fact, there seemed to be some peculiar inverse relationship developing: the worse Daly's golf got, the more the Cambridge Sports office phone seemd to ring. The latest backer to find some space on Daly's increasingly crowded bag was the Mark Christopher Auto Center, a major car dealer based in California. As specialists in Chevrolets, they wanted Daly to drive their cars – only not, presumably, in the same way he had after that night out with his brother in 1989. 'I've always been a Chevy guy,' Daly would say of the deal, 'so it was a great combination,' although you suspect that if a bra manufacturer or a diaper company had given him enough money he would have said much the same thing.

The Mark Christopher deal was testament to Daly's enduring popularity among his blue-collar constituency. Their reckoning – in fact any sponsor's reckoning – was that Daly was always going to be high profile no matter what he did. Whether he was winning a major or missing the cut and bending his putter over his knee, you were virtually guaranteed exposure. The only real question for potential endorsers was whether they could live with the occasional, and almost inevitable, episode of bad press.

Back Daly went to Australia, stopping off in Singapore on the way to take eighteenth place in the Johnnie Walker Classic, then taking fifth in the Heineken Classic in Perth. Surprisingly, after three rounds he was even sharing the lead with the eventual winner, Ian Woosnam. The highlight of the trip, however, was the $250,000 he picked up at the casino one evening. It was a welcome tonic: he had lost $200,000 just a few days earlier. Still, the display in Perth was a timely reminder to those who were writing off Daly. Sure, there were the age-old problems with his performance (strong start, weak finish), but two top-twenty finishes in as many weeks was as good as he could have hoped for.

For whatever reason, Daly left his confidence behind in Australia. On his return home, he simply took up on the PGA Tour where he'd left off, struggling to make cuts and flattering to deceive with a couple of top-twenty finishes, all of which was strangely reminiscent of the state of his game going into the Open at St Andrews in 1995. This year, however, Daly had things on his mind, things beyond chocolate muffins and contract discussions. Over the course of the last twelve months, a year which had seen Daly garner more wealth than he could ever have imagined, he had discovered more than a grain of truth in the maxim that money can't always buy you happiness. But then Daly never did shop in the same places as most folk.

There were changes to be made, and fast. The first thing that needed rectifying was his living arrangements. Although he had bought the house in Rogers over six months ago, it was still sitting empty as Daly tried to find the time to make the move. Staying in Southwind was no longer a viable option. The longer they lived there, the more Daly would be tempted by the ever-increasing number of casinos that were springing up in Memphis. In Rogers, there were no casinos, just peace, quiet and perfect facilities for practising golf. In short, significantly less temptation.

Two weeks before Daly flew to the UK to defend his Open title, he rolled up at the Motorola Western Open in Chicago. During the tournament at the Cog Hill, Daly found himself subjected to another pseudo-psychological interrogation by Bill Blighton, who had now taken up a new position at the *Sunday Mirror*. As they talked, Blighton couldn't help but notice that the Open champion was looking 'longingly at the free bar in the locker room'. When he pressed him on the point, Daly was as open as ever, and began talking to him as if he had swapped jobs with Thomas Henderson. Temptation, said Daly, was everywhere he looked, and the more his golf game deteriorated the more he thought about what he was missing out on. Of course, the temptation had been there in 1995 too, but in the madness and mayhem of winning the Open Daly had found himself too busy and too popular to notice.

Had John Daly been an office worker or shop assistant, he might have found resisting the temptation to drink or gamble somewhat easier. If, say, at the end of a hard day pushing pens his colleagues invited him out for a drink, all he would have to say was no. He could then go home and nobody would mind. But the problem with being a professional golfer on the PGA Tour was that alcohol was everywhere – in the hotels, in the clubhouse, in the locker room. Every night there was some champion's banquet or sponsor's dinner or pro-am party to attend. What's more, you couldn't really say no. Why, if a man wasn't careful, he could quite easily get himself a problem. 'It's just so tough with so much alcohol around,' he complained. 'I smell it and get shaky sometimes. It's real tough to go to these functions. It used to be easy. I was drinking and socialising. But I'm not a very good socialiser since I was sober.' Alcohol wasn't the only thing Daly had given up. Sober as a judge but crippled by embarrassment, he admitted that without the stimulus of booze the man who once silenced an unsuspecting Australian audience with his version of 'Wild Thing' could no longer cut the rug at the PGA's pro-am parties. 'It's like I don't want to dance ever again. I feel I look like a total idiot. When I was drinking I didn't care. I'm just real low-key now. I don't get excited about going a lot of places and doing a lot of things.'

In late July, Daly arrived at the Hilversum Golf Club near Amsterdam as the former Open champion. His defence of the crown he had won at St Andrews had, at times, been surprisingly spirited, but still nowhere near good enough to live with the eventual winner, Tom Lehman. For the seventh consecutive event, Daly had made the cut, but he never once troubled the scorers, his tie for 66th the result of a sloppy 77 in his final round. As the press were extremely keen to point out, Daly was being paid a reported $100,000 to play at Hilversum, but judging by his rather forlorn expression and his lethargic gait, it looked as though the promoters could have given him ten times that amount and he still wouldn't have looked remotely interested. Midway through another swine of a season, it was painfully clear that here was a player going through the motions. His eyes, so blue and bright just twelve months ago, now bore the kind of lifeless demeanour more commonly seen in banks or bus queues.

A first round of 75 did little to mollify Daly. But if he considered his opening round to be unworthy of comment, he really should have thought twice about turning up for the second round. To call it a nightmare would be a gross understatement. In perfect conditions – gorgeous sunshine and hardly a breath of wind – he reached the turn in an horrendous 51 which included an unthinkable quadruple bogey at the 9th. He picked things up on the inward nine, coming home in just 38, but the damage had been well and truly done. Daly's two-round total of 164 left him a mind-boggling 33 shots off the leader, Des Smyth, not to mention embarrassed beyond words and on the verge of tears. The last time he had shot anywhere near this was back in Maine in 1990 when he ended up in hospital in an alcohol-induced coma. Mercifully, this time Daly would merely sign his scorecard, walk silently to the courtesy cars office, order a vehicle and leave the course without so much as a backwards glance.

Daly's final stop on his sorry European Tour was Sweden and the Volvo Scandinavian Masters at Forsgardens, near Gothenburg. They liked Daly in Sweden. With his shock of blond hair, he was just like one of them, only fatter (and maybe his grasp of English wasn't as good). It would prove to be a mediocre end to a less than memorable trip. With a level-par total of 288, Daly tied for eighteenth. It was, after the horrors of Hilversum, a better than anticipated result, but it did nothing to improve his spirits. When he returned to his hotel suite, he was joined by Mascatello, Rita and Donnie Crabtree. As the quartet chatted, Daly stood up and ambled over to the minibar. Opening the fridge door, he pulled out a bottle of beer and returned to his seat. Mascatello stared at John, then looked at Rita and Crabtree to gauge their reactions. They looked as nervous as he felt. Nobody said anything. With the open bottle between his legs, Daly sat there staring at the beer and contemplating whether or not to drink it. Five minutes later he picked it up and took a gulp. Three years, seven months and four days of sobriety had come to an ignominious end.

Once Daly had drained the bottle, he picked up the phone and called Paulette back in the States. When she answered, she asked John how he had played and what he was up to. 'We're just sitting around having a beer,' he said, as if it was the most innocent thing in the world.

'That's not funny, John,' snapped Paulette. 'Don't play games with me.'

'I'm not playing games. I'm drinking a beer,' he insisted.

Paulette told John to put Mascatello on, and the agent confirmed that Daly wasn't joking.

With his wife sat at home contemplating just what kind of husband would now be returning home to her and Sierra, Daly moved on to his next beer. Although he would stop after his third bottle, his decision to resume drinking would have grave consequences. Later that year, he endeavoured to explain exactly why he had given in to temptation. 'The whole time I was going through sobriety, I was thinking, "Man, it would be great to have a beer." It was something that was always over my shoulder. I had to find out.' Perhaps the saddest thing about that day in Sweden, though, was that in his hour of need neither Crabtree, Rita nor the man hired to look after his interests took it upon themselves to walk right over to Daly and take the bottle out of his hand.

Back in the States, John and Paulette sat down and talked about what had happened. She told him she didn't care if he never broke a hundred again, just as long as he stayed away from the booze and carried on being a great dad for Sierra. Daly agreed, but maintained that just because he had a beer or two on his travels didn't necessarily mean an immediate and life-threatening descent into the kind of mess he had found himself in so many times before. As long as he wasn't drinking whiskey, he insisted, there really was no need to be too worried. Paulette wasn't convinced, but she took her husband at his word.

Certainly, the standard of Daly's play after his return from Europe suggested that he was back on the booze: four missed cuts in his first four tournaments back on the PGA Tour. Of course, the extent of his dependence on alcohol had never been an accurate barometer of how he was playing. From the day he'd started drinking, he could shoot 64 with a killer of a hangover or shoot 74 after a cup of cocoa and an early night. In purely golfing terms, there was no way of telling just where he was at in his life. But that made little difference to the tour gossipmongers. Soon word spread that the Wild Thing had buried the hatchet with his old buddy the bottle. Inevitably, Daly himself learned of the hearsay. Faced with growing speculation about his condition, he decided to take some pre-emptive action. On Saturday, 5 October 1996, he issued a statement through the PGA Tour to the *New York Times* designed to quell any rumours about the extent of his relapse. It read, in part: 'It is true I have had a few beers on several occasions this summer, but I have not been involved in any alcohol-related incidents. I have not been drinking to excess, and this has not been the reason the level of play lately has been below my usual standards. In fact, I have put more time and effort into my game than I have at any time.' Mascatello agreed that Daly had 'been drinking socially, not to excess' and denied that he had returned to the kind of problematic binge drinking that had seen him hospitalised in the past. 'The thing we don't want is for this to be portrayed as John falling off the wagon,' he stated. 'John believes he can handle this.'

The problem here, however, is that alcoholics nearly always believe they can handle it. It is part and parcel of their denial. Indeed, Daly's denial went further. Despite a wealth of incidents and accidents that suggested otherwise, he still wasn't sure that he could actually be called an 'alcoholic', suggesting that the root of his ongoing problem lay in some mystery allergy. 'I don't know if "alcoholic" is the right name for my case,' he said. 'Am I really an alcoholic? Or am I just allergic to alcohol? Is it the same thing? That's something I'd like to find out.'

Though Daly's statement concluded with a pledge to 'continue my counselling program', which as far as anyone was aware meant the occasional phone call to Thomas Henderson, it was apparent that he had still singularly failed to grasp the most basic tenet of dealing with alcoholism, i.e. that you can't drink alcohol. Until Daly learned to understand and accept that alcohol was bigger than him, he was always going to be helpless against it.

Predictably, the tabloids seized on Daly's admission. Virtually every Sunday newspaper in the UK and the States carried a report of his shock confession. Typical was the line taken by Britain's the *News of the World*, which ran a piece by Ken Lawrence under the headline DALY'S BACK ON THE BOOZE featuring a less than flattering picture of Daly at St Andrews in 1995 stuffing a huge chocolate muffin into his mouth. It listed the now obligatory rap sheet of all Daly's misdemeanours and was at pains to remind everyone that when Daly had entered Sierra Tucson in 1993 he had said that if he ever had another drink he would be history. Now that he had, 'he may once again be an accident waiting for a place to happen'.

The 1996 PGA Tour came to an end in mid-October when Tiger Woods won the Walt Disney tournament in Orlando. For Daly, it was a wholly appropriate event at which to conclude his Mickey Mouse season, although if he was honest with himself his year had really ended when he had lost his Open title in July. What had really ruffled Daly's feathers, though, was the cold, hard facts of his annus horribilis, and the breakdown made for depressing reading. In the 23 events he had played, he had missed nine cuts and had scraped just one top-ten finish when he nicked a tie for tenth at the Kemper Open in May. His return of $173,557 (121st on the money list), meanwhile, was the worst tally of his PGA career. But the malaise ran much, much deeper. Though he retained his mantle as the PGA's longest driver, he had a woeful stroke average of 72.3, he was fourth from last in the percentage of birdies made on par-threes, he was 174th in greens made in regulation, and having hit only 57 per cent of fairways he was 188th and last in the driving accuracy category. John Daly's game, it seemed, was in free fall.

Daly's form might have stunk, but as a two-time major winner he was still receiving invitations to a raft of contrived, end-of-season competitions so beloved by the TV networks and players looking to make some easy money. At the first of these events, the Sarazen World Open in Atlanta, Daly openly admitted that he was having a few beers again, enjoying himself and not getting involved in any of the 'alcohol-related' incidents that had so characterised his old relationship with the bottle. Indeed, since that afternoon in Gothenburg, Daly claimed to have hardly even touched a drop. 'I've had maybe twelve beers since August,' he claimed. 'Basically, I've stopped drinking but I haven't quit. That means for ever, and I don't know if I can do that.'

But the story at Atlanta was that Daly had fired Greg Rita. Unbeknown to Daly, Rita had secretly met with the game's superstar-in-waiting, Tiger Woods, and offered him his services. He'd been in the game long enough to know a rare talent when he saw one. After all, it was he who had approached Daly at the Skins Game back in 1991. In Woods, however, he saw something quite unique. Tall, athletic, and seemingly blessed with the complete golf game, he was longer and straighter than Daly and had already won twice on tour in his first year. He was even being touted as the man finally to challenge Jack Nicklaus's record of eighteen major titles. For Daly, a player who had always preferred to surround himself with people he knew and trusted, Rita's manoeuvring was like a stab in the back. 'He had to go,' he said. For Rita, however, the plan backfired: Woods decided to stick with his regular caddie, Mike 'Fluff' Cowan, leaving Rita out in the cold until veteran Scott Hoch gave him a job.

Daly gave his old friend Brian 'Wedgie' Alexander a call and asked him if he wanted a job. Wedgie was an old drinking buddy from the Bettye days, and he had worked at Chickasaw Country Club as an assistant professional. Since the late 1980s he had caddied for Daly on an occasional basis and had received his nickname when he had given Daly a wedge for every second shot he faced in a round at the 1989 Chattanooga Classic.

Still angered by Rita's networking (and, perhaps, by his tied-for-42nd finish in the tournament), Daly headed off to the Kapalua International in Hawaii, the scene of his now infamous walkout in November 1993. With Paulette along for the ride, Daly established base camp at the exclusive Ritz-Carlton Hotel and enjoyed an activity-packed week, even though he could only scrape a finish of 43rd. On the Thursday evening, Daly hooked up with his rock buddies Hootie and the Blowfish once more, joining them on stage with his Stratocaster and playing the introduction to Bob Dylan's 'Knockin' On Heaven's Door'. After a 75 in his second round, Daly then joined fellow tour players Jim McGovern, Billy Andrade, Woody Austin and Brad Faxon for two full-court games of basketball before returning to the hotel to watch Evander Holyfield upset Mike Tyson. With energy to spare, he then rounded off the night by taking Paulette to see country star Vince Gill in concert. It had been a great week – off the golf course. 'The golf game will hook in,' he insisted. 'Now I have the chance to prove to myself and to others that, hey, a bad year was all it was, and come back strong next year. I know this about me: when I get in the hunt, I'm going to win or somebody is going to have to kick my butt. I just got to get there. The good news is, it can't get any worse.' Perhaps the most telling remark Daly made before he left Maui, however, was that he didn't think he had 'had fun on the golf course since I won at Atlanta' – and that included the Open win at St Andrews.

17. IF YOU LEAVE ME, CAN I COME TOO?

'Reporting I'm drunk is like saying there was a Tuesday last week.'
Grace Slick, Jefferson Starship

There was a sign in the window of the John Daly Golf Shop; it read: SORRY WE'RE CLOSED. After six years in business, the store on Highway 22 was to cease trading. Despite Daly's worldwide renown, it had transpired that there was about as much demand for golf equipment in Dardanelle as there was for snowshoes in Dakar. And besides, Mama Lou needed a break.

Of course, not everyone was distraught at the shop's demise, least of all those who lived nearby. Over the years, the store had become a focal point for Daly's energetic social life whenever he returned home; memories of the rock music blaring out of the premises at 3.00 a.m. would live with the residents for many years to come. Now, though, tranquillity had finally returned to the neighbourhood. All that was left to remind them of the revelry was a few crushed beer cans lying on the shop floor.

Notwithstanding the passing of the shop, Daly had enjoyed a productive break away from the tour. Over the Christmas period he had eschewed the kind of calorie-packed, carbohydrate-loaded diet he usually enjoyed at that time of year and had actually started working out. Whereas once the only vegetable to pass Daly's lips was the small slice of gherkin they stuffed in Big Macs, now he had even been seen eating salad, the net result being a weight loss of some fifteen pounds.

In mid-January 1997, in his first tournament of the new season, the five-round Bob Hope Chrysler Classic in Indian Wells, California, Daly emerged looking fresh and ready for battle. He looked well, very well, and his much-vaunted experiment with 'social drinking' – as opposed, presumably, to 'unsocial drinking' – seemed to be having no adverse effect on his game. On his way to shooting 65–73–64–66–69 he played, at times, some imperious golf, and his eventual finish of seventh was his highest placing for over a year. In terms of his reputation on the PGA Tour, the performance was the best possible riposte to those who had said that his golf, like his drinking, was only social as well. It meant he was back. Well, kind of. On a personal level, though, the result couldn't have been worse. Now, with some kind of warped justification for his relapse, Daly could kid himself into thinking that he had his problem under control, when he patently had not.

For 1997, Daly had had a rethink on the number of non-tour appearances he was going to make, the theory being that he was spreading himself too thinly around the golfing world and neglecting his bread and butter, the PGA Tour. Apart from the Open at Troon, there were only two events in Australia he intended to play outside the United States. He arrived on the Gold Coast nursing a troublesome hip. For two months he had been struggling to cope with an inflammatory ailment called bursitis, and the long flight from the States had done him no favours at all. While the problem would force his withdrawal from the celebrity event that preceded his first appointment, the $1.4 million Johnnie Walker Classic, Daly would, however, still take his place in the main event, and despite the injury he was remarkably upbeat about the season ahead of him, especially since the top-ten at the Bob Hope. Daly had a feeling that 1997 was going to be his year. 'Maybe I'm jinxing myself by saying that,' he added, 'but that's the way I feel right now.'

After a day confined to his hotel room, Daly eventually teed it up at Hope Island but was still clearly in some pain as he limped, literally, to rounds of 77 and 79 and missed the cut. Luckily, there was a six-figure guarantee on hand to help ease his discomfort. He then headed to Perth for the Heineken Classic, but again his form eluded him. He laboured to make the cut, and on a sweltering Saturday he overheated in the kind of pig-headed manner only John Daly could manage. As he had the previous year, Daly had decided to keep his driver in his bag and navigate his way round the Vines course using long irons off the tee, much to the annoyance of the galleries, and just like the previous year, the idea had proved to be utter folly. Indeed, as soon as his tee-shots began to compromise the safety of the spectators, Daly decided he had had enough and set about racing through the round like he was cutting up Sawgrass with Calcavecchia again. For someone whose track record in the country was less than exemplary, it was a curious strategy and one which suggested that he wouldn't really lose any sleep if he never got invited back again.

The 10th hole was typical of Daly's round. Having played the front nine unspectacularly with his driver tucked safely in his bag, he unleashed the big dog and promptly drove his ball right behind a cactus plant. Then, at the par-five last, he tried to hole his 141-yard second shot to claim the half-a-million-dollar prize for an albatross. 'I wanted to be the only man to shoot in the eighties and win $500,000 for an albatross in the same day,' he explained. He didn't, by the way. He found the water. Just two hours and ten minutes later, Daly was back in the clubhouse with a face as long as a horse's and thousands of paying fans outside feeling thoroughly cheated. He then found himself, not for the first time, having to explain his actions. 'When I get an appearance fee,' he countered, 'I'm damn sure I'll give a hundred per cent.' Which was perfectly true, of course, so long as you were playing speed golf.

As yet, John Daly and his policy of social drinking hadn't upset anyone on the PGA Tour. A few foreign promoters and several thousand Australian golf fans maybe, but nobody who could hit him with a fine or a suspension. As long as that was the case, then the PGA and their wait-and-see line could be said to be working.

Outwardly, there was no sign that Daly had upped his alcohol intake. After all, it wasn't like his form had suddenly slumped when he had resumed drinking; it had been in the doldrums for months. Behind the closed doors of his new home in Rogers, however, there was increasing discord between John and Paulette, and now that alcohol had entered their relationship it was crunch time for their marriage. Ever since Paulette had learned of John's relapse she had been convinced that the only way he could make amends was by returning to rehab, preferably before he did something both of them would regret. But as John's drinking escalated – by March 1997 he was back to drinking a fifth of whiskey a day – he had grown increasingly hostile towards Paulette and had taken to verbally abusing her with alarming regularity. 'At times,' he would concede, 'it was pretty bad.' After one altercation too many, Paulette laid it on the line: either John went back to rehab or some serious decisions would have to be made. Faced with the starkest of choices, Daly agreed with his wife that rehab was the place to be.

In the meantime, the tour rolled on into Florida for the Players' Championship, the game's unofficial fifth major. While everyone on tour knew that Daly was drinking again, nobody quite appreciated the extent of his relapse. Only Paulette really knew. With her words ringing in his ears and the PGA keeping tabs on him, Daly set out early that Thursday morning for his first round. By 11.00 a.m. he was back in the clubhouse with a shabby 76 making an unholy mess of his scorecard. He was in a foul mood. Returning to his suite at the Marriott Resort, Sawgrass, he informed Paulette that he was popping out to get some lunch. Critically, there were two salient pieces of information he omitted to relay to his wife: the first was that this was going to be a liquid lunch; the second was the elastic nature of that term 'popping out'.

Daly grabbed Donnie Crabtree and headed to Jacksonville Beach. The pair shared a couple of beers before Crabtree made his excuses, leaving Daly in Hooters with a couple of caddies – always the most willing of drinking partners – and, later, some members of the NFL's Jacksonville Jaguars. At 5.00 p.m. the party moved on to Sloppy Joe's just a block from the Atlantic Ocean where, foolishly, Daly switched from beer to Seagram's whiskey. Jeff Taylor was working behind the bar at Sloppy Joe's that night. 'It was very crowded,' he remembered. 'He [Daly] was very nice, signing autographs and buying drinks for people. He drank a lot, but he was not a problem.' It's a view backed up by Taylor's colleague Tara Raichel, who was also working that night. 'He got up with the band and sang some little redneck songs, some Lynyrd Skynyrd,' she recalled. 'He was a perfect guest.' Even the manager that night, Jeff Goss, found him totally charming. 'John Daly,' he maintained, 'would be welcome here any time.'

It was gone midnight when Daly returned to Room 1713, and no longer was he the happy, cuddly drunk. Paulette was sleeping in the bedroom with Sierra and was woken up by what sounded like someone falling over. When she went to investigate she found her husband hauling his bloated body off the floor and wailing like some caged bear being baited. He had collapsed against the kitchen door and both Daly and the door looked the worse for wear. Paulette was terrified. 'I had seen him drunk quite a few times, but I had never been so frightened before,' she recalled. 'I had never felt physically threatened by him. But that night was really scary.' As Paulette tried to shield Sierra, Daly began furiously pulling the phone lines out of the wall and demanding that his wife and child stay put. 'He knew I wanted to leave and he was just trying to make me feel guilty,' she added. As John's rage deepened, Paulette managed to escape with Sierra to the relative safety of the hotel lobby where she found John's tour colleague Mark Brooks and his wife Cynthia, who took them back to their room. Shortly after 1.00 a.m., Paulette called Fuzzy Zoeller, who was also staying at the Marriott, and told him that John had lost it. Then came a knock at the door. It was the police. Someone had heard the commotion and had already dialled 911.

Zoeller led the police to Daly's room and found his friend in a rage. 'That's the worst I've seen him. He needs help. He was out of control,' he would later tell the press. 'He has definitely hit rock bottom. All I can do is talk to him; you cannot lock a horse in a barn.' With the help of several police officers, Daly was eventually subdued and loaded on to a stretcher. As he was carried to the ambulance, he turned to Fuzzy and said, 'Take that cop's gun and shoot me in the head.' With Zoeller by his side, Daly was taken to the local Baptist Beaches Medical Center where he was diagnosed with acute alcohol poisoning. Another whiskey overdose. So much for growing up.

Years later, Daly would claim that the whole sorry episode had been blown out of proportion by a media intent on sticking the knife in. 'I fell into the kitchen door, and they said I trashed the room,' he sighed. It must have been an expensive door. According to Kevin Kelshaw, spokesman for the St Johns County sheriff's office, Daly did over $1,000 worth of damage to the hotel room before being hospitalised for chest pains (a settlement was later made). 'The Marriott did not want to press charges,' added Kelshaw.

The morning after the night before Daly emerged from hospital with a thick head and a heavy heart. Later that day he 'withdrew' from the Players' Championship citing the same sore hip that had forced his withdrawal at the Honda Classic earlier in the month. Strangely, he didn't mention his sore head. Paulette, meanwhile, had taken Sierra and flown back to Palm Desert, California, to be with her mother. 'I couldn't believe what my life had become,' she said. 'That night was like something out of a bad movie.'

Daly was at a crossroads, albeit a tediously familiar one. He could carry on drinking, carry on wasting his talent and everyone's time, or take steps to get his head straight. For once, he made the right decision. With his marriage on the ropes and his place on tour in jeopardy, Daly pre-empted any further punishment by calling Tim Finchem and telling him he was checking himself into rehab once more. It would mean missing out on the Masters, his favourite tournament, but he had to do something. He then issued this statement through his agent John Mascatello: 'As part of my ongoing battle to overcome alcoholism, I have decided to immediately enter the Betty Ford Rehabilitation Program. In August of 1996, I suffered a setback in dealing with my disease. Until that time, I felt that I had won the battle alone by simply stopping the act of drinking. I've come to realise this terrible disease is much tougher than I thought and have decided with the support of my family and friends to let others help me. I apologise to others who struggle with me in fighting this disease. I'm going to do my best and hopefully we will prevail together.' Mascatello went on to explain that his client was approaching this particular spell in rehab far differently from the three-week stay at Sierra Tucson in 1993. 'There is no set timetable for how long he stays,' he said. 'He knows that now. Stays there can be anywhere from three to four weeks to six to eight weeks. John is not rushing to come back. He's only going to come back to play when he's ready. It's a hard deal. He's got to find out what makes him happy away from golf. How do you find inner peace? That's a question he can only answer for himself.'

Daly's decision to seek immediate help for his drinking certainly found favour with Finchem, who, convinced that John was determined to change, opted not to impose any suspension. 'It is an important step for John to continue to recognise and acknowledge his disease and his relapse. We fully support his decision to enter the Betty Ford program, and we admire his courage in taking the action he has to find the best professional help he can. John is doing what is best for him, and we wish him well in this effort.' And there was more genuine sympathy for the Wild

Thing's plight from the players. 'I really feel for John,' offered Brad Faxon during the practice rounds at the Masters. 'I have a parent who is an alcoholic, and so I know what he has to do to get well. It's a lifetime thing, and he has to take care of that before he takes care of this [the Masters].' Tom Lehman also voiced his concern. 'If I could talk to him, I'd tell him that I'm proud of him for doing what he's doing. His not being [in Augusta] doesn't take anything away from the event. John needs to do what's best for John. The Masters will always be here. Tournaments will benefit from a healthy John Daly. No one benefits from a John Daly who's sick.'

With his lifelong buddy Donnie Crabtree at the wheel, Daly drove back to his home in Memphis, packed a suitcase and then drove all the way through to California and the Betty Ford Clinic in Rancho Mirage. Just before he entered the clinic, Daly gave a telephone interview to the *Commercial Appeal* to give his version of the catastrophic events of Thursday night. Initially, he employed humour. 'I just thank God the bars close early in Florida. I could have been dead.' Then he explained just what had happened. 'When I got back to my hotel room, I stumbled into the kitchen, and I kind of fell into the door . . . The next thing I remember is waking up in the hospital. I was scared. I was told I was lucky . . . that my blood alcohol level was .25 and that was a couple of hours after I was admitted. They said when they found me on the bed [in the hotel] that I wasn't breathing.' Daly was determined that this time he would give this rehab thing his all, for the PGA Tour, for his family and, most importantly, for himself. 'The first time it was because the tour forced me; this time I'm doing it of my own will. Doing it this way, maybe I'll understand it more. I've got to get better . . . sober again.'

He checked into the clinic as an outpatient – it was the only way he could carry on playing some golf – and underwent a stringent medical. The prognosis wasn't good. When he had entered the Sierra Tucson rehab clinic in 1993 the doctors had told him that as he'd drunk beer since he was eight and Jack Daniels since he was fourteen, his liver was black; now the experts were saying that his liver was on its last legs, raising a white flag. If he didn't stop drinking, they said, it was only a matter of time before he sank his last bourbon. The medicine men scared Daly into action. It was time to get serious, which meant getting up every day at the kind of time he used to get in at, and making his way to the clinic for his daily 5.30 a.m. AA meeting. And, for once in his life, it also meant actually listening to people.

The programme went well. After completing the fourth of the Twelve Steps to recovery, for which the alcoholic is asked to give a 'fearless moral inventory' of all the screw-ups he has made while under the influence, Daly even found there was enough time to squeeze in a little golf in the afternoons, too. There were no hacks sticking tape recorders under his nose, no PGA Tour officials wagging their fingers at him, and no temptations leading him astray. It was just him and a bunch of folks who were in the same shit as he was. 'The people in that group saved my life,' he would later maintain. 'They were like me, people who were fighting alcoholism every day. They understood me and I understood them.'

But as Daly came to terms with his new-found sobriety, he was hit by two hammer blows. When he had entered the Betty Ford Clinic at the end of March, he had spoken of his regret for what he had put Paulette through. 'I love her to death,' he said. 'I hope when I get out she'll be there for me.' But less than a fortnight after his now infamous fourteen-hour drinking spree, Daly learned that Paulette had applied for a divorce. The papers, filed in the Circuit Court of Shelby County in Memphis, Tennessee, alleged that Daly was guilty of 'inappropriate marital conduct' and said that for Paulette and Sierra to continue living with him would be 'unsafe and improper'. The petition gave the date of the final separation as 27 March – the actual day of Daly's drinking binge in Jacksonville.

As Daly reeled from the prospect of another failed marriage, bad news came on the professional front, too. On his 31st birthday, John opened a gift from his parents. It was a wooden plaque that read, 'God, grant me the serenity to accept the things I cannot change, the courage to change the things I can, and the wisdom to know the difference.' While the gift was a touching show of support from his family, the present from his sponsors, Wilson Sporting Goods, was less welcome: this latest transgression was one too many for them and they announced their intention to terminate their ten-year equipment contract with Daly (it still had over six years to run). 'Through all of his trials and tribulations, Wilson has always stood behind John,' explained Jeff Harmet, director of marketing for Wilson Golf. 'This was by no means an easy decision. But after reassessing our relationship, we have decided to bring it to a close.' And Wilson weren't the only sponsor to give Daly the corporate finger. Soon afterwards, Reebok brought an end to a deal that had given Daly up to $500,000 a year plus all the shoes, shirts and trousers he could spill beer on. 'It was a really difficult decision,' said John Morgan, senior vice president for Reebok's golf division. 'John's been a part of the Reebok family for six or seven years, but we want to take the golf division in a different direction.' For 'different direction' read 'finding a golfer who won't make the CEO wake up in the middle of the night in a cold sweat'.

It was yet another kick in the teeth for Daly, and he couldn't even have a beer to drown his sorrows. 'The low point of all aspects of my life', he called it. Still, it was difficult to feel sorry for him. After all, his problems were entirely self-inflicted. He had been given last chance after last chance by virtually everyone he knew and he had thanked them all by nearly drinking himself to death. His response was to jump in his car and speed off to a mountain top between Palm Springs and San Diego with the intention of ending his and everyone else's misery. 'And I was going to drive that son of a bitch off a cliff,' he recalled, 'but for some reason I called Thomas Henderson, and then Donnie. I said, "I just want to say goodbye. You've been my friend since first grade." ' Just as he'd done in 1993, Crabtree talked him round and persuaded him that there were too many people pulling for him, too many folk who wanted John Daly alive, for him to go and do something so stupid. So Daly drove back down the cliff and returned to the Betty Ford Clinic, where he was placed under suicide watch.

Not that he felt any better. As he sat in his condo and reflected on the world crumbling around his ears, Daly realised that without the comfort zone of his lucrative contract with Wilson and with two ex-wives in tow picking away at his earnings, the prospect of insolvency had become very real. With the help of his Wilson cash Daly had been endeavouring to clear some $2.6 million in gambling markers he had accrued over the years, but he still had $1.8 million to pay back. It was a burden compounded by some ongoing IRS debts which were also costing him 'close to $350,000 or $400,000 a quarter'. In short, Daly was up to his neck in it and sinking fast.

But there was one man who felt the Wild Thing deserved a break. His name was Ely Callaway. As the founder and chairman of Callaway Golf, the 78-year-old had seen Daly claim the long-driving title on the PGA Tour for five of the previous six seasons and saw in him the living embodiment of their famous 'Big Bertha' woods. He figured Daly needed a helping hand, so he arranged for him to visit their company HQ in Carlsbad and let him try out a few clubs. On his third visit, John finally met Ely. The two hit it off immediately. If Fuzzy Zoeller was John's big brother on tour, Ely Callaway would become his old man.

On 27 May, Ely presented Daly with a contract to use Callaway clubs. The offer was a generous one: $10 million over five years, and they would also write off Daly's gambling debts. But there were stipulations attached to the deal, conditions that tied 'his ongoing affiliation with Callaway to his successful maintenance of sobriety and stable behaviour'. It was also top-loaded with financial incentives in the later years of the contract, making it financially prudent for Daly to stay sober for at least the length of the deal. 'John Daly,' said Callaway, 'is one of the most skilful professionals in the world of competitive golf and he is also a very likeable and charismatic young man. We share with John an enthusiasm and optimism for the success of our partnership throughout the term of our relationship.' Daly shared Ely's confidence. 'It will be nice to be part of the Callaway family,' he said, 'which cares not only about my golf, but my personal life and wellbeing. As for my commitment to sobriety, I have an outcare program in place and plan to live one day at a time. I hope and believe this approach will be successful.'

With the ink of Daly's signature drying on the contract, Callaway employed the advertising agency Daily & Associates to create a new campaign which they intended to launch during the tournament broadcasts of the forthcoming US Open at Maryland's Congressional Golf Club, the course where Daly had pursued Jerry Pate as a kid. The theme of the ad was 'Keep It Straight, John'. It worked, as they say in advertising circles, on many levels. 'John suggested the theme for the ad campaign,' Callaway explained. 'We all wanted a slogan that would be encouraging. It fits with his conviction that our product can help him win.'

Daly returned to action at the end of May in the Mystic Rock Pro-Am event near Pittsburgh with a view to using it, the Memorial Tournament and the Kemper Open as a warm-up for the US Open. With the new Callaway ad campaign due to start at Congressional, Daly felt obliged to play in the Open even though all his new friends at Rancho Mirage were advising against it. 'They told me it was too soon. They thought I needed to go through the summer, take it easy, and not play in the majors. They thought I should play in tournaments with less pressure, not the ones with more.' It was sound advice, but it fell on deaf ears. Daly finished last at the Memorial and the Kemper Open, and when the US Open came round the shakes he had been suffering on and off for months were becoming too much for him. He even contemplated pulling out of the competition but felt he owed it to Callaway to give it a shot. 'I honestly thought I was going to get better each day,' he said.

On the first day, Daly carded a 77, but walking up the 9th during the second round he felt he couldn't continue. He was walking around in a blur, his body was shaking like it was midwinter, and the sweat was pouring off him. He looked like one of those ill-prepared marathon runners who has hit the wall at twenty miles and can barely walk any more, let alone run. Without so much as a word to his playing partners, Paul Azinger and Payne Stewart, Daly walked off the course after completing the hole. Even Wedgie was left standing at the 10th tee wondering where on earth his boss had got to. Shortly after his abrupt withdrawal, a spectator saw Daly sitting on the bonnet of a car 'sweating profusely, his face flushed scarlet'. Within half an hour, he was gone. He had jumped in his car and driven to Memphis, then pointed the car in the direction of Rancho Mirage – a sign, at least, that while he might not have totally conquered all his demons, he had them in his sights. By way of explanation, Daly issued a statement the following day: 'Even though I thought I was going to be strong enough to come right back and play three straight weeks on tour, I found out I was wrong.' Not that the United States Golf Association was impressed. As the organisers of the event, they were furious. Just when they thought Daly had got a grip on all his issues, there he was up to his old tricks; to compound matters, he'd done it during one of the most prestigious, high-profile tournaments of the year. Callaway pulled the 'Keep It Straight, John' ads.

Daly's premature exit from the US Open set tongues wagging on the circuit. The widely held assumption was that he was suffering from delirium tremens, but the truth was far removed from the rumour. In a bid to quench his apparently endless thirst, Daly had taken to drinking vast amounts of Diet Coke during his time at the Betty Ford Clinic, sometimes consuming as many as seven cans during a round of golf and up to twenty cans over the course of a day. What he hadn't realised, what nobody had realised, was that the sweetener used in Diet Coke, the chemical additive aspartame, was now in his blood in such quantities that it was clashing head on with the vat-load of anti-depressants he had been prescribed, producing an adverse reaction and quickly turning him into a physical wreck.

By the end of July, five weeks after the walkout at Congressional, a new 'nutritional programme' had helped Daly lose nearly 40lb. Thanks to this new regime free from Diet Coke, beer and cheeseburgers, Daly returned to the tour at the Canon Greater Hartford Open looking leaner and seemingly more relaxed. During his lay-off he had taken to swimming and playing tennis and had been attending as many as five AA meetings each week. Apart from golfing equipment, all his golf bag carried now was the slogan 'God, Serenity, Courage, Wisdom'.

He'd arrived in Cromwell, Connecticut, after a nineteen-hour, 1,215-mile drive from Rogers with Donnie Crabtree and his caddie Brian Alexander. As usual, flying was out of the question. Instead, he had got himself another new motorhome and had decided to hit the road. 'I can eat when I want, listen to music that I like, and I don't have to sit down and buckle up when the light goes on,' he said. A tie for 21st that week was a respectable finish to his latest comeback. Moreover, there were no un-scheduled departures, no half-cut quarrels, and no off-course high jinks – just a 'really sweet week', which is all anyone, Daly included, ever wanted. Even the press agreed that Daly was now an altogether nicer interviewee. He was open, approachable and back to his amusing, self-deprecating best. Never was this more evident than during a celebrity long-driving competition he took part in a couple of days before the event got under way. When the time arrived for ESPN broadcaster Chris Berman to take his shot, the organisers found that he was too busy signing autographs to make it to the tee. Instead, Daly stepped up and took his place, prompting the MC to ask him if he had taken a wrong turn somewhere. 'No,' he replied with a smile, 'I'm just a drunk who got lost.'

What fans and commentators were now witnessing was a John Daly more at ease with himself than he had been in years. Thanks largely to the backing of Ely Callaway and the positive steps he had taken at the Betty Ford Clinic to address his alcohol dependency, Daly was now able to strike some semblance of a balance between the demands of the tour and those his mind and body were placing on him. He pledged not to play more than two consecutive weeks for the remainder of the year, giving himself much more time to work on his game and his wellbeing. It was a policy that would pay dividends.

In the PGA Championship at Winged Foot in mid-August, Daly, wearing his Callaway flat-cap with the 'Keep It Straight, John' slogan emblazoned across the back, amazed everyone, including himself, by blitzing his way to a first-round 66 and a tie for the lead with Davis Love III. It was an extraordinary round of golf, each birdie, each dead-eye iron shot greeted with the kind of reception usually reserved for the President or Bruce Springsteen. There were even whispers that Daly might just go on to emulate his PGA success of 1991. For Daly, though, it was one day and one round at a time. 'I believe I've had fifteen chances in life,' he explained. 'I guess I am scared to screw up again, but I'm doing good today, and that's all I can say about it.' The early promise didn't last. A second-round 73 was followed by a dispiriting 77 and another charge on the Daly rap sheet, though this time, thankfully, it was a minor indiscretion. Standing on the 12th tee, Daly blocked his drive way right, over some trees and on to the 17th fairway. Turning away in disgust, he hurled his driver – his new Callaway Biggest Big Bertha – over an out-of-bounds fence and into some woods. As an act of petulance it was almost as good as Tommy 'Thunder' Bolt chucking his driver in the lake at Cherry Hills during the 1960 US Open, but not quite. As Daly marched up the fairway, a couple of marshals went looking for the errant club and found it in a patch of poison ivy. By the time Daly got to the next tee, the driver was back in his bag.

Daly wised up in his final round and shot a respectable level-par 70, this time with no juicy stories for the press gang to get their teeth into. His four-round total of 286 gave him a tie for 29th, but after everything he had been through since his last major championship appearance it was a satisfactory outcome, even if he had thrown his shiny new driver away.

18. STAND BY YOUR MAN

'Has it ever struck you there's a thin man inside every fat man, just as they say there's a statue inside every block of stone?'

From *Coming Up for Air* by George Orwell

The PGA Tour keep statistics on everything. From sand saves to scrambling, from birdies to bounce-backs, there is barely an aspect of the game that goes unrecorded. Indeed, their predilection for number-crunching is such that it would come as no surprise were the powers that be at Ponte Vedra to introduce a divot distance table or a cuss count for those players whose games are failing.

When John Daly examined his report card for 1997, the stats made for depressing reading. He had played in just seventeen Tour events. He had had only one top-ten finish and there were six missed cuts and two withdrawals to his name. He had earned just $106,762 – his lowest ever return on the PGA Tour – and was languishing at 166th in the money list. He had also lost another wife along the way. But there was one chink of light amid the gloom. With an average drive of 302 yards – the first time any player had ever achieved a 300-yard-plus average – Daly remained far and away the longest hitter on tour. Say what you like about Tiger Woods, there was still no one out there who could kill a ball like John Daly.

Without Paulette and Sierra by his side, Daly retreated to the condo in Palm Springs for the winter to do some serious thinking.

With nothing to distract him – no family, no alcohol, no thirsty buddies hellbent on leading him astray – he decided to concentrate on putting his golf in order. After all, it was the one thing he had some trace of control over. With a renewed vitality and a determination to prove everyone wrong (yet again), Daly threw himself into practising, hitting up to 700 balls a day until his hands were covered in calluses. He would phone Rick Ross and talk technique, and then call Thomas Henderson and discuss his progress at AA meetings.

Crucially, Daly had accepted in the wake of his second stint at rehab that a structured aftercare programme was vital if he was going to have any chance of remaining sober. It was long overdue. 'When I entered the Betty Ford Clinic for the second time I listened to people for the first time. I let myself find out how many people have this disease – it's a lot,' he explained. 'Then I started to get the letters. I don't know how many I got, all I know is that I've still got 1,500 of them to open. I go to meetings and hear other people's stories and tell them mine, I go to schools and hope that kids learn from my experience. I suppose some will, some won't. They'll just be crazy like me. But the truth is that I now can't live without those people. The only way I am going to stay sober is to surround myself with them. You know, alcoholism is a tough disease. If I want to kill myself then I go to a bar and have a drink. It's that simple. Instead I read some of those letters when I feel an urge.'

When the new season arrived in January 1998, Daly took his place among the guys but with none of the fanfare or hullabaloo that had greeted his recent returns. Though nobody said it, there was a feeling that after the disturbing events of the previous season his role on the PGA Tour was now merely that of clown-cum-curio, a kind of warm-up act before the serious business of professional golf began. A tragicomedy in spikes, if you like. But Daly had other ideas. He hadn't busted a gut all winter to come along and make another exhibition of himself. If you want a laugh when you're watching golf, go watch Peter Jacobsen. John Daly's here to play some golf.

In the first three months of the year, Daly's form was a revelation. As coaches and commentators the world over are wont to say, he was 'in the zone', whatever and wherever that is. Back-to-back fourth places at the Nissan Open and the Honda Classic were his best results, and by mid-March he had already won nearly three times his entire winnings for 1997. Was this really the same John Daly who couldn't hit a clubhouse wall from ten yards in 1997? Could it really be the same John Daly who had almost drunk Jacksonville dry less than a year ago?

The answer, of course, was no. Outwardly he looked the same, but inside he was as far removed from the 1997 model as was possible. On the course he was focused, thoughtful and patient; off it he was considerate and humble. For once, Daly was the talk of the tour for all the right reasons. Indeed, the papers he had long since stopped reading were gradually becoming a little more interesting. They were calling him a 'reformed character' and describing his return to form as a 'miracle'. They were actually saying nice things.

'Golf pro. Love amateur'. Not the title of John Daly's autobiography, but the tagline of Ron Shelton's 1996 golf comedy *Tin Cup*. The movie, starring Kevin Costner and featuring a clutch of cameos from PGA professionals, is the story of washed-up golf pro Roy 'Tin Cup' McAvoy, a one-time tour player who sets about qualifying for the US Open in a desperate bid to win the heart of his painfully smug rival's girlfriend. Unusually, it is one Costner vehicle that actually met with a modicum of critical acclaim, not least because (a) it wasn't four hours long like most of his other movies, and (b) it wasn't *Waterworld*.

Those who have seen the film will recall the denouement; for those who haven't, it goes something like this. With victory at the US Open in his sights, McAvoy arrives at the par-five final hole and is faced with a shot across water to reach the green. Ignoring the advice of his caddie to play safe and take the easy option of the lay-up, McAvoy goes for the green and watches as his ball drops lifelessly into the lake. Determined to make it on his terms, he then hits ball after ball into the water until, with the very last ball in his bag and his chance of victory long since gone, he knocks one on to the green, much to the joy of the galleries. It's all about being true to yourself, apparently.

On 22 March, life imitated art at the Bay Hill Invitational. Playing with Paul Goydos and Tom Watson in the final round, Daly reached the par-five 15th (actually his sixth hole of the round because he'd started at the 10th that day). For the final day, the tees had been moved forward in a bid to tempt the longer hitters into going for the green in two. When John Daly stepped on to the tee box and tore the head cover off his driver, it was like watching a fox size up a nearby snare and then walk headlong into it. Crunch. Off went the ball in search of the fairway. It didn't make it. It came up a few yards short and took a dip in the lake that bisects the hole. Unperturbed, Daly strode forward to the drop zone, swapped his driver for a three-wood and gave the new ball another almighty lick. Wet. Reload. Wet again. Reload. Wet again. By the time Daly finally cleared the lake, sections of the crowd had begun chanting 'Tin Cup! Tin Cup!' and Daly was down to the last ball ('other than a couple of shag balls') in his bag. 'When I finally got on the green,' Daly said, 'I had a 30-footer for a seventeen. Tom Watson said, "Knock it in" – like it meant something. He was serious, too. We both just started to laugh.' When he finally coaxed his ball into the hole, Daly walked off the green the not-so-proud owner of an eighteen. Even for John, thirteen over par for one hole was uncharted territory.

Lesser players would have crumbled, been treated for shock or just fallen on their putter with the utter shame of scribbling '18' on their scorecard. Not John Daly. At the very next hole, the par-three 16th, Daly knocked a five-iron to twelve feet and drained the putt for a birdie two. Extraordinary. He also parred the 17th and 18th before walking off in search of a calculator. The end result, an 85, might have done for Daly in years gone by, but sober, and perhaps more importantly happy, he just laughed it off with the press and fellow pros alike. 'I just kept toeing the thing,' he joked. 'I was trying the whole time, but by my seventh swing I was pretty wasted.'

It is this kind of so-bad-it's-good golf that guarantees Daly the biggest galleries on the tour. The sheer unpredictability, the not knowing whether he's going to shoot 62 or 82, or even if he's going to see out the round, are part and parcel of his game and golf fans the world over love it. Hundreds of fans turned out to see him in action the following week on his return to the scene of the most depressing and destructive episode of his life. A year on from the night he drank Florida dry, Daly was worried about the reception he would get when he returned to the TPC at Sawgrass. He needn't have been. As he stepped on to the 1st tee, he found not fury but favour among the players and spectators. They recognised that Daly had made a genuine and sustained effort to get himself straight. So did Alcoholics Anonymous, who gave John a medal on the Saturday of the tournament in recognition of his twelve months of sobriety. 'This time last year I was a walking drunk,' Daly said. 'Hell, I don't even remember last year. When I get that medal . . . it will be like winning my third major.' But while turning his back on alcohol had given Daly's liver a much-needed rest, his lungs weren't so lucky. Driven by a compulsion to keep his mouth occupied at all times, Daly had upped his Marlboro intake to four packets a day, saying that it was 'that and eating a load of chocolate' that helped keep his mind off the Jack Daniels.

It would prove to be a successful return to Sawgrass; but for a 76 in his third round, Daly would have challenged for the winner's cheque. Instead, he settled for tied 16th and $66,000, which, for all John knew at the time, was what he might have spent in Sloppy Joe's a year earlier.

Despite the ongoing divorce proceedings, Daly maintained regular contact with Paulette, just so he could have some time with Sierra. Privately, he was more than a little disappointed that Paulette hadn't shown any real interest in how his rehabilitation was going, but in mid-May, as he prepared to make the trip to Texas for the Byron Nelson Classic, he received a call from his estranged wife. As the couple spoke, Paulette told John that she had indeed been impressed by his efforts to stay sober and that if he wanted to try for a reconciliation she was willing to give it a go too. But just as Callaway had taken on Daly with a list of conditions as long as his driver, Paulette too had a clear-cut proviso so simple even John could understand it: 'If you have one more drink, I'm out of your life.' Daly knew where he stood. 'I know now that if I drink again I will lose my wife and my daughters,' he said, 'and there is a good chance I'll end up dead. I know how lucky I've been. I've had support from people I probably didn't deserve. I hope I'm going to get it right this time.'

When he arrived in Irving, Texas, for the Byron Nelson Classic, Daly walked through the Four Seasons Resort with Paulette at his side looking every inch the contented family man once more. 'Being together again has made me more happy and relaxed,' he said. 'It's awesome, and I'm very happy.' That word again – awesome. He had employed it to describe his victory at the 1995 Open Championship, and would doubtless use it again if he enjoyed, say, a particularly good steak or a new line in Hershey bars. For the most part, though, Daly is a man of few words.

When he is dry and playing well, he is pleasant, affable and surprisingly quick-witted; catch him after a stinker of a round, though, and he is quite capable of swearing for an entire minute without ever once repeating himself. But with Paulette and Sierra back in his life, John had no need to curse anything, least of all a final round of 79 that dented any lingering chance he had of a decent finish.

A distinct and familiar pattern was developing. When Paulette was temporarily out of his life and he was free from the day-to-day responsibilities of family life, Daly had rediscovered his hunger for the game and played some of the best golf of his tempestuous career. Personally, the return of his family was the best thing that could have happened to him. As a dad, he was a natural – kind, loving, and above all fun. It was a role he felt truly comfortable with, and Paulette couldn't fail to recognise that. But with his personal life on what appeared to be an even keel, he had a tendency to take his eye off the day job. Examine the facts. After his tied-for-33rd finish at the Masters in April, Daly had earned a little under $350,000 in just ten events. If he could maintain that kind of form over the course of the year it would almost certainly mean a top-five finish in the money list. However, as the frequency of the meetings with Paulette and Sierra increased and the couple moved ever closer to their reconciliation, Daly's form suffered: in five events after Augusta he finished 76th and 77th in two and missed the cut in the others.

None of which augured well for the US Open in San Francisco. The competition was to be held at the historic Olympic Club, the very course where, after a disastrous round one day, Mark Twain had famously declaimed that golf was 'a good walk spoiled'. It was the kind of tight, undulating course that did not suit Daly's game. With its narrow, tree-lined fairways and less than generous greens, it took his favourite weapon, the driver, out of his hands. Not that Daly was worried; he was just happy that Paulette was there with him. 'I believe you only truly love one person in your life, and for me that is Paulette,' he told Bill Elliott of the *Observer*, forgetting that he had said much the same thing about Bettye Fulford back in 1993.

Despite his sobriety and contentment, it was evident from Daly's ever-expanding girth that the compulsive side to his nature was still getting the better of him. With chocolate and Coca-Cola taking the place of Crown Royal and Coors, his weight was getting out of control. 'I'm fat, but I'm happier,' said Daly, who was weighing in at 237lb (a shade under seventeen stones). 'A couple of weeks ago I was 245, but hey, when you're carrying as much blubber as I am then you only have to miss one meal to lose ten pounds.'

In the past, with alcohol flowing through his veins and that irrepressible self-belief taking charge, Daly might well have taken the big dog out and carved his own path through the Olympic course, but now, with a clear head and a reputation to rebuild, he was prudence personified, knocking three-woods and two-irons down the fairway instead. Gradually, it seemed, he was learning to accept that the only reason other players didn't flail away with their driver all day long wasn't because they were intimidated by him or because they were chickenshit, but because they simply preferred going home on Sunday evening with a sizeable cheque rather than on Friday night without a bean.

On Thursday, Daly's caution paid immediate dividends with a first-round 69. In the press conference he was asked what it had felt like to leave the very club that had made him in the trunk of his car. 'I think it sucks, man,' he joked. 'People want to see us hit the ball miles, want to see birdies and that stuff, but this is the US Open and they do what they want to do. That's OK too. I just have to adapt.' Patient and unflustered, Daly would fade after his initial promise and settle for a tied 53rd, but that was by the by. All that really mattered to John now was that Paulette and Sierra were back. He was getting to see Shynah, too. Life, his turbulent life, was sweet.

A bulldog licking his own piss off a nettle. Mrs Doubtfire. Fat bastard. Just three of the many sobriquets hurled at Colin Montgomerie over the years. With his ruddy Caledonian complexion and his less than perfect physique, the man who won an unprecedented seven consecutive European Order of Merit titles has become the prime target for some of the most vile and vicious abuse any golfer has had to endure on the course. And more often than not, it usually happens when he's playing in the USA. It's the New Yorkers that are on his most-wanted list. Renowned as the most raucous, brash and downright offensive galleries in the game, they make Millwall football fans seem like missionaries. *Newsday* columnist Johnette Howard once argued that a New York sports fan 'will boo his own mother if she burns the breakfast toast'. They're just that kind of crowd.

Montgomerie discovered just how accurate Howard's words were when he played in the 2002 US Open at New Jersey's Bethpage State Park Golf Club. Prior to the tournament, American magazine *Golf Digest* had handed out 25,000 'Be Nice to Monty' badges in a bid to ease the growing tension between the Scotsman and his adversaries. Monty joined in too, grabbing a handful for his caddie to wear. But it was like tackling a chip-pan fire with a gallon of unleaded. Soon, even the badge wearers were getting it in the neck. One tale, possibly apocryphal, sums up the kind of abuse Montgomerie has to suffer when he takes a trip across the pond. As he stood on a tee box at Bethpage waiting to take his shot, Monty was pursued by a determined fan desperately trying to attract his attention. Initially, his attempts were familiar, though not at all insulting. 'Hey Monty!' he shouted. No joy. 'MONTY!' No response. Time for a more formal approach. 'Excuse me, Mr Montgomerie.' Assuming that for once this wasn't just one of the Budweiser boys, Monty relented and turned to see what he wanted. With his undivided attention, the fan struck. 'NICE TITS!' he shouted, before running away, giggling like a schoolkid after one too many ciders.

The problem for Monty and similarly big-boned golfers is that with the notable exception of darts and sumo wrestling, golf remains one of the few sports where a pair of breasts are of little hindrance to a player's success (equal rights in the clubhouse may be more problematic, but that's another issue). It is a game where the peak of physical fitness is less important than what's between your ears. Think about it. You never saw any golfers on *Superstars*, did you? Gymnasts, boxers, footballers, they could all hold their own on the programme, but golfers? Conspicuous by their absence. Today, you are more likely to see pro golfers on *Celebrity Fit Club* than on shows requiring anything approaching physical exertion. Why? Because, with a few exceptions, they're arguably the least fit of all sportsmen, or rather they require a very different kind of fitness. Look at some of the big names on the European Tour. Lee Westwood, Darren Clarke, Ian Woosnam – they could all do with losing a few pounds. And the least said about Russell Claydon the better.

Over the pond, where the prize funds and the portions are much bigger, the problem is even worse. According to the PGA Tour's official website, Tim 'Lumpy' Herron weighs in at 210lb (fifteen stone), even though he looks like he's been attacked with a bicycle pump. Duffy Waldorf, no stranger at the sweet trolley, is said to be 225lb (sixteen stone). At the time of writing, Daly's official weight was 220lb (bigger than Monty) – surely one of the biggest fibs since Jeffrey Archer took the stand. Ever since his childhood, Daly has struggled with his weight almost as much as he has with his drinking. From the days when his mother watched him eat buckets of cookies to his all-too-frequent super-sized excursions to McDonald's and Taco Bell, his size has fluctuated not between slim and fat but between fat and morbidly obese.

At the 127th Open Championship at Royal Birkdale in July 1998, with his drinking temporarily in check, it was the issue of Daly's ballooning weight that became the talk of Southport in Lancashire. When he set out for his practice round on Wednesday he looked like a walking heart attack. He was big and bloated; his neck was nowhere to be seen. Everyone knew Daly was a big guy, but this big? The following day, the *Sun* carried a full-length photograph of Daly, complete with trademark Marlboro in mouth and bottle of Diet Coke, waddling along a fairway. The headline read GIVE ME MY DALY BREAD (and steaks, burgers, pizzas and chocolates, says food junkie John). It was a tad cruel, especially as the fresh coastal wind had clearly got inside Daly's waterproofs and puffed him out even more, but in Daly's new spirit of *glasnost* he was only too keen to spell out just why his weight had risen so dramatically. 'I've gone from one addiction to another,' he said, matter of factly. 'Right now, it's food. It makes me overweight and out of shape, but all I want to do is eat. I'm eating burgers, pizza, steak and all kinds of chocolate – anything I can get my hands on. The only thing I won't eat here is ice cream, because I'm too darn cold. Being off alcohol has left me with a craving for sugar, and that can only be satisfied by sweet things like chocolate. Hopefully that will change after a few years of sobriety, but as for my weight, I guess I'm just meant to be fat.'

But there's fat and then there's obese. Daly was now tipping the scales at over 240lb (seventeen stones plus); all those years of six cheeseburgers a day, large fries with everything and rivers of Mama Lou's chocolate gravy were finally catching up with his 32-year-old body. Not, again, that he was overly concerned, for Paulette was back in his life. As long as he steered clear of the booze and there was sufficient room for the two of them in the marital bed, she would love him even if he weighed 500lb. Indeed, Daly's determination to prove to everyone that he had finally turned the corner was such that he was even actively looking for an AA meeting to attend while he was in Southport. 'I'm going to find one,' he insisted. 'There's drunks all over the world, man. We're everywhere!'

Paired with Payne Stewart and Bernhard Langer, Daly fought his way to a respectable 73 in his opening round as the wind threatened to take centre stage, but it was what happened at the last hole of Daly's second and final round that not only stole the headlines but could have had him asking the locals directions to the nearest off-licence. Needing just a bogey five at the 18th to make the cut, Daly pushed his drive into a bunker on the right-hand side of the fairway and succeeded only in splashing out into the bunker ahead. He then tried to reach the green with his third shot when the more prudent option would have been to chip it out and try to make bogey. In Stewart's words, he then took 'five swishes at the ball' before escaping and watched in horror as the ball nose-dived into the greenside bunker. Another sand shot and two putts eventually gave Daly a ten and an early flight home.

Daly's head had gone. When the trio arrived in the scorer's cabin, Stewart, who had been marking Daly's card, asked him what he had scored on eighteen – and he wasn't trying to be funny. Like Daly, he had lost count of the shots as John had hacked his way to the finishing line; they had to enlist the help of Langer so that they could agree on a score. 'What difference does it make?' moaned Daly. 'Put down whatever you want.' After his eighteen at Bay Hill, Daly had left the course laughing and joking with anyone who cared to listen; now, though, he simply kept his own counsel and left as quickly as his huge frame would carry him. There was no press conference, no interview and definitely no comment, just a discarded putter, a ball lobbed angrily against the clubhouse wall and a volley of overheard expletives. It was left to Stewart, again, to comment on Daly's latest lapse. 'He was in good shape. He was going to make the cut, he just hit the wrong shot. When you hit it in those bunkers you just have to take your medicine. He was not a happy camper when he left here.'

Daly talked over what had happened with Paulette and they agreed that while missing the cut was less than ideal John could at least look at himself in the mirror and know that the real reason he had stormed away from Birkdale had had nothing to do with drink (or the lack of it) or any of the issues that had monkeyed around with his mind for so long. Rather, it was simply the frustration of not being able to play the game the way he wanted, or the way he knew he could.

He took two weeks off, although he wanted to take more. After the terrific performances of the first four months of the year, his form had nose-dived. The last thing he wanted to do was tee it up in the St Jude Classic. But, you know, it was close to home, and there were a bunch of old friends that wanted to say hello, and everyone would be so happy to see him again. Come on, John, they said, what's the worst that could happen?

Eager to please, as ever, Daly took his place in the Memphis tournament and after a second-round 68 seemed to be at ease with himself again. By the time he reached the turn in round three there was even a suggestion that he was actually enjoying himself, despite his initial reluctance to participate. He was three under par for the day and playing as well as he had done in months. With just two holes to go, he must even have been harbouring thoughts of a decent finish come Sunday. Then back-to-back double bogeys at seventeen and eighteen (and a snapped five-iron) not only wrote off any chance he had of making a real challenge in the final round, they also triggered another trademark tantrum. Visibly incensed, Daly exchanged cards with playing partner Loren Roberts, but after his calamitous finish he was in no mood for the small talk of the scorer's cabin, let alone totting up the damage of the final two holes. With typical haste he vanished from the course, flanked by three armed guards, without even signing his scorecard. The penalty was the usual one, and Daly suddenly found himself with a day off on Sunday.

The following week he reflected on this latest disappearance. 'That was stupid,' he concluded. Nobody disagreed.

19. STRANGERS IN THE NIGHT

*'Being a golf wife is a terribly secondary existence. You're always
orbiting around an enormous star. You're never shining on your own.
You exist only as a satellite.'*

Melanie Rockall, ex-wife of Nick Faldo

Shanae Chandler was a looker and no mistake. A journalism
student at the University of Texas, she was pretty, pert and, as
a star member of the college track and field team, extremely fit.
On the evening of Tuesday, 27 October 1998, after three years of
study, the 22-year-old Texan had just twelve hours of tuition left
before her course finished. She was looking forward to her
graduation in the new year.

Chandler had ventured into Austin for a night out, but had
dropped by the Four Seasons Hotel to catch up with her friend
Sammy Irwin. Sammy was the lead singer in Duck Soup, a covers
band that had acquired quite a reputation on the PGA Tour. Six
or seven times a year they would get a gig at an after-tournament
party and entertain players and fans alike with their extensive set
of rock classics. Irwin was also an Austin resident and was back
home for a charity golf tournament that he and the band had
helped organise. They had even got themselves a star guest, too –
John Daly. Chandler was excited. She had worked at a golf course
during her high school years and had heard all about him. 'I knew
he had blond hair. I knew he hit the ball further than anyone else

and I knew he had one or two big tournaments,' she explained, before adding, 'though I didn't know which ones.' As Irwin chatted with Chandler, he told her that, believe it or not, Daly was actually staying at the hotel and that the so-called 'Wild Thing' had just gone to bed. She didn't believe him. After all, it was only 9.00 p.m. Irwin told her to wait there while he made a phone call. Moments later, he walked back into the bar with a smile on his face. Daly had been persuaded to make an appearance.

Ten minutes later, Daly entered the room. He greeted everyone, glanced at Shanae, then looked at Irwin. 'Boy, you weren't kidding,' he said, 'she is beautiful.' Chandler was stunned. Here was an internationally renowned and wealthy sportsman coming on to her. He sat down, and the pair began talking. There was an immediate spark and Chandler, herself a recovering drug addict, knew that they were kindred spirits, somehow destined to be together. 'In the next twenty minutes, I knew I had found the soul I wanted to spend the rest of my life [with],' she said. 'By that Saturday, four days later, I had already flown to Palm Springs [where Daly was living at the time], and school and everything else was a thing of the past.'

By now, Daly knew his marriage to Paulette was all but over. For five months they had tried to make things work but they'd been forced to concede that the damage done by that night in Jacksonville had been irreparable. Now, as the partnership wilted, he had become convinced that his wife had lost all interest in him and his career. Sensible adult conversations about their future would descend into quarrels, and whenever tempers flared Paulette, with the memory of John's fury at the Sawgrass Marriott still fresh in her mind, was never quite sure how it would end up. With Sierra's interests to the fore, John and Paulette had discussed the idea of separation, and now that a new, younger model had entered Daly's life the writing was on the wall for their marriage. By the end of the year, the reconciliation would be over and Daly would have filed for divorce.

Despite the pleasant distraction of Shanae Chandler and a slightly clearer picture of just where his life was heading, Daly made his way to New Zealand for the World Cup of Golf in a decidedly surly mood. Reporters covering the event at the Gulf Harbour Country Club in Auckland recall him as cranky, bad-tempered and, at times, irrational. Well, more irrational than usual. After his rounds, he gave journalists and fans alike the brushoff. Not giving reporters the time of day was no big deal for Daly – they only wrote rubbish anyway – but rarely did he refuse an autograph or a photo with the fans, no matter how down he was. Among the press, the verdict was that Daly had fallen off the wagon again and had landed in the arms of the only person that really understood him – Jack Daniels.

It was a long way to travel to act like an idiot; he could have done that in his back yard in Dardanelle and spared himself the bad press and the air fare. Certainly, it wasn't his golf that was bugging him. Teamed with compatriot Scott Verplank, Daly claimed third place for the USA, and but for the eleven shots he and his team-mate dropped in eight holes in the third round they would have won.

While there was a wealth of circumstantial evidence mounting up, it would transpire that Daly had not, in fact, turned to drink; the reason for his erratic behaviour was the unsettling combination of his pending divorce from Paulette and the effects of antidepressants. Later, Daly would list the sideeffects of the medication, from diarrhoea to migraines, from lack of libido to uncontrollable vomiting. He was flagging badly. It was a miracle that he'd even had the energy to hold a golf club, let alone fly across the world and play in a four-round tournament.

Despite having some justification for his conduct, the press were nevertheless critical of Daly's attitude, some writers insisting that tough love from the PGA Tour was the only way he was ever going to get better. 'Now is the time for Finchem to put his foot down,' demanded Richard Mudry of *Golfweek*, as if Daly had been found guilty of mass murder. 'He should – make that, he must – suspend Daly indefinitely with the stipulation that he cannot return until such time that an outside third party – a respected health care professional – deems him mentally and physically fit to play in the spotlight of professional golf. It may, in the end, be the only way to save John Daly's life.'

Truth was, all John Daly really needed was a break.

As usual, Daly threw himself headlong into his affair with Shanae Chandler with about as much caution as a hedgehog crossing a motorway. Chandler had already moved in with him and was always on hand whenever he needed a Diet Coke on the driving range or yet another pack of Marlboro. Remarkably, she would also indulge Daly in one of his favourite pleasures. As one source revealed, the reason why Daly still chose to drive from tournament to tournament was not purely down to his chronic fear of flying: up to three times a day, Daly would take the wheel of his car and head off down the highway with his girlfriend buried in his lap fellating him. It was, he maintained, the only thing that kept him going on those long journeys. Like everything else in Daly's life, there were no half measures, not even in matters of the flesh.

Chandler wasn't the only one pulling for him. Still the galleries turned up in their thousands, willing him on whenever he played, waiting for his golf game to catch up with the breakneck pace of his life. Commendably, Daly did his utmost to repay their faith and, just as in 1998, he started the 1999 season well, registering two decent pay days in the Bob Hope Chrysler Classic (tied 21st) and the Phoenix Open (tied 14th). That said, there was the occasional glitch, and the less said about the Masters the better. Daly made the cut but hurt his ankle playing basketball the night before his final round and struggled to make an 81 for a tie for 52nd place, or next to last. 'He got dunked on,' was caddie Brian Alexander's view of the incident.

But how Daly needed a good year. With a battalion of ex-wives and a couple of kids to support, and having run up $500,000 markers in a variety of casinos in Las Vegas and Tunica, it was imperative that he keep his nose clean and dedicate himself to regaining his reputation as one of golf's true stars. The last thing he could afford, both psychologically and financially, was to incur the wrath of his saviour, Ely Callaway.

While Daly was, undeniably, finding it hard to make ends meet, there was another drain on his already limited resources waiting in the wings. Having so publicly declared how much he had earned (and then squandered at the casinos), it was almost inevitable that eyebrows would be raised at the Inland Revenue Service, and Daly would confess that his quarterly tax bills were now running between $350,000 and $400,000. Even with the Callaway millions, Daly was still living way beyond his means. He would need to play like Tiger Woods to live in this manner, and given that even Shanae was hitting the ball better than him, that wasn't going to happen. With the taxman breathing down his neck, Daly set about making some much-needed cutbacks. By the spring he had been left with no option but to sell the house in Palm Springs and engage in a cull of his fleet of cars. Indeed, the situation was so perilous that he even considered selling his house at Southwind as well. If matters didn't improve, and fast, Daly would soon be down and out in Dardanelle.

In early June, after several more calamitous rounds, missed cuts and forgettable finishes, Daly travelled to Dublin, Ohio, to an event that was close to his heart – the Memorial Tournament. This was Jack Nicklaus's very own tournament and it was held at the Muirfield Village course Nicklaus himself had designed in the 1970s. Despite the respect he so publicly held for Nicklaus, it was clear from the outset that for Daly the event was fast losing its appeal. When he reached the 18th green he was already four over par and looking entirely disinterested. Faced with an eight-foot uphill putt for his par, he rolled his ball two feet past the cup, then quickly stroked the return putt four feet back down the hill. It is at moments like this when you want Daly to step back and consider his options, or at least to give a passing thought to what he's doing. But with the red mist descending, with that who-gives-a-shit attitude to the fore, he rushed his next putt and knocked it a couple of feet past again. On his fourth putt, Daly feigned to kick the ball while stabbing at it with his putter and sent it racing past yet again. Finally, he managed to two-putt from five feet for a six-over-par ten and a total of 82.

Many of the game's greatest players have encountered problems at Muirfield Village's closing hole, but nobody had suffered as much as John Daly: his ten was the highest score on that hole in the tournament's 24-year history. As he lumbered off the green, he was approached by one brave fan who handed him a hat to autograph. He paused, scrawled his name on it, then threw it away before walking off in search of the scorer's tent. He withdrew from the event as soon as he got through the door.

In the wake of this latest record-breaking effort, Daly admitted that his form over the past two years was now so bad '[that] if I wouldn't have been exempt, I wouldn't still be playing'. Unusually, he also set himself a target, although few in attendance took him seriously. Genuinely aghast at the downturn in his fortunes, he indicated that if he failed to finish in the top 125 or to win again between now and 2005 (when his exemption expired) he would, in all probability, quit the game. 'Win two majors and have to go back to qualifying school? No way,' he insisted. 'I'd be too embarrassed. That's one case where my ego would get in the way.' And what of the six-putt at the last? 'The saddest part of it was that I was actually trying on the first four.'

Daly's exit from the Memorial was greeted with about as much amazement as one greets nightfall. Everyone knew he was on the slide; nothing short of eating himself to death on the 18th green could have provoked a reaction anything other than mild surprise in golf circles. Yet he was right about the state of his golf game. Without his exemptions from the victories in the 1991 PGA and 1995 Open, Daly would have been back at Q-School playing with the wannabes and the has-beens.

The following week, as Daly exited the $2.5 million FedEx St Jude Classic without earning a single cent, there were rumours that Ely Callaway was considering tearing up the contract of his most notorious endorsee. At the time, the story, in the wake of the withdrawal at the Memorial, was that Callaway had grown weary of Daly's ever-lengthening rap sheet; when pressed on the matter, however, Callaway was quick to refute the notion that his company and Daly had reached the end of the road. 'We are not reviewing his contract,' he insisted. 'Sure, he's had his ups and downs, but it's not affecting his contract or anything. We would rather the six-putt [at the Memorial] not happen, but it was a signal that he was a little bit agitated about something.'

Callaway's remarks were doubtless designed as a fillip for a player at a low ebb, but he might have had an entirely different opinion if he'd learned of Daly's reaction to the latest in a long line of missed cuts. Make no mistake, the St Jude Classic was by no means Daly's worst performance of the year, but this missed cut, on his own patch to boot, was one missed cut too many. Now, as he slid into his jeep to head back to Dardanelle, he found himself faced again with the moment all recovering alcoholics encounter sooner or later. It had been 26 months since Daly had last touched a drop of alcohol, 26 months in which he'd lost another wife, had been pushed from one psychologist to another with no discernible results and had found himself on the brink of insolvency and insanity. What rankled most, though, was that his golf game, his seemingly God-given golf game, had deserted him at precisely the same time he had given the bottle the boot. Daly might never have been the brightest kid in the school yard, but even he could figure that equation out.

As he left Memphis, he parked his car outside the nearest liquor store and went inside. When he returned to his vehicle there was a twelve-pack of Miller Lite riding with him. By the time he reached Dardanelle, it was gone. Of course, he had been here before, back in August 1996 when he sank a couple of lagers after the Scandinavian Masters and prompted the beginning of the end of his marriage to Paulette. Now, as the weeks passed and Daly tried to make up for over 26 months of sobriety, Shanae Chandler found their relationship was also in grave danger of disintegrating. 'When I first met him, he went to bed early, didn't drink, basically didn't do the things I considered fun,' she said. 'We had this beautiful storybook relationship, never fought. Then things began to change. We were constantly having spats. What changed? Alcohol was introduced into the relationship. When I drink and John drinks, its like nitro and glycerine.'

With Daly back on the booze, the tiffs between the two escalated and the chance of them conducting anything resembling a normal relationship was remote. It was a situation compounded by a seemingly ubiquitous army of Daly fans clamouring to hang out with the Wild Thing. 'Everybody wants to buy John a drink,' Chandler added. We'd go out and people would send over wine. And I was invisible. I felt like I was the most important thing to him when we first met, but then it seemed like he had a lot more things to occupy his time. When he was drinking, he certainly had a lot more friends.'

The problem with Daly, indeed most alcoholics, is that when he is under the influence his behaviour becomes increasingly erratic. Clearly, this also presents a problem for those closest to him in that one never knows just how to approach the situation. 'I've been with a happy one, a sad one, a mad one, a depressed one,' Chandler explained. 'But if you take a professional athlete and he's not playing up to his standards and he's not mad about it, if he's Happy Merry Sunshine, then something is wrong.'

20. I FALL TO PIECES

'I resent performing for f***ing idiots who don't know anything.'

John Lennon

The legendary American golfer Bobby Jones once called the Pinehurst Country Club the St Andrews of US golf, but if the Old Course could well have been designed with John Daly's game in mind, Pinehurst was the one to finish him off. Set amid lush North Carolina woodland, it is truly a golfer's paradise. There are eight courses alone at the country club resort, and scores of others in the area. In June 1999, however, it was Pinehurst No.2, the creation of celebrated course designer Donald Ross, to which the USGA gave the US Open.

Traditionally, the USGA prepare their Open courses to harsh directives: the fairways are tight, the rough heavy and the greens Teflon-coated. But Pinehurst No.2 represented something of a change in direction. For once, the fairways were wide enough to hit a driver (and therefore wide enough to tempt Daly into playing, after he had initially considered skipping the event) and the rough nowhere near as ugly as usual. That said, any player who thought he was in for four free and easy days of laughs and low scoring was in for a terrible shock. Without the lean fairways usually seen at US Opens, the USGA were relying on a combination of Pinehurst's infamous domed greens and some wicked pin placements to keep the best players in the world at bay. The plan worked. After the practice rounds on Wednesday, players were already likening the greens to putting on the back of a spoon. And things were destined to get much, much worse.

'I'm about as much in shock as everybody else,' said Daly after his first-round 68 left him two under par and just one shot off the lead. 'It's kind of scary, but I want to soak this day in and pat myself on the back for a round that I very much needed for myself and my self-esteem.' He had started his round with birdies on the first three holes and had looked like he was back in the groove. As he walked up the 18th, orange-tinted Oakley sunglasses perched on his nose and cigarette dangling from his lips, it was just like the old days – the days when he used to win things. 'The fans were awesome,' said Daly, who admitted that the encouragement he had received throughout his round had almost made him cry. 'They've been that way throughout my career, through all the ups and downs. It was nice to show them the old John Daly. I'm not saying it's going to happen every day. But I owe it to them. I owe it to myself.'

Still pinching himself, Daly retired for the day and celebrated by helping himself to six cheeseburgers in rapid succession, a man-size bag of Oreos and, strangely, a carton of milk. And as he sat in his room watching the sports highlights on TV, waiting for his round to show up, they tasted pretty damn good.

On Friday the wind picked up and everyone, Daly included, struggled. His round of 77 might have been in marked contrast to his opening-day exploits, but it was just enough to make only his second cut in his last seven events. At five over and bottom of the pile, his chance of a high finish had receded, but at least he had made it through to the weekend and for once his name wasn't the talk of the tournament. That honour went to the reigning Masters champion Jose-Maria Olázabal. The mercurial Spaniard, who had recorded a woeful first-round 75, withdrew from the event after having punched the wall in the locker room and broken a bone in his hand. It was a fit of pique straight from the John Daly Book of Tantrums – not that the big man himself was impressed. Asked if he had ever punched a wall in anger, Daly replied, 'Most things I punch, it goes right through the thing. In South Africa, I punched the TV and it kind of fought me back. I did it one time in Swaziland; I think I'd just gotten my first divorce. I was just in a great mood, was drunk off my butt and wound up shooting 23 under and winning the tournament.'

It had been a while since Daly had played competitive golf at the weekend, and to do it in a major felt pretty good, even if he was at the rear of the field. As he sat with the press, he reflected on what had turned into an increasingly typical Daly display. 'This game is crazy. I think, with my ability and talent, if I could get off to a decent start and hopefully find some confidence, there's no telling what I could do. Sooner or later, I hope to put four rounds together. It hasn't happened yet, but now the goal is to put three out of four together here.' But Saturday ended with a morale-sapping 81, and Sunday brought a whole new bunch of crap.

The trouble flared at the 8th. Daly had overshot his approach and was faced with a formidable putt up the steep slope at the rear of the green. The look on his face said it all – it was a devilishly difficult shot. A fraction too hard and he would end up on the other side of the green; too soft and he would be back where he started. Taking his putter, he rapped it up the hill but watched in disgust as it simply rolled straight back down again. He putted again. As the ball approached the apex, it slowed to a halt, turned round and once more began rolling right back towards its owner. That was it. Daly strode forward to meet the ball, swung his putter at it in the same way a polo player might swing his mallet, and smacked it back across the green and 30 yards up the fairway. In a career pockmarked by episodes of puerility, this was up there with the best of them. Strangely, nobody looked that surprised. Warned to behave himself by a USGA official, Daly headed for the exit, but as he contemplated another walkout he heard voices in the crowd pleading with him to give it another shot. 'Don't do it!' they yelled. 'Don't do it!' For once, he didn't. He walked over, made it up with his ball, chipped it back on to the green and took three putts to hole out for an eleven (including a two-shot penalty for hitting a moving ball). He completed his round without further incident and received a standing ovation as he walked up the 18th fairway. With a final total of 309, he finished a massive 30 shots adrift of the winner Payne Stewart.

With the humiliation at an end, Daly took the opportunity to vent his spleen. 'Yeah, it was frustrating and I lost my patience,' he told NBC-TV after signing his scorecard. 'But they have too many unfair pins. The US Open is not John Daly's style of golf. I'm not going to Pebble Beach [venue for the 2000 US Open] next year and watch the USGA ruin that golf course too.' The interview was brief, but then Daly was in no mood to shoot the shit with anyone. As he brushed off a waiting band of reporters, he stormed away in search of his courtesy car but still managed to spare a few moments to squeeze in another rant at the USGA. 'This is my last Open,' he said, with no small measure of melodrama. 'In fact, this isn't even one of the majors to me any more. From now on, my four majors are the Masters, the British Open, the PGA Championship and the Players' Championship. [The USGA] is just trying to embarrass the golfers ... I'm just speaking up for the players. They [the PGA] can fine me if they want. I'm not going to make a scene. I'm just not going to return.'

Despite his contention that he had only done what he had done to stand up for the guys, few actually saw it that way. Daly's playing partner that day was Tom Kite. He certainly didn't interpret John's actions as some altruistic act of defiance. 'People have different breaking points,' he said, diplomatically. 'Everybody does, and John just reached his.' Still, as the rest of the field finished their rounds and took their seats in the press room, it quickly became clear that others had also suffered at the hands of Pinehurst No.2. 'I played this as a par 88,' said John Cook, who carded a 77, while Brandlee Chamblee declared the course to be 'Augusta on steroids'. Perhaps Daly had a point after all.

The following Wednesday, the other John Daly turned up at The Club at North Creek in Southaven, Tennessee, to host his sixth Make-A-Wish Celebrity Golf Classic, an event aimed at raising funds for children with life-threatening illnesses. This was the flip side of John Daly. Here was a genial host with a smile for everyone and none of the scowling irascibility the world had witnessed three days earlier. 'Today, I'm a salesman,' he said. 'It's great trying to raise money for the kids. I've been on the phone every day for the past twelve months trying to get money and teams together. I've told the organisers of the event that the reason my golf game is so bad is because I've been working for this tournament the past year.' Excuses, excuses. But as he spent the day meeting and greeting, Daly also revealed that in the wake of his outburst at Pinehurst he had written a formal letter of apology to the USGA executive director David Fay, asking for forgiveness for his 'stupid' comments. 'I kind of regret what I said about the USGA,' he explained. 'They [the media] kind of caught me in a weak moment. I hope that the USGA will accept my apology. I think it was nine weeks of horrible play and I took it out on the USGA. I can't apologise enough.' Clearly, it had dawned on Daly that biting the sizeable hand needed to feed him and, for that matter, his three ex-wives, two kids and a new girlfriend wasn't the smartest idea he had ever had. Moreover, it would also transpire that Callaway Golf were none too impressed with his antics at Pinehurst and had marked his cards as to his future conduct. 'I just want to try and stay out of trouble,' he pleaded. 'That would be nice.'

As Daly helped raise a couple of hundred thousand dollars for the foundation, he could have been forgiven for sticking his hand in the bucket and helping himself to a large slice of it. Lord knows he needed it. After his first round at the US Open, he had spoken at length about just how perilous his financial position was. Claiming debts of $13.8 million, Daly staggered everyone with the sheer scale of his gambling debts. 'From 1993 to 1996 I won $42 million from casino gambling but lost $51 million for a total loss of $9 million,' he said, with all the charisma of a qualified accountant. 'You name it, I bet on it. It was fast action. I always liked it . . . but I haven't recovered from all the losses.' Those losses came as a result of some spectacular visits to casinos all around the globe. Five-hundred-dollar slots and blackjack were his undoing. Indeed, there were several occasions when Daly had over $200,000 riding on a single card, and he had lost $500,000 in a night and $1 million over a weekend, a fact tempered only by the occasional big win, such as the $900,000 he banked in one lucky night on The Strip. It was, of course, all relative, and Daly believed that as he had been earning exceptional amounts at the height of his gambling addiction, losing a million over a weekend wasn't really that big a deal. It was like a $30,000-a-year construction worker dropping a couple of thousand – annoying, but hardly likely to have the bailiffs beating at your door.

While the gambling liabilities were taking their toll – he still had an estimated $3 million to clear in a variety of casinos – he was also finding that the true cost of all those lost loves was much more than just a broken heart and some shattered memories. 'I am financially strapped,' he confessed. 'I'm not earning the money I used to and then there's the divorce payments . . . they're killing me.' With three divorces now behind him, Daly revealed that his alimony and child support were now costing him close to $40,000 every month. It was enough to have any rational man reaching for the bottle. As for an overweight alcoholic with a gambling addiction and a promising career sliding rapidly down the pan . . .

As yet, the word hadn't spread that John Daly was back on the booze. Sure, some people had their suspicions, but Daly was nothing if not honest and if he said he wasn't drinking again, well, who were they to argue? But since that first golden sip of Miller Lite nearly three weeks earlier, Daly had continued to tell everyone that his life remained one perpetual struggle against a mind and body craving alcohol. At the US Open he had told reporters that he was tempted by drink now more than ever because he didn't have any money to gamble with. Of course, he neglected to tell them that he had already fallen off the wagon. That said, confessing to a relapse would have been brainless in the extreme, even by Daly's extraordinary standards. Having earned under $30,000 in the last three months on tour, he barely had enough money to pay his way, let alone sit at the slots. Moreover, were Callaway to discover that he had been drinking again, it could spell the end of his only real financial lifeline and send him spiralling headlong into insolvency.

Daly needed cash, and fast. Thankfully, the good people at Druids Glen in County Wicklow came through. Daly had played in the Irish Open before and he enjoyed his spells back in his ancestral homeland. Ever since his win at Crooked Stick, like most other professionals he had become used to flitting overseas whenever a promoter was willing to stump up the cash. Indeed, it seemed that whenever there was a decent offer on the table Daly's fear of flying always managed to subside just long enough to pick up the cheque. This time, the offer was $150,000. It said a lot about Daly's phenomenal box-office appeal that a player standing 127th on the US money list and at 89th in the Ryder Cup points table could still command six figures.

Daly arrived at Druids Glen looking like a tourist in search of the craic. Which, to all intents and purposes, he was. Dressed in knee-length shorts and wearing sandals and sunglasses, he carried a sports holdall in one hand and a briefcase in the other, presumably to stash his appearance fee in. As the tournament's biggest draw, Daly's image was plastered all over the course and had been featured prominently on the poster campaign promoting the event. Surprisingly, however, nobody had cottoned on to the distinct lack of tact displayed by the adverts' slogan 'One good round deserves another'. With bumper crowds and a palpable air of anticipation for Daly's round, it was as if the circus had come to town. Not that the chief clown was overly concerned. 'I've never looked at myself as an entertainer,' he said. 'It's not a bad thing to be classed that way, but when tournaments start, I'm very serious. When I play good, I smile. When I play bad, I don't smile. I'm very angry. That's the way I have always been. I don't hide my emotions like a lot of guys do.' Happily, Daly seemed in good spirits, even though a reporter had told him that as they were in the wilds of County Wicklow he would struggle to locate any cheeseburgers. Daly, though, was undaunted. 'I *will* find them,' he insisted.

For his first round, he was placed in a trio that included the equally wayward Seve Ballesteros; sales of tin hats and crash helmets went through the roof. And if the posters bearing Daly's name were a little close to the bone, so too were the tee markers – replica pints of Murphy's Stout. Daly would later claim that those pints were staring back at him when he was trying to tee off.

Despite the fanfare that heralded his arrival and the warm reception he was afforded at Druids, Daly's golf followed a depressingly familiar pattern. A heartening start of 69–72 was followed by a rotten 81 and a final-round 74. The only scrap of consolation from his trip to the Emerald Isle, aside from his $150,000 and a couple of thousand bucks in prize money, was that for once he didn't finish last. He was one place higher than that.

21. I'LL NEVER GET OUT OF THIS WORLD ALIVE

'They can take their shit and keep it. I've never kissed an ass or licked a boot and I won't ever compromise what I believe in for nobody. I won't live by their rules. I'll do whatever I damn well please.'

Donald Lytle, aka country music star Johnny Paycheck

In the aftermath of the Irish Open, Daly withdrew from the Open Championship at Carnoustie citing a lack of confidence. Considerately, he also explained that he didn't think it was fair for him to take up the place of someone else who would be genuinely glad to be there and would give it their very best shot. A little over a month later he also pulled out of the PGA Championship, again with no real reason other than a festering feeling that he just couldn't do himself justice.

Clearly, for Daly to miss out on two of the most lucrative tournaments in the golfing calendar when he patently needed every cent he could lay his hands on meant he was suffering from a slump of career-threatening proportions. And the facts were there for everyone to see. In the nineteen PGA Tour events that year, Daly had missed seven cuts, had withdrawn from three events, and had finished in the top 50 on only four occasions. The last thing he needed was to enter a major and find himself embarrassed, humiliated and ridiculed once more. Better to save everyone the trouble and not even turn up.

The truth – the sad, unavoidable truth – was that alcohol had wormed its way back into his life and was threatening to wreak havoc not just on his game but on his not-so-private life too. Prior to the US Open Daly had once more met with Bob Rotella in a bid to clear his mind and help regain some focus in his life. Now, as his game went from bad to worse, he sought help – or rather Callaway sought help – from another sports psychologist, Jay Brunza. A former caddie for Tiger Woods, Brunza had once set up an alcohol rehabilitation programme for the US Army, and now, thanks to the intervention of Ely Callaway, he was looking to get to the root of Daly's problems.

The pair met several times, but to no avail. Daly listened to what Brunza had to say. It was straight-talking, common-sense stuff, but Daly was growing increasingly wary of all the people Callaway was surrounding him with. He needed to find his own space. 'He is just very stubborn,' explained Donnie Crabtree. 'He's the most stubborn person I've ever met. He's been to rehab twice and thinks it didn't work. He thinks the next time will be a waste of time. He has a tough time with authority, where there are rules and regulations and people say, "You've got to do this." John is not physically or mentally in shape to play competitive golf. Based on the history, he's headed downhill.' Unintentionally, Crabtree's sentiments might have had a more beneficial effect than any of those drummed into Daly's head by the sports shrinks Ely Callaway had hired. When your best friend since first grade is marking your card, you should realise that it's time to wise up. Instead of carrying on, piling up the quadruple bogeys and making the headlines for all the wrong reasons, Daly elected to take a break from the circus of the PGA Tour and head back to Dardanelle, where the folk liked him and the living was easy.

It was another beautiful August evening in Arkansas. Despite their recent troubles, John and Shanae were, for the time being, getting along just fine. With the top down on Daly's Corvette, the couple were enjoying a country run when, out of the blue, John turned to Shanae and said he wanted to drive somewhere special. Shanae agreed. Ten minutes later, the couple were 1,800 feet up at the top of Mount Nebo looking out across the sprawling Arkansas countryside. Daly wrapped his arms around Shanae and the two of them watched the sun set together, just like lovers do in the movies.

Before they left for home, John looked Shanae in the eyes and asked, 'Will you love me for the rest of your life?'

'Yes,' she replied.

'Will you marry me?'

Shanae was taken aback. 'Between the shock and crying, I blubbered yes,' she explained. 'John is like any other man – clueless when it comes to romance . . . I was so shocked when he proposed, and it remains the most special, romantic moment in my life.'

Clueless he might have been, but like most men Daly could still manage the occasional moment of soft-focus Hollywood romance, in addition to the five-carat marquise diamond ring he slid on to Shanae's finger. According to Chandler, Daly was much more than just some golf guy who could belt a ball until it vaporised. 'In three years, he brought me breakfast in bed every morning,' recalled Chandler. 'He was a morning person and I am not. He got breakfast every morning, and I cooked dinner every night.' Together, they shared baths in John's hot tub, filled with Chandler's favourite scented bubble bath from the lingerie chain Victoria's Secret; he would lavish gifts upon her; they would even play golf together. Indeed, Daly would teach Chandler with the kind of patience he almost never displayed on tour and was bowled over when his pupil once drove her ball 240 yards straight down the middle. 'In disbelief he said, "I would never have believed it if I weren't standing here," ' Shanae recalled. 'He was very proud.' Shanae paints a picture of a man who when away from the pressures of professional golf was capable of 'extraordinary kindnesses' on the one hand and inflicting 'so much pain' on the other. Life with Daly was a maddening mix of laughter, loving, beers and tears. 'There was never a dull moment. It was much like riding a roller coaster,' she added, 'up and down and up and down.'

In late August, with his new fiancée in tow, Daly returned to the PGA Tour for the first time in two months and teed it up in the Reno-Tahoe Open. On reflection, you have to question the wisdom of a man who having taken a two-month hiatus from his profession in a bid to deal with his addictions, including gambling, decides to return to action in an event in Nevada, the state with almost as many casinos as there are residents. Daly played badly, really badly. With two days to kill, he did what any gambling addict who found themselves in Nevada would do. He made tracks for Vegas.

The slots were great. When Daly started shovelling $500 chips in like they were dimes, and with a crowd gathering behind him, he got the same buzz, the same intense frisson, he did after hitting a 350-yard drive in front of a packed gallery, or from sitting down to that first beer of the day. Working a line of machines, he said, was like he was on some 'long, lonely cross-country drive'. He could put that first token in, look at his watch, and 30 hours had passed by. That weekend, Daly walked out of the Mirage, then Caesars Palace, shattered and shell-shocked. Over the course of a marathon 36-hour session he had lost $530,000, and his debt in the world capital of self-indulgence now stood at $1.5 million.

As speculation mounted about his renewed relationship with alcohol, Daly decamped to Carlsbad, California, to work on some test clubs with his sponsors Callaway. Nobody at HQ suspected anything. Daly was his usual cheerful, apparently carefree self. He was eager to see what Callaway had in store for him and keen to get out on the practice range and hit some balls. It was only when their day's work was done that trouble reared its head. With testing finished, Daly drove the 300 miles back to Las Vegas and into the waiting arms of Caesars Palace where he 'gambled, had a few pops and had a great time'. It would turn out to be another costly night for John, not simply because he blew another $150,000 on the slots.

The occasional clandestine rendezvous with a ravenous one-armed bandit, coupled with a few looseners, was all well and good so long as the paymaster didn't find out. Trouble is, when you're John Daly, there's about as much chance of a quiet night at the casino as there is of George W. Bush finding Albania on a world map. The following day, Daly's phone rang. It was Ely Callaway. 'I guess somebody at Caesars must have called Mr Callaway and told him I was in there gambling,' said Daly. 'He said, "Well, you know that's a problem." I said, "Yes, sir, I do. But I'm not happy with the way things are going. I hate the medication. I feel bad. I haven't played good for you. I want to win." ' A meeting was convened. Daly showed up with his entourage and, eventually, a deal was struck. If John agreed to go back to rehab, he could remain part of the Callaway family; if he refused, then his contract would be terminated and he would be free to do whatever he wanted. Reluctantly, Daly agreed to seek help, but only if he could take Shanae with him. 'I was extremely concerned for his health,' she said, 'to the point that when he told Mr Callaway he would only go to rehab if I agreed to go with him, I did it.'

Faced with the very real prospect of losing his last financial lifeline, Daly took Chandler and drove back to another faceless rehab clinic, this time in San Diego. Once inside, though, he knew he wouldn't be able to hack it. Within hours, patients were approaching him and offering him booze and cocaine, reefers and heroin. Anything he wanted, all he had to do was say the word. After just one sleepless night at the clinic, Daly decided to discharge himself and damn the consequences. 'I figured, screw it. I knew what was going on,' he explained. 'They took away every choice, even the little ones. Really, the hardest part for me was they wouldn't let me have Diet Coke. Cigarettes, yes; Cokes, no. It made no sense. At Betty Ford, at least they tried to teach you. This place was the opposite. They said they had their reasons, but I had just had it. People think I walked out because I couldn't handle it. I just didn't respect the method. Not there, anyway.'

As John got into his car, he picked up his car phone and called Ely Callaway. He told him that he was leaving the centre.

'Turn around, John,' pleaded Callaway.

'I can't do it, Mr C,' said Daly, his voice wavering. 'That place just isn't for me.'

Callaway repeated himself. 'Turn around, John.'

Silence. The line was dead. Daly had gone, and the moment he hung up and put his foot on the gas he kissed goodbye to the remaining $4.6 million of his deal. It was mid-September 1999, and Ely Callaway had reached the end of his tether. Try as he might, he had not been able to keep John on the straight and narrow. Daly had taken his cash, and all the faith, trust and goodwill that came with it, and pissed it up the wall. He and his company had done their utmost to accommodate their errant star and Daly had thanked them by ignoring all the advice they had given him and ordering another Jack Daniels. A statement was issued: 'We care a great deal for John as a person, a golfer and a friend, and we are grateful for the period of time he successfully supported the Company and its products as a member of our Professional Staff. Regrettably, we cannot continue to have John as a Company representative when he is not prepared to take the future steps that we and our expert advisors feel are necessary to deal with the alcohol and gambling problems facing him. We congratulate John for being the longest driver on the PGA Tour during his association with us and for his period of sobriety for more than two years. We wish John the very best and hope that someday he listens to those who love him and gets the help he needs.'

A little over eight years since John Daly had burst on to the pro golf scene like a brick through a window, he now found himself up to his neck in debt, oppressed by antidepression medication (he often described himself as a 'lab rat' during this period) and as the only player on the PGA Tour without a major sponsor behind him. But Daly knew best, or at least he thought he did. Over the years, he had convinced himself that his self-devised programme of AA meetings and replacing alcohol with food or tobacco rather than a handful of pills every day was infinitely more effective than anything Callaway could invent. Not that Callaway agreed. 'John keeps thinking he can do it all on his own, but his own does not work,' he sighed. 'He is a very practised manipulator, but I don't think he realises that the person he most manipulates is himself.'

At the heart of Daly's problems was the so-called 'Team Daly'. As one who had never been the greatest of listeners, apart from when his demons were doing the talking, Daly had found it difficult to absorb the never-ending stream of advice heading his way and had responded by kicking his medication into touch. 'Lithium, Prozac, Xanax, Paxil . . . I was on everything you can think of,' he would explain later. 'Everybody was saying I was manic-depressive. I was bloated. I was tired. I didn't want to do anything. I had headaches, diarrhoea, no energy. You don't want to have sex. You're just bored. There are no emotions in your life at all.' It was a sentiment echoed by Daly's father Jim, who felt that his son's continuing woes had nothing to do with issues with authority and everything to do with the invasive regime thrust upon him by his corporate backers. 'They had weight-lifting trainers. They had a doctor to keep him on drugs. Must have been a dozen of them,' he recalled. 'All to straighten out John. And you ain't gonna straighten out John until he's ready to straighten out . . . When you get out on the road, there are a lot of sophisticated people and I'm sure it was good intentions when they told John, "You gotta go to AA every day. You gotta exercise every day. You gotta take Prozac every day." [But] it's just too much pressure and they're controlling your life. Here's a guy who really doesn't have any problems, except that he likes to drink. OK, John had a few drinks and hit some golf balls maybe where he shouldn't. Because of that, they put him in rehab? Reminds me of pipe fitters I used to work with. Whenever they wanted a vacation, they'd say, "I've got a problem," and they'd send 'em to rehab.'

But while those closest to Daly attributed the bulk of his problems to the pressures of being at the centre of some vast, sprawling network of advisers, gurus and would-be Samaritans, it should be noted that whatever Callaway did was (a) designed with Daly's best interests in mind, and (b) aimed at protecting the considerable investment they had made in him. After all, Daly's contract never once stipulated that he had to actually play well or hit the ball further than anyone else, merely that he make a genuine attempt at sobriety. And as for insisting that Daly take medication – rubbish, according to Callaway spokesman Larry Dorman. 'A company cannot prescribe medication,' he insisted. 'We wanted to do whatever it took for John to get healthy. He had his own doctors who did prescribe medication for him. However, those medications were prescribed by doctors, not by Callaway Golf. The only things we asked John to do specifically were to attend AA meetings and to avoid gambling.'

John Daly had got what he wanted. He was free, or as free as a man crippled by debt and a ceaseless desire to drink could be. Without the shackles of a multi-million-dollar contract hanging around his neck, he could do what the hell he wanted. The Tunica riverboats were calling him.

22. ALONE AGAIN (NATURALLY)

'That man [Daly] has as much talent as anyone who has ever played this game. In terms of pure physical ability I would rank him with Sam Snead and Seve Ballesteros. The tragedy, of course, is that he will never come close to realising his potential ... because he so clearly dislikes himself.'

Five times Open Championship winner Peter Thomson

At home in Arkansas and unavailable for comment, Daly's official response to the split with Callaway came via his gripitandripit.com website. It read: 'My commitment to live a sober life remains strong. Alcoholism is a disease which will continue to challenge me the rest of my life. I accept the difficulties presented and hope that I will overcome whatever obstacles I face. While I am extremely disappointed to part ways with Callaway Golf, I can only hope that long-term success with my personal life will assist me in efforts to succeed as a professional golfer. To my family, friends and fans, I can only say that I still love you and I appreciate your continued support.'

While Daly lay low in Dardanelle, news of his separation from Callaway spread and virtually everyone, from fellow professionals to close friends, expressed deep sorrow for the decision he had made. Coach Frank Broyles, his old athletic director at the University of Arkansas, was dismayed, especially as his own brother Bill had died from alcohol-related illnesses in the early

1970s. 'I'm bitterly disappointed to hear about this, because I've been pulling for John and trying to encourage him to get over this hurdle. I don't exactly know what happened, but I know this – I'm not giving up on John. He still means a lot to me personally and I'm going to do everything I can to help him win this addiction battle. I worked with my brother as hard as I could, and we failed, although the effort was there. That experience makes me want to keep helping and encouraging John. I think he needs encouragement from the people of Arkansas, too. That would be the biggest boost he could get to help him rehabilitate himself, for the Arkansas people to stay behind him. I hope and pray that they will.' While Broyles was understandably disturbed by this latest turn of events, Daly's occasional coach Rick Ross had, sadly, seen it all before. 'He's at that point in his life where he has to get things right before he can communicate with the rest of the world,' said Ross, now the director of golf at Hot Springs Village golf complex in Arkansas. 'He has a tendency to hide. If I look at history when he has had problems, he doesn't call or write or anything until it's too late. Then it's like, "Bail me out." '

But if anyone knew what was going on in Daly's head, it was his friend from first grade, Donnie Crabtree. As his pal, driver and confidant, Crabtree had witnessed virtually all the fits and flare-ups Daly had endured over the years and he was growing tired of it. 'If anything motivates John, it's money,' he suggested. 'For him to turn away all those Callaway millions shows the despair his life is in now. Maybe he needs to hit rock bottom before he realises he threw it all away. Everybody in his inner circle has exhausted all efforts to help him. He has rejected those closest to him by saying he can handle the problems by himself in his own way. Sadly, he's not at the point yet where he thinks he needs help. He's in obvious denial about where he is at in his life. He continues to make bad decisions.'

When Daly finally emerged from his house, he gave his first post-Callaway interview to *Golf World* magazine. It was a typical Daly feature, focusing on the extent of his now legendary gambling debts, on exactly why the split from Callaway had come about, and on the apparently never-ending turmoil in his life. That said, there was nothing else for journalists to write about. Daly's golf game was dying a death, and why would anyone want to read about some bloated guy who missed the cut every week when they could read about Tiger Woods rewriting every record in the book?

All things considered, Daly sounded remarkably upbeat about his situation, but there were worrying signs that after two years of sobriety he was now intent on making up for lost time. 'It's sad, but I think it's great to be free,' he said. 'Granted, I could go out and lose everything [by] gambling and drinking, but there's no sense in denying it. It's in my blood.' When asked if he thought he could stay sober on his own, his answer was undoubtedly distressing for those who knew and loved him, but brutally frank all the same. 'Honestly?' he said. 'Probably not. I want to gamble and I want to have a few drinks now and then. Basically, it [trying to stay sober] had taken over my life, and I was miserable. It's like I've said before, there's no way I'd never drink again.'

Daly's freedom was, of course, relative. In the wake of his departure from Callaway Golf, Ely Callaway had taken the opportunity to set the record straight on Daly's debts. When Daly had signed his contract with Callaway, it had been widely reported that the company had cleared his gambling liabilities for him as part of the new deal. This, however, was not the case. The $1.7 million used to pay off the debts was, in fact, a loan, and Callaway confirmed that they would be asking for it back in due course.

In mid-October 1999, Daly picked up his biggest cheque of the year ($60,000) when he partnered Karrie Webb and Hugh Baiocchi to a tie for fifth in the eight-team Gillette Challenge in Tuckers Town, Bermuda. It was a knockabout, made-for-TV cash bonanza that required very little effort for considerable return, and in that respect it was right up Daly's street. But if the atmosphere at the Gillette Challenge was relaxed and convivial, the Las Vegas Invitational (LVI) tournament, up next, would prove to be a severe test of Daly's resolve.

Over the years, Las Vegas had become a second home to Daly, and his return to the gamblers' paradise did not go unnoticed by the media. DEATH-WISH DALY ran the headline in the *Daily Mail* over a piece by Lauren St John that argued that Daly was going to the one place virtually guaranteed to speed his journey towards self-destruction and probably oblivion. Daly's agent, John Mascatello, agreed that Vegas was possibly the worst place on earth for John to compete. 'Obviously it's a tough venue for John, but hopefully he's going there to play and not for the distractions,' he said. 'I can only hope he gets through the week without any more problems.' St John's piece described how Daly had set up camp on the Strip with a pile of $100 chips at one side and a bottle of Jack Daniels at the other, but Daly insisted that he spent just one hour in the casinos during the entire week he was in Vegas. 'I hardly gambled ... I threw a little bit into the slots but not anything like I used to,' he maintained. 'The good news is that I don't have millions of dollars to gamble right now. It's just nice to go there and play the $100 slots or $25 slots for an hour and then go to bed and get up and practise.' Go to bed and get up and practise? Maybe this was a new John Daly after all. The evidence from the LVI, where a switch to Titleist clubs helped him to three rounds in the sixties and a tie for 37th, certainly suggested that he had found a new order in his life, now that he was free from the intervention of others. He had even been seen smiling

Reinforcing Crabtree's belief that John would go anywhere for money, Daly left Las Vegas and flew to Belgium. The promoters of the Belgacom Open had offered him $150,000 to play at the event at Royal Zoute, and feeling more positive than he had done in years, Daly was only too happy to accept. The bookies were even talking of Daly as one of the dark horses in a 108-strong field that included the likes of Lee Westwood, Darren Clarke and Bernhard Langer. As Daly prepared for the tournament, he gave freely of his time and spoke at length about his reasons for going it alone. He was candid and cheerful, and looked as though his recent trials and tribulations had been erased from his memory. 'I made a decision about two months ago: I'm going to drink a little and I'm going to play golf. That's what I do. The other option was never to gamble, try to stay sober and never play golf again. I didn't want to go that route. Golf is my life, it always will be. It's what got me here and what puts food on the table for my children.' An alcoholic who allows himself a drink and a gambler who still plays the slots. It was certainly a novel approach to dealing with his addictions. Indeed, all he need do now was try to shed a few pounds on a double cheeseburger and fries diet. But then this was all Daly ever wanted – the freedom to tackle his problems in the way he saw fit, the responsibility to live or die by his own methods. Two days later the all-new John Daly was on his way home from Belgium having missed yet another cut.

Daly's ongoing problems were put into some kind of tragic perspective on 25 October when a plane carrying the reigning US Open champion Payne Stewart from Orlando to Dallas crashed, killing all six people on board. The twin-engined Lear 35 lost cabin pressure soon after taking off, rendering everyone aboard unconscious, and then cruised at 45,000 feet on autopilot for four hours before running out of fuel and nose-diving into a South Dakota field. He left a wife, Tracey, and two children, Chelsea and Aaron. For a man with a lifelong fear of flying, the untimely demise of 42-year-old Stewart merely reinforced Daly's belief that man wasn't meant to take to the skies. To that end, he elected to drive the six hours from the Dallas area rather than hop on a one-hour flight to reach Madison, Missouri, for the Southern Farm Bureau Classic. 'I'm really not even wanting to get on a plane to go anywhere right now,' he said during his practice round. 'I know they are safer and it's the best way to travel, but I've always said I like my chances in a car wreck before I do a plane crash, because nobody is going to live.' What compounded Daly's fears was that Stewart, so often at his side during his many moments of madness, died in a Learjet. 'You expect some other kind of plane to go down before a Lear. It was the only plane that I really felt safe in because of all the safety features it had. It was just like it was crash-proof.' With play at the 54-hole event suspended until Saturday as a mark of respect for Stewart, 40 of the 131-strong field took the opportunity to fly to Florida for Friday's memorial service. Others, like Daly, chose to have a quiet round at Dancing Rabbit, an exclusive new course at the Silver Star Casino on the Choctaw Indian Reservation about an hour from Annandale.

Despite the tangible air of sadness around the venue, Daly's mood some six weeks after the split with Callaway was noticeably more relaxed. Insisting that he was more at ease with himself than at any time in the last two years, he was quick to point out that while everybody who didn't know him had expected him to descend headlong into some bacchanalian nightmare, the reality was a little different. 'I haven't even hardly drunk to tell you the truth. It's not something I want to do every day. Knowing that I can now and knowing that most everybody knows that I can, I'm not really doing it. The pressure's kind of gone. Now I can just go out and practise and play golf, and that's all I've got to worry about.'

During the final round, Daly seemed set for his first top-ten tour finish since the Honda Classic in April 1998, but it wasn't to be. Despite back-to-back birdies at ten and eleven that took him to eight under, he dropped seven shots in three holes and closed with a 76 for a three-day total of 214 (two under par) and a tie for 36th place. It was Daly's last tour event of the year, and it couldn't have come sooner. Perhaps the only positive he could draw from an otherwise soul-sapping season was that despite everything, including the emergence of Tiger Woods as the main threat to his driving-distance crown, Daly had won the category yet again, this time with an average drive of 305.6 yards, which was over twelve yards longer than Woods' average. Clearly, Callaway's Big Berthas had added yet more length to his drives, but they had patently failed to improve the rest of his game: he finished 158th on the money list with just $186,215 to show for his efforts. It might sound like a fortune to the average Joe, but it should be remembered that when you are a professional golfer you are, for the most part, responsible for all your expenses, including air fares and accommodation. Factor in the cut of your caddie, agents and managers, your lawyers and accountants, the IRS and, in Daly's case, an all-consuming gambling habit and enough alimony and child support payments to break a man, and you're soon left with barely enough cash for a round of blackjack. For the record, Tiger Woods topped the money list in 1999. He played in one fewer event than Daly and won $6,616,585.

There were still a couple of potentially lucrative events to compete in, though, and much to Daly's surprise they would turn out to be extremely profitable. The first of these was Greg Norman's Franklin Templeton Shark Shootout, a pairs event for which Daly teamed up with tour veteran Chip Beck. With the Callaway clubs no longer in his bag, Daly decided to use the competition to road-test a selection of drivers and irons. It made sense. Nobody really took these events seriously, and if Daly did find himself in one of his more wayward moods there was always Beck on hand to pick up the pieces. Aside from a couple of errant tee-shots from Daly, the pairing proved to be a useful partnership, and Daly was more than content with their tie for seventh place and a cheque for $47,000.

His assessment of his form as he arrived at the JCPenney Classic, however, was undeniably accurate. 'It pretty much sucks right now,' he said. 'I've been working really hard on my game and I'm not getting anywhere with it and it is really frustrating. But if I can get something here, something there. Just get a little confidence. I think that's what I need the most. I'm just taking baby steps, trying to get anything I can out of my game.' Daly was hoping that his regular partner for this mixed-pairs event, England's Laura Davies, would arrive at the course at Innisbrook near Tampa, Florida, at the height of her powers. Daly had first met Davies in September 1995 when they teamed up with Jack Nicklaus to play in the Wendy's Three-Tour Challenge at Muirfield Village. 'Far from being loud, he was one of the most shy and unassuming professionals I have ever met,' she recalled. 'We got on like a house on fire. So well, in fact, that at the end of the day he asked me if I would partner him in the JCPenney tournament.' Daly and Davies had been a fixture at the JCPenney Classic since 1996, and there were definite similarities in terms of style. Both were huge hitters, longer than all their contemporaries, and both had all the deftness of a heart surgeon around the greens. But while Daly, waylaid by all his many problems, had struggled to fulfil his true potential, Davies was unquestionably one of the biggest stars the women's game had ever produced, as scores of tour titles, including five majors, on both sides of the Atlantic proved. This was to be their fourth time in the JCPenney, and it would be their last as the event would cease to exist once the final putt had dropped. To date, their best finish had been fifth in 1996, and despite Daly's protestations about the state of his game, Davies wasn't in the slightest bit worried. 'John can play fantastic at the drop of a hat,' she insisted. 'I never worry about how he's hitting it.'

Going into the final round five shots behind leaders Paul Azinger and Se Ri Pak, Davies and Daly clawed themselves back into contention, the LPGA star making birdie at eighteen to force a play-off. It was then that Davies came into her own. After holing an 8-footer at the second play-off hole to keep them in it, she then drained a 30-footer at the next for an unlikely victory. Daly was astounded. 'If she ever says she can't putt again,' he threatened, 'I'm coming after her.' After a year that had seen another divorce, possible financial ruin and an end to his sobriety, Daly had astonished everyone by ending it not on a mortuary slab, as many had expected, but by winning a tournament again. The triumphant duo split the winners' cheque of $440,000, Daly's share enough to cover six months' alimony or a bad night at Caesars Palace.

23. THE DEVIL MADE ME DO IT

'Golf inflicts more pain than any other sport. If you're the sort of person whose self-worth is tied up in how you play, golf will cut right to the core of who you are. When a person like that performs poorly, it's another indication to him that he's a bum.'

Dr James Loehr

After six months of trying and almost 200 telephone calls, Tom Chiarella finally got through to John Daly. As they spoke, Chiarella, a writer for *Esquire* magazine, explained to Daly that he wanted to meet him so he could write a piece about his ongoing struggles with his golf and his life. Taken with the idea, Daly invited him down to Dardanelle for a few days.

Having found a photographer at short notice, Chiarella flew to Memphis then drove to Yell County. When he eventually arrived at the house he was greeted by an unshaven Daly in his underwear. He had just woken up after a long, drunken poker session the night before and he had lost again. Ninety bucks, for the record. Chiarella had expected to find a huge hulk of a man with a beer in one hand, a Marlboro in the other and a gut spilling over his shorts; instead, he found a softly spoken gentle giant, extremely hospitable and eager to please. Also there for the weekend were Shanae Chandler and Bud Still, Daly's friend and aspiring tour pro. With the introductions made and the obligatory tour of *chez* Daly complete, Chiarella sat down at 3.00 p.m., whereupon he was presented with what he would later describe as an 'absurdly large' whiskey. It was the green light the journalist in him had been hoping for.

Five hours later, Chiarella was smashed. He had fought a running battle with Crown Royal, an inexpensive Canadian blended whiskey, mixed with Coke – Diet, obviously – and it had won hands down. Daly, meanwhile, was just getting warmed up. When dinner time arrived – that's to say, when the host felt hungry – Daly strode into the kitchen, took a giant eighteen-inch bowl of cheese dip out of the refrigerator, stuck it in the microwave and served it up to his guests.

As the night wore on and the booze kept flowing, Daly's guard gradually dropped. Confident that Chiarella wasn't just another reporter out to assassinate his character, he left the room, returning moments later with a pile of photographs in his hand. As he started showing them around, Chiarella's jaw hit the floor. 'He had Polaroids of himself f***ing some woman in town,' he recalled. 'I said, "John, you're crazy. You know I'm a journalist?"'

'You won't take them,' Daly replied, before adding, 'That's why they call me Long John.'

Later that evening Daly passed out on the couch. There, right next to his slumbering frame, was the incriminating evidence. Chiarella looked at the stack of photographs, sorely tempted to help himself, but his good nature got the better of him. After all, the two of them were getting along famously, so why ruin things? 'I could easily have taken two or three,' he said, 'but he had given me more access than he'd given any reporter in ten years. He'd given me a break.' While Chiarella concluded that Daly's decision to show him the photographs was an act of faith on his host's part, he was still left with the overriding impression that Daly was a man who was 'incredibly proud of the size of his penis', adding that 'he's hung like a racehorse. He looks like a f***ing donkey.'

The Polaroid incident was just one of many eye-opening episodes during his two days in Dalyville. There was also a trip to McDonald's, where to Chiarella's amazement Daly ate four Big Macs in quick succession ('You can be addicted to meat,' Daly claimed). Then there was breakfast with Jim and Lou Daly and his introduction to the wonders of chocolate gravy (with bacon); an impromptu gig with Daly and his ever-increasing collection of guitars; and a midnight trip to Tunica to play the slots, aborted when they couldn't find a sober driver. While Chiarella's piece in *Esquire* revealed a person very much at ease on his own territory, it was nevertheless a depiction of a man in his mid-thirties who with his cheap whiskey and cheese dip, his heart-to-hearts and his hangovers, was still behaving like a fraternity boy. 'He is more of a boy than a man, and we like boyish ... They can be very charming,' added Chiarella, who has since quit drinking. 'The problem is that they get themselves into trouble.' Crucially, Chiarella found none of the desperation or anxiety he had anticipated, 'none of the fearful hunger of the inveterate boozer'. Instead, just a resolute denial of any suggestion that he was an alcoholic. He was, Daly insisted, just someone who liked to drink. 'The worst mistake I ever made was admitting I was an alcoholic because I gave them [the rehab centres] all the power,' he claimed. 'According to them, there's only one way to go. Now, I either go that way or everybody writes me off.'

Daly's long-standing declaration that he was absolutely not an alcoholic was greeted with the level of scepticism he had come to expect. At the Phoenix Open at the end of January 2000, where he tied for 72nd, he said that despite pleas from virtually everyone he knew, he would never be going back to rehab, no matter how serious his condition got in the future. The reason, he maintained, was not denial or some rampant self-belief in his ability to beat his demons on his own terms, but money. That is to say, they charged too much, and he didn't have any. 'They are only in it for the money,' he said, revealing that his three visits to clinics had cost between $12,000 and $30,000 each. 'While AA meetings are much better, I don't think I need to go to them any more. Besides, I'm not an alcoholic. I have four or five beers if I go out to dinner and a twelve-pack if I stay home.' There can't be many people who would regard sitting at home and devouring a twelve-pack of beer every night as entirely normal. That Daly thought it was acceptable behaviour suggested that his notion of what could be termed 'moderation' differed markedly from the received belief.

When Henry Kissinger was awarded the Nobel Peace Prize in 1973, the American author Gore Vidal marked the occasion by arguing that it was the day satire died. Much the same could be said of John Daly's decision on 2 March 2000 to sign a deal promoting the benefits of the ironically named soft drink SoBe. 'We've used "grip it and lip it" as a slogan for SoBe, so moving to "grip it and rip it" with John Daly made a lot of sense to us,' said Norman Snyder, chief operating officer of the South Beach Beverage Company. 'We relate to people like John who have a fun, edgy attitude.'

In all of his years on the PGA Tour, Daly's attitude had been called everything from impetuous to irresponsible to downright dangerous, but 'fun' and 'edgy' were two words conspicuous by their absence. Still, it was an unexpected bonus for Daly at a time when he needed every cent he could lay his hands on. The base salary alone was worth $150,000 for the first year, and he would receive an additional $2,500 every time he made a cut in a PGA Tour event. Daly's duties for the company were the standard requirements placed on contracted players. As well as appearing in advertising campaigns for the drink, he would have to wear SoBe branded clothing when he played and use a SoBe umbrella whenever it rained; he also had to carry the SoBe logo on his golf bag, which, some of the press wags remarked, was the first time anything resembling a soft drink had ever been near his bag. Yet Daly's response to the new deal was not exactly the ringing endorsement Snyder wanted. When he was asked what he thought of SoBe, Daly claimed that it 'tasted good with vodka'.

The sponsorship deal with SoBe wasn't the only source of income Daly had been chasing. With the help of Shanae, he'd also set up John Daly Enterprises, a company dedicated to selling a new line of Daly merchandise bearing his latest brainwave, 'The Lion' logo. The Lion range encompassed a wide range of products for aspiring Wild Things: there were T-shirts and golf tops, umbrellas and head covers, caps and hats, all with the gaudy cartoon Lion logo. There were also 'Cub Clubs' for kids and a line of Lion lighters that would finally bring him some success in the casinos: he sold them at a profit in gaming-house gift shops. In time, the range would, somewhat inexplicably, also include jewellery, the fourteen-carat gold and diamond Lion pendant yours for just $2,395.50. 'I try to think of myself as a lion, bringing down the kill, controlling the jungle,' he said. 'A lion controls his jungle. I control the jungle. That's the way I see my days now.'

Control, or the patent and long-lasting lack of it, however, was one of the main reasons why Daly was still without an equipment deal. Indeed, he was now the only player on the PGA Tour without one. It was a shambolic situation, although one which was entirely self-inflicted. But then why would any manufacturer want to touch Daly with his track record? By the time he teed it up at the Honda Classic at Coral Spring in early March he had taken to playing with the new Tommy Armour 845 irons, Taylor Made's Firesole driver and the Inergel ball. In a bid to get a feel for his new clubs, he was also taking to the range more than he had in recent months, hitting balls for several hours and going through four buckets at a time. 'That used to be my quota for the year,' he joked.

Daly had always performed well at the Honda Classic. The TPC at Heron Bay was a wide, open course with little danger for the more aggressive players like Daly who liked to flail around with their drivers and call on parts of the course they weren't really meant to. There was also the small matter of Honda's hospitality, too. Over the years, Daly had grown particularly enamoured with the home-baked chocolate-chip cookies they served in the players' locker room and was quite capable of eating a dozen of them in one sitting. He even had an arrangement with the locker-room attendant whereby the biggest ones in the batch were placed directly into his locker. This year, though, the cookies were strictly off limits. In a bid to shed some of his excess baggage, Daly had been following a diet – nothing drastic, mind, just a few less visits to the Golden Arches each week and less chocolate. He had done well, losing twenty pounds in two months, and he was determined to lose another twenty. For once, his golf improved too. His finish, tied for sixteenth, represented his highest placing in six events that year.

While Daly was scrabbling around cutting deals with drinks companies, trying out some new clubs and figuring out novel ways to subsidise his golf hobby, one of his friends was enjoying the kind of fortune he could only dream of. On 23 March, Daly's rehabilitation counsellor and erstwhile Dallas Cowboys star Thomas 'Hollywood' Henderson discovered that he had won the Texas Lottery, his prize an inconceivable $28 million. 'I'm the winner,' he told the press. 'I am the only ticket holder here in Texas. It's a blessing.'

Daly could certainly have used some of Henderson's luck off the course, and he was desperate for some on it, too. As he approached the Masters, he was 22 over par for his last eight rounds on the tour. One of those rounds, a closing 87 at his nemesis event the Bay Hill Invitational, was typical of the way things were deteriorating. 'It's embarrassing,' he said. 'I feel great physically but I'm a feel player and I don't feel it out there. I usually know what I'm doing out there, but nothing looked good or felt good. I don't know where the ball is going to go. I try to hit a draw and it cuts. I try to cut it and it draws.' The millennium Masters was the final year of Daly's five-year exemption to the tournament. With his form at an all-time low, he had to face up to the very real prospect that if he didn't finish in the top sixteen that week (or in the top fifty of the world rankings by the end of the year), then in 2001 he would not be back at the event he lived and died for. Daly's behaviour that week suggested that even he didn't believe he had what it took to win another automatic qualifying spot. Before he played his first round, for example, he was spotted spending thousands of dollars on official Masters merchandise at the gift shop for his family and friends back in Dardanelle. He bought six boxes of Masters shirts (twenty per box at $60 per shirt), then lugged them from the pro shop to his van. It was as if he knew he might not be back for some time. 'There goes my prize money,' he said.

What prize money? While the National course was its usual resplendent self, its magnolias and azaleas in full bloom and the white dogwood catching the eye, Daly's golf stank as much as the groundsmen's top-quality fertiliser. After bludgeoning a drive at the very first hole that landed in the pine straw to the right of the fairway bunker, Daly looked wistfully at the pristine fairway and said, 'I wouldn't know what it's like to hit off that pretty green stuff.' By the time he holed out at eighteen, Daly had taken 80 shots to negotiate Bobby Jones's baby and he knew in his heart of hearts that he would not be returning to Augusta. After signing for a 73 the next day, he simply walked off to the locker room refusing all requests for interviews. He then placed his belongings in a plastic bag, headed to the parking lot, jumped in his van with its PGA 91 licence plate and drove off down Augusta's fabled Magnolia Lane. As the vehicle disappeared into the distance, the golf world wondered whether they would ever see the Wild Thing back at the tournament again.

The following Tuesday, Daly re-emerged across the state border in Auburn, Alabama. After another celebrity bash he could have done without, he sat down for an interview with the local newspaper, the *Opelika-Auburn News*. Yet again, the subject of his drinking came up; nobody, it seemed, wanted to know about his golf any more. Politely, Daly trotted out the stock responses about drinking in moderation and taking each day as it comes. When he stood up after the interview, however, he left three empty beer bottles on the table in front of him.

With Shanae in tow, Daly carried on drinking well into the night, the memory of Augusta still playing on his mind. Shortly after 10.00 p.m., a drunken Daly decided he wanted to eat and the couple repaired to a local branch of McDonald's. When they had eaten their meals, they walked out to the van, whereupon Daly, who had gone on record that year claiming that he would never drink and drive, decided he was going to drive home. Not surprisingly, Shanae was having none of it, knowing full well that he was way over the limit. John screamed at Shanae that he could drive if he wanted to. Shanae, no shrinking violet herself, countered, saying that if he wanted to kill himself then that was fine but there was no way he was taking her with him. Scared that he was losing it, she then shoved him in an attempt to keep him away from her. As the slanging match escalated into an ugly and all-too-public incident, the chances of their ever walking down the aisle together ebbed away.

At 10.25, the police arrived to find Daly hurling Shanae's clothes out of the van. Somebody had called from McDonald's and told them that things were getting out of hand. Daly and Chandler were taken to separate hotels and interviewed about the altercation. Neither was arrested, but the damage it had done to their relationship was immeasurable. Three years on, all Shanae Chandler will say about the incident is that 'it began over who would drive the car home', adding that 'he was too intoxicated to do so, and we were arguing over the fact'.

The mood in the Daly camp remained distinctly bleak into the summer. It was like living through some lengthy eclipse and waiting for the sun to emerge. Trouble was, it never did. On the course, Daly continued to feel the pinch of a season played without the backing of a major sponsor, and so too did Brian Alexander. Wedgie had stuck with Daly through thin and thin (there had been no thick), but now, as his boss struggled to make ends meet, Wedgie decided to take up a new position as Tour representative for a new equipment company, just so he could carry on working with Daly and at least get a steady pay cheque in the meantime. 'I just needed some stability,' he explained with a shrug.

* * *

On 20 June 1999, John Daly had told the world that he was through with the US Open, that he no longer considered it to be a major championship. Twelve months on, in spite of having missed three of his last four cuts, Daly rolled into Monterey, California, to take his place in the 100th US Open Championship at Pebble Beach. Wedgie couldn't make it, though, sidelined by a slight strain. His place was taken by a mutual friend, the one-time NFL star Dan Quinn.

The first round was going nicely. Daly coped well with the foggy conditions and arrived at the 18th at three over par. Ahead of him was a 543-yard par-five, with the ever-receptive Pacific Ocean waiting for any balls that strayed left. Playing safe, Daly thrashed his ball way right off the tee, but when he traipsed down the fairway to find it he discovered that it had scuttled under a fence and into the back yard of one of the exclusive homes that border the hole. Returning to the tee, he then proceeded to hook his next two tee-shots into the waves on Carmel Bay. Hitting seven from the tee, Daly ditched his driver and opted for the safety of a five-iron. Finally, he managed to get a ball in play. On his eighth shot, Daly laid up short, 115 yards from the green, then pulled his ninth into the water again. Forced to drop into the bunker (where his ball had last crossed the margin of the hazard), Daly then found he had to play his shot left-handed as his stance was impeded by the sea wall. Unable to shift the ball with his first swing, he took another whack at it and succeeded in finding the green. After two putts, Daly walked off with a fourteen and a twelve-over-par 83. After signing his scorecard, Daly rushed to the locker room where again he simply gathered together his things, walked to a waiting car and said, 'Get me to the airport, fast.' By the time journalists reached the dressing room, he was gone.

Dan Quinn will never forget the events on the 18th that day. 'It's amazing how quickly it went,' he recalled. 'I was real excited. It was fun through sixteen or seventeen holes. He was playing good. He just got all beat up at the end. One little swing and it was like, "Oh, my God!" ' Among the players, however, the reaction was anything but surprise. They had seen Daly self-combust so many times in the past that they would have been more shocked had he finished off at eighteen with a steady round free from incident or accident. 'I think he forgot that you're trying to get the least amount of shots on a hole, not the most,' joked the Australian Stuart Appleby, before adding, 'I don't understand why he has to keep doing that to himself. He's not doing it to anyone else. He needs to be a bit kinder to himself.' It was a sentiment echoed by Jack Nicklaus. 'No one knows what is going through his mind. I like John. He's a fun guy to be around, but obviously he's his own worst enemy. He's not going to get better until he gets those demons out of his head.'

The press reaction to Daly's latest implosion was less forgiving. Dan O'Neill of the *St Louis Post-Dispatch* argued that after his outburst at Pinehurst twelve months earlier the USGA should never have allowed Daly to play in the first instance, and suggested that had he been employed in any other profession he would have been struck off a long time ago. 'Imagine Daly was a surgeon and things started going poorly during a quadruple bypass. Imagine he turned the scalpel upside down and started swinging it left-handed. Would he keep his license? Say Daly was a plumber. Say he was having a bad day and started connecting toilets and installing shower heads in a careless, haphazard manner. Say he finally just picked up his tools, hopped in the truck and went home. Now pretend he wasn't in a union. Do you think he would keep his job?'

It was a ludicrous argument to make. For one, Daly wasn't a surgeon or a plumber, he was just a professional golfer whose sole aim in his day job was to get a small white ball measuring 1.68 inches into a hole in the ground measuring 4.5 inches in as few shots as possible. Nobody's life, or plumbing, depended on him. Second, if anyone was at fault it was the USGA for allowing him back after what he had said and done at Pinehurst. All they had to offer, though, was sympathy for Daly's plight. 'It is always unfortunate when a contestant withdraws prior to completion of his regulation rounds,' said USGA spokesman Marty Parkes. 'We are very sorry that John's struggles at the end of his round caused him to withdraw.'

In the wake of his walkout, Daly gave an interview to the *New York Post Sports Week*. 'I know there's a lot of doubt in a lot of people's minds and stuff,' he admitted. 'If I didn't think I still had it, I wouldn't be here [on the PGA Tour]. I don't know when [the breakthrough will come] but as hard as I've been working, it's going to happen. And when it does, it's going to be fun again after all the stuff I've been through.' Perhaps the most intriguing aspect of this latest confessional, however, was the noises he made about the direction in which his career was heading. While other, more level-headed players would have earmarked records to break or titles they longed to win, Daly's ambitions had sunk to more modest levels. After his worst season to date, he confessed that he just wanted 'to be Chris Farley and play golf'. Worryingly, Farley was a 290lb (twenty stones plus) comedian who had battled drink and drug problems and died of a cocaine overdose in 1999, aged 33.

Throughout the summer the malaise persisted, Daly lurching from one tournament to the next endeavouring to eke out what he could from his wreck of a career – which, as it happened, was nothing. He missed the cut on his return to St Andrews for the Open Championship, and things got no better at the PGA Championship in Louisville, Kentucky. After Daly shot 74–82 at the notoriously taxing Valhalla course, he was making his way to the locker room when a fan leaned over the ropes and screamed, 'We don't care if you miss the cut, John! We love you no matter what!' Daly was touched. He was playing like a jerk and still people were pulling for him.

Later that evening, as he sat with Shanae in his rental house making his way through a Pizza Hut delivery, he scribbled down the lyrics to a song on the back of the box. It was called 'Mr Fan', and in time his friend Daron Norwood would set it to music:

Hey, Mr Fan, I'm doing the best I can.
Got my eye on the fairway and a driver in my hand,
Gonna grip it and rip it, that's what you want me to do.
Wish I could change things, as my eyes swell up with tears,
Haven't seen my name on top of the leaderboard for years.
But I've still got you,
Got you, Mr Fan.

Bob Dylan was unavailable for comment.

24. OLD RED EYES IS BACK

'John Daly could draw a crowd in Saskatchewan.'

PGA Tour player Rocco Mediate

Another tournament, another missed cut, this time at the Reno-Tahoe Open. Six on the bounce, and not a nickel to take back to Dardanelle. At the end of that horrendous summer of 2000, and with a heavy heart, John sat down with Shanae and reviewed what was becoming an increasingly desperate situation. He was unhappy. She was unhappy. There were tax bills to pay as well as alimony and child support for Dale, Bettye, Shynah, Paulette and Sierra. The Lion range had largely failed to capture the public's imagination, let alone their cash, the drinking was up, the income was down, and his future was in the balance. The players and promoters were turning their backs, too. Where once he could rely on a glut of invitation-only events at the end of the Tour to help keep the ex-wives in jewellery, now he didn't have a single offer on the table. He was the Forgotten Man of the PGA Tour. 'A lot of the players wanted me to play in their tournaments when things were going great. Now I can't get invited to shit. What hurts most is being left off the year-end "fluff stuff" like the Wendy's Three-Tour Challenge,' Daly moaned, before adding, 'I love Wendy's. I eat there all the time.' He even considered bankruptcy as a way out.

After sacrificing her schooling and throwing herself headlong into the relationship, Shanae was also considering her future with

Daly. The quarrel in Auburn had brought into sharp focus the kind of volatility she was dealing with. Moreover, since that fight in the McDonald's car park, Daly's drinking had increased to the point where not only was he virtually incapable of behaving himself properly on the golf course, he was also having severe difficulties when it came to conducting his relationship with Shanae, and he would often accuse her of cheating on him. 'People don't understand why I don't leave him,' she said. '[But] if you don't have loyalty, what do you have? You don't know pain until you have witnessed someone ruining their own life. Not only can you not help them, they will fight you at every turn and corner.' Tom Chiarella was less convinced of Shanae's commitment to Daly's recovery. After spending time with the couple in Dardanelle that January, Chiarella concluded that Daly's fiancée was a less than positive influence on him. 'I think she would have put drugs in his nose right in front of me,' he claimed. 'He didn't do any drugs, but she didn't seem to care at all.'

Irrespective of Chiarella's viewpoint, John and Shanae pledged to make a go of their relationship, and on the evening of 28 August something remarkable happened. The couple were having another tête-à-tête when, apropos of nothing, Daly stood up and announced that he had had it with being one of life's losers. 'He said, "I'm going to live my life straight, take care of business, get my priorities in order and work on my game," ' Shanae recalled. 'That was the day everything changed.' According to Chandler, there was no incident that prompted Daly's epiphany, no blinding light from the heavens above. 'If it was a big deal, you would have read about it in the paper,' she added, 'and if you know John, you would know that he literally is the type of person who can walk in and say, "I'm changing my life." '

First to go was the booze. Playing professional golf, he decided, was difficult enough without the fuzz of a hangover picking away at your brain all day. Then the medication went; it was just another kind of poison anyway. He set himself up at the practice range again, rising at 6.00 a.m. and hitting thousands of balls each week on the newly installed 124-yard practice hole in his back yard. And when he went back on Tour he sought out sobriety meetings with all the vigour with which he used to seek out trouble.

In mid-September Daly's hideous, humiliating run of missed cuts came to an end at the Texas Open at LaCantera. Although he could only tie for 76th, the placing at least represented a modicum of progress, and when he picked up his cheque for $4,862 after three barren months without earning a single cent, he felt like Hollywood Henderson picking up his lottery millions. Slowly, Daly's feel for the game returned. The next week he went to the Buick Challenge in Pine Mountain, Georgia, and finished 63rd. Two weeks later, after a trip to Scotland for the Alfred Dunhill Cup (the USA were eliminated in the first stage but Daly's behaviour was described as 'exemplary'), he bagged a tie for 51st at the National Car Rental Golf Classic, followed soon after by a tie for 50th in the final tournament of the year, the Southern Farm Bureau Classic. Obviously nobody was suddenly marking Daly down as a potential major winner again, but the very fact that he had made four consecutive cuts on Tour and improved his position with each event was proof that maybe John Daly was finally clawing his way back to some kind of respectability.

Though Daly pronounced himself happy with this slight upturn in his fortunes, it was clear from the season-end statistics what a terrible year he had endured. Despite claiming a ninth driving-distance category win, he found himself at 188th on the money list with just $115,460 in official earnings. Yet it was only when Daly scanned the listings for the end-of-year Sony World Rankings that the extent of his decline really hit him. There, at the top of the tree, was the precocious kid he had beaten back in 1989 at the Texarkana tournament, Tiger Woods; several chapters later, Daly finally located his own name on the list, and he couldn't believe what he was reading. John Daly, winner of the 1991 PGA and the 1995 Open, was now ranked at 507. That there were actually more than 500 professional golfers in the world was enough of a shock for him.

Embarrassed beyond words, Daly decamped to Dardanelle and used the winter months to work on his game. For up to eight hours a day he would crank up the stereo and hit balls on the range, pausing occasionally for a smoke and a slug on some water. Three weeks before the new season began, he headed out west to Palm Springs to practise in the more temperate Californian climate. During the trip he worked on his takeaway, slowing it down in a bid to improve his accuracy. He also switched to steel shafts on his irons for the first time since high school, the result being a marked increase in control and a lower trajectory. Feeling fitter and stronger – he was down to a little over 210lb (fifteen stones) from 260lb at the beginning of the year – Daly discovered that his game was coming back to him like some long-lost family pet that had been missing for months.

His dedication in the off-season had not gone unnoticed. In early December, British-based club manufacturer Hippo Golf contacted Daly's management to discuss a possible equipment deal. They had been developing a revolutionary new driver, the Giant, and had earmarked Daly as the ideal man to front the launch. They had just been waiting for him to turn the corner. A three-year deal was struck. Daly would play with Hippo clubs in return for Hippo clearing the remaining $1.5 million of his outstanding debt to the Callaway company. 'John Daly,' said Brent Dornford, marketing manager for Hippo, 'will be our official leading Giant player because we believe he represents our image of being available to the masses rather than the elite.' Certainly it was a sentiment Daly identified with. After all, he had once claimed that the only reason golf fans loved him so much was because he shopped at WalMart. With one less burden to worry about, it seemed like another fresh start for Daly. 'It's awesome,' he said, employing his favourite adjective yet again. 'It gives you an extra motivational boost. I have people behind me who still believe I can do it, and it's starting to make me believe.'

The 2001 season started in promising, if unspectacular, fashion. After a tie for 48th at the Tucson Open in early January where he reached the 690-yard 9th hole in just two shots, Daly travelled to Hawaii for the Sony Open at the Waialae Country Club in Honolulu. As one of the more exotic stop-offs on the Tour, this was the first time the majority of the heavyweight golf writers had seen the new slimline Daly, and after a first-round 64 the unavoidable consensus was that Daly's bleak midwinter of toil and temperance had been worth all the effort. It was a remarkable round, with seven birdies and just one bogey, and it gave him a share of the lead with Larry Mize and Brad Faxon, the first time he had enjoyed such a lead since the 1997 PGA Championship. Key to his success was the rare restraint he showed. He hit the driver just five times during the round, preferring to play for position with one- or two-irons off the tee. In his post-round press conference, a surprised Daly told reporters that he couldn't actually remember the last time he had had a drink or the last time he had felt so good about himself. What's more, he couldn't remember the last time he had shot a 64 (it was at the Honda

Classic in March 1998). The rest of Daly's week in Honolulu failed to live up to the magic of this opening round, but he left the islands knowing that now he wasn't the only person who felt like he was making genuine progress.

A week later, he was back in Arizona for the Phoenix Open where he built on the good work. Shooting 67–70–70–66, Daly, with his new caddie Mick Peterson, was a picture of patience, thinking his way round the course with a hitherto unseen maturity and claiming a tie for ninth and a cheque for $104,000. Daly had already won more in the first month of 2001 than he had in the whole of 2000. What people were now witnessing wasn't the Daly of old. Far from it. This was an older, more savvy John Daly, a golfer who accepted his limitations and played to his strengths. There was none of the carefree, cavalier golf of his twenties, none of the bravado he was renowned for. It was a new year and an entirely new attitude.

Which was fine, as long as things were going his way. At the Pebble Beach National Pro-Am, playing with the actor Joe Pesci, Daly clocked back-to-back 69s in his first two rounds and looked set for another high finish. Starting the third round on the first day of February at six under par, he then had a catastrophe at the very first hole. Having blazed his tee-shot out of bounds, he put his next shot in play, but only just. Then, in an attempt to give himself more room, he uprooted a white out-of-bounds stake, an infringement of the rules which cost him a two-stroke penalty. Four shots later, Daly walked off with a quadruple-bogey nine. Worse was to come. He carded a triple bogey at the next hole and then played pinball with the trees at the 3rd for another triple bogey. This was the first real turbulence Daly had encountered since his return to form, and everyone in attendance waited to see just how he would react to the setback. A year ago, you wouldn't have seen Daly for dust; now, however, he simply walked down the fairway with his arm round Pesci's shoulders, laughing it off as if his partner had played an air shot. On the back nine he recovered well, scoring four birdies in the last six holes. 'I've been through so much stuff,' said Daly afterwards, 'I can't let my golf game get me down any more.' If anyone had any doubts about exactly how far Daly had come in the last six months, the Pebble Beach Pro-Am was proof that he was now working his ample butt off to make amends.

* * *

Masters week, and only the second time in ten years that Daly had missed his favourite tournament. With an expired exemption and a place off the rankings radar he was no longer eligible to take his place at Augusta, but that didn't stop him trying to squeeze in through the back door. Audaciously, Daly contacted the Men of the Masters suggesting that as he was in rehab in 1997 he had only actually played in four of the five years he was entitled to, and therefore he still had one year left on his exemption. It was a noble effort but one that was doomed to fail. 'They were very nice about it, but they said no,' he said.

With his last chance of playing at Augusta gone, Daly headed home. Rather than watch Tiger Woods stroll to victory on television, he opted to take to his practice range and imagine that it was lined with azaleas and tall pines. Then his old coach Bill Woodley paid him a visit and the two enjoyed a quiet round at Bay Ridge. As the pair played, Woodley noticed how clean Daly's ball striking was and how he was continually working on cutting the ball from left to right. It was exactly the kind of shot you needed in order to be successful at Augusta.

'Man,' said Woodley, 'you are stroking it!'

Daly looked up. 'Coach,' he said, 'I want to do one thing.'

'What's that?' asked Woodley.

'I wanna get back in the Masters.'

Woodley smiled. It had been years since he had heard such determination in his student's voice, and as Daly pounded another drive into the distance, Woodley knew that he was on his way back.

As summer dawned, Shanae Chandler decided to return to Austin and finish school. She would attend class from Monday to Friday and then fly out at the weekend to meet up with Daly at whichever tournament he was playing in. While she headed back to Texas, Daly drove to Memphis to take his place in his old home-town tournament, the FedEx St Jude Classic. It was as if he had never been away. As he set out on his opening round he was pursued by a crowd of some 300 bawdy fans with little or no respect for the QUIET PLEASE signs held by the marshals. That is to say, exactly the kind of gallery Daly loved playing to. Carried along on a wave of goodwill, he played solidly, and his two-under-par 69 left him in a cluster of players near the top of the leaderboard. The highlight of the round, however, had come at the 10th tee. As he waited to take his turn, Daly's eye caught that of a pretty young woman in the crowd. He smiled. She smiled back. Then he carried on with his round, assuming it was just a rather pleasant distraction.

After the round, Daly was milling around the clubhouse when an old Arkansas buddy of his, Ken Holland, walked over and told him there was someone he wanted him to meet. Step forward 26-year-old local girl Sharon Miller – Sherrie to her friends. It was the bottle blonde from the 10th tee. Daly smiled, and once again she returned the gesture. It was like he was fifteen again. Holland laughed and left them to it.

With a fanatical crowd cheering his every move, Daly raced to a six-under-par 65 in his second round. A good week had just got better. It was time for a little light relief. Just two hours after his round, Daly was sat in front of the slots at his old haunt, the Horseshoe Casino in Tunica, spinning $100 tokens into a machine 'until the sonofabitch hits'. A week earlier he had scooped $85,000 in one afternoon at the Horseshoe ('Just like coming fifteenth [in a tournament],' he said) but still he denied that his gambling was anything other than a way of killing time between rounds. 'I used to gamble to try to make money, but I don't do that any more,' he maintained. 'I come here to enjoy myself.'

On Saturday, Shanae arrived for the weekend, blissfully unaware that Daly had been flirting with another woman, and as her fiancé got back to business on the golf course she followed him around, her five-carat engagement ring sparkling in the sunlight. 'I washed it this morning,' she said. 'I'm blinding the competition.'

Daly continued to take the TPC at Southwind apart in his third round. He had estimated that he needed to shoot a 64 to stay in touch with the leaders, but cheered on by a rowdy Memphis crowd he managed to go one shot better, birdieing four of the first five holes and finishing off with another fist-pumping birdie at the last. It was only the third 63 of his career, and the first time he had gone that low since the Las Vegas Invitational ten years earlier.

For the last round, Daly found himself in the final pairing of the day with the Texan pro Bob Estes, the tournament leader. Estes was a formidable opponent. Solid, super-fit and monotonously consistent, he was always in the upper reaches of the money list come the end of the season and while he was only a couple of months older than Daly, he had the kind of mature outlook that suggested he had twenty years on his playing partner. He was also unique on the PGA Tour as he was the only player who didn't wear a golf glove when he played. Daly failed to claim what he had said would be his 'greatest win', finishing three shots behind Estes in a tie for fifth – his best placing since the victory at St Andrews in 1995. 'It would have been nice to have won for my family and friends,' said Daly, who added another $127,750 to his season's earnings, 'but it feels good to play well and have a chance.'

The St Jude Classic was another turning point in the renaissance of John Daly. All year he had found it relatively straightforward to record scores in the late sixties, but what he'd failed to register were those super-low scores that the Tigers and Ernies could seemingly conjure up whenever they really needed them. Now, with his lowest Tour round in a decade under his belt, Daly had proved to himself that he could still produce the kind of golf that could put him in contention come Sunday. Moreover, he had now moved up to 62nd on the Tour's money list, his world ranking was heading ever upward, and he announced with a smile on his face that he had 'fallen in love with golf again'. Unbeknown to Shanae Chandler, he had also fallen in love with another woman.

Still, on Tuesday, 19 June, Daly called Chandler and asked her if she wanted to set a date for their long-overdue wedding. One of the main reasons for their procrastination was Shanae's reluctance to have a Las Vegas ceremony; it just wasn't her style. But they had been engaged for nearly two years now and she was, understandably, beginning to question whether she would ever become Mrs Daly. So when John suggested they tie the knot during his personal appearance at Bally's Casino on 29 July, Shanae gave in and began to make plans. That Friday, she left university and flew to meet Daly in Arkansas. He sent a limo to pick her up, and when she climbed in the back there were a dozen roses waiting for her. As the weekend progressed, however, she noticed that Daly was in an increasingly dark mood. He was silent and edgy, surly and short-tempered. By Sunday, Shanae had had enough of Daly's behaviour and asked him just what was bugging him. Daly turned on her and out of the blue accused her of seeing someone else. Shanae had no idea what he was talking about and told him to stop being ridiculous.

The following Tuesday, Daly called Chandler in Austin and informed her that they were through. What was the point, he said, when there was no trust left in the relationship? Still Shanae had no idea where John was coming from. After reassuring him that nothing was going on, she hung up.

Two weeks passed with no contact from Daly. This time, Shanae was worried. Then she received a call from Donnie Crabtree. He had some news that she ought to know: Daly was getting married to Sherrie Miller. The date? The twenty-ninth of July. The venue? Bally's Casino, Las Vegas. Chandler was beside herself. 'I never got a chance to speak to him again,' she explained. 'I don't know why we broke up or why he did this. I just know the facts.'

Later, press reports of how Daly and Miller had first met would emerge; Daly would talk at length about how he had seen Sherrie on the 10th tee at the St Jude Classic and how he'd decided that one day he would marry her. 'She said, "I don't like blonds, I don't like golfers, but I do like fat boys." So I knew I had a chance.' While Daly made light of the situation, Shanae Chandler failed to see the funny side. 'You do the math,' she suggested. 'I left for school on Tuesday, 5 June, the Classic began on 7 June. He was saying this about some woman while his fiancée was down in Austin wearing an engagement ring. We didn't break up until the end of June, but he was saying this about Sherrie during a tournament that took place 7 June!' Despite the manner in which Daly had clearly engineered an end to their relationship, Shanae harbours no resentment towards him. 'People ask me if I regret leaving school to spend three years of my life with a man I never married. Given the chance a million times over, I would do it again without hesitation.'

On 5 July, as Daly was preparing to leave for the UK, he received some sad news. Ely Callaway, his 'father figure' on the PGA Tour and the man who had given him a break when no one else wanted to know, had died of pancreatic cancer at the age of 82. It was in a sombre mood, then, that Daly made the trip across the Atlantic. He had committed himself to the $2.2 million Scottish Open at the picturesque Loch Lomond course as a warm-up for Royal Lytham & St Annes, and for once his good form made the trip too. Daly scored successive 68s, leaving him just three shots off the lead at the halfway stage. As he played with his partner Darren Clarke, he and the similarly big-boned Ulsterman spoke about everything from Clarke's love of Cuban cigars to their shared passion for cars. After the round, a reporter asked Daly whether he could match Clarke's fleet of seven vehicles. 'Hell,' Daly retorted with a laugh, 'if you count all the cars my ex-wives are driving round in, I've probably got around thirty.' Curiously, Daly also told reporters that following the recent split with Shanae he was now 'looking for a good woman', even though he and Shanae knew there was one already waiting for him back home. An almost effortless 66 followed in the third round, but just as the golfing world waited for Daly's breakthrough victory the rug was pulled from under his feet by the new US Open champion Retief Goosen. 'I had my chances,' said Daly, who tied for third and had now shot par or better in twelve of his last thirteen rounds. 'I can't hit the ball better. I just need to find a way to get the ball in the hole.'

Although Loch Lomond provided the perfect shot of confidence for Daly, it was far from an ideal venue to prepare for the Open. While it is undeniably beautiful, it is more akin to the flat and faultless courses on the American PGA Tour and favours those players more accustomed to target golf. By comparison, the Royal Lytham course is like playing golf in the Himalayas. It is a set-up suited to conservative, accurate iron-play, rewarding those with an imaginative short game and offering little advantage to the game's big hitters. Certainly the breezy Lancashire links did for Daly that week, though he can't have mulled too much over his rounds of 72 and 76 as he flew back to the States to make Sherrie his wife, having decided that marriage was a par-four.

25. KING OF THE ROAD

'I didn't come into this to look after John. He's old enough to look after himself.'

Sherrie Daly

On Sunday, 29 July 2001, Sherrie Miller became the newest Mrs Daly. During a whirlwind weekend in Las Vegas, Daly not only tied the knot in the ceremony at Bally's Casino, he also emerged a preposterous $630,000 richer after three days of unparalleled good fortune at the slots. For Miller, it was a wild welcome to the world of John Daly. For Daly, it was a year's alimony in one fell swoop. And this time he'd finally wised up: a prenuptial agreement had been arranged. Not that Miller minded. A Memphis girl through and through, she was a car saleswoman on the verge of completing a nursing degree. She was honest (for someone in car sales), level-headed and down to earth. She had a two-year-old boy, Austin, from a previous marriage, but there were no other dark secrets waiting in the wings, and virtually the only baggage she had was a make-up case.

Back in Dardanelle, Daly's mother, Lou, was sure that her son had found the love of his life. Again. 'We feel good about this one,' she said, as if clutching a lottery ticket. It was a sentiment echoed by one of Daly's closest friends on Tour, Dudley Hart. 'She seems a lot different than any girl he's been around, which is a good thing, more stable,' he said. 'John doesn't need a wild and crazy girl, which he seems to have had in the past. He's wild and crazy enough as it is.'

At least, he used to be. The new John Daly was a sober, more reflective soul, keen to put his chequered past behind him and concentrate on re-establishing himself in a game he clearly loved. The fact that he had found a new wife on the road to recovery, well, that was a bonus. On 30 August, with Sherrie in attendance, Daly registered his second 63 of the year on the opening day of the BMW International in Munich. It was a faultless round, with seven birdies and only the second hole-in-one of his professional career. It came at the 153-yard 12th when he ripped a nine-iron that pitched a foot beyond the hole and spun back into the cup. Daly's only regret was that it hadn't come at the 17th, where there was a brand-new BMW on offer for any player achieving the feat. 'I'll have to try and win it now and then I'll be able to afford one,' he laughed (despite having already pocketed a six-figure appearance fee). The following day, Daly cemented his impressive start, carding ten threes and two eagles in another scintillating round of 64. Prior to the tournament, the bookmakers had earmarked twenty under as the likely winning score; at the halfway stage, Daly was already four shots clear at seventeen under par. It was, by some distance, his best ever start to a competition.

Daly always enjoyed his trips to Europe. The fans were every bit as appreciative as those back home, and they tended to allow him more space to practise and go about his business. It was an altogether more laid-back atmosphere, and one which clearly benefited his game. Moreover, it made sense for Daly to play more tournaments outside the States: the rankings system meant he gained more points for playing in Germany than he would have done for playing in the PGA event in Vancouver that week. And if Daly was going to get back in the Masters, every point was vital.

Daly surrendered his lead during a rain-affected third round when the Irishman Padraig Harrington sprinted past him with a course-record-equalling 62. Daly's 68 meant that he would go into the fourth round trailing Harrington by a stroke. It was a tense, nervy affair. While Daly was looking to end his six-year drought, Harrington, a qualified accountant, was looking to register his first European Tour victory in five years, having finished second a bewildering fourteen times since his win at the Spanish Open in 1996. As the round progressed, the Irishman found it difficult to pull away, and Daly hung in with a rare tenacity. With three holes to play, the pair were locked in the lead at 25 under par. Crucially, though, the remaining holes favoured the bigger hitters. It was advantage Daly.

At the 319-yard, par-four 16th, Daly drove the green; Harrington, to his credit, succeeded in getting up and down from the rough to match his birdie. At the next hole, the par-three 17th, the Irishman had a chance for a two but slid his twelve-foot putt past the hole and, like Daly, had to settle for a par. Level going down eighteen, ahead of them a 568-yard par-five. It was an ideal hole for Daly: long, left to right and out of reach for most mortals. Daly let the big dog eat, cutting the corner and leaving himself a gentle four-iron into the green. Harrington also found the fairway, but knowing he needed to reach the green in two to have a chance he cut his second shot, a three-wood, into the water. From just off the green, Daly chipped up to two feet and tapped in for a birdie to bring to an end a losing streak that stretched back 2,231 days to a blustery Sunday evening in Fife.

It had been six years of turmoil, six years during which Daly had been up and down more times than a new bride's nightie, had squandered millions of dollars, had gained and lost hundreds of pounds, and had been laid low by caffeine, glucose, nicotine and alcohol. The victory was a vindication of all his endeavours over the past year and, perhaps, his decision to end his relationship with Shanae Chandler. Now, just 35 days into his fourth marriage, he had picked up a cheque for $270,000, the biggest of his professional career. But as he celebrated his victory, there was none of the violent fist-pumping or outward show of emotion you would expect from a player who had gone 151 tournaments without a win. Instead, he simply hugged his wife, his caddie Mick Peterson and his agent Bud Martin, smiled, and walked off to the scorer's cabin. It was relief rather than elation.

As Daly received his trophy and his winner's cheque, someone foolishly presented the sporting world's most famous teetotaller with a magnum of champagne. He laughed and gave it away to a journalist. 'I'm sure a lot of people gave up on me, but I hadn't. I'm a fighter,' he said, dragging on a cigarette. 'I just want to thank everybody around the world who's been rooting for me, because it has been a long time, a long six years. This trophy belongs to all of them as well.' Certainly Daly had deserved his victory. He had strung together four sublime rounds and his putting had hit the same fluent rhythm he'd displayed at Crooked

Stick all those years ago. The scorecard didn't lie. His total of 261, 27 under par, tied the record for the lowest-ever score recorded in a European Tour event and brought hearty praise from the magnanimous runner-up. 'John deserves to be back in the winner's enclosure,' Harrington said. 'He did all the things he did when he won the two majors. He hit it long and he hit it straight. At the same time, he putted beautifully.'

Having not succumbed to the pleasures of alcohol for over a year, Daly found it easy enough to resist the allure of Munich's impending Oktoberfest beer festival and head back home. Quite what was going through Sherrie Daly's mind as they flew home, though, was anybody's guess. A little over a month into their married life, she had been at Daly's side when he had won $630,000 at Bally's and now she had watched her husband win his first golf tournament in six years and take another quarter of a million. Add on the appearance fee for the trip to Germany and it was over a million bucks in a month. In any showroom in the world, that was a hell of a lot of motor cars.

While John's ex-wives club scanned the sports pages and doubtless choked on their cornflakes, Daly's implausible run of good fortune continued. He began to wonder whether he had married Sherrie Miller, car saleswoman, or Lady Luck herself. He played at the Canadian Open and fired book-end 66s to tie for fourth and net a cool $182,400, and then, in a bid to improve his chances of qualifying for the 2002 Masters, he turned down a £75,000 appearance fee from the World Matchplay at Wentworth to take his place in the $4.5 million Invensys Classic in Las Vegas. It was a good call. Not only would Daly finish in a tie for seventh place there and add another $135,000 to his tally, he would also shoot a course-record 62 at the TPC at the Canyons – his lowest-ever round as a professional golfer. He also shoehorned in another trip back to Germany for the Lindt German Masters at the Kut Larchenhof course in Cologne. Indeed, in the wake of the 9/11 terrorist attacks, Daly became the first golfer to end the self-imposed ban on overseas travel by American players when Bernhard Langer let him use his private jet for the journey. It was another good call: he trousered a $250,000 appearance fee and $200,000 for coming second.

Daly had turned his career around in a manner nobody, himself included, could have possibly predicted. It was, without doubt, the hottest streak of his professional career. Surprisingly, the final cash total of $828,914 and another record PGA driving title with an average of 306.7 yards didn't mean that much to Daly. Why would it when he could win more than that in a weekend on the Strip? What really mattered to him was his new world ranking, his position on the money list and whether he had done enough to earn a return to the Masters. Sadly, 61st on the latter would not be enough as only the top 40 gained a place at Augusta. But having started the year ranked at a perplexing 507 Daly had now improved by nearly 460 places and had managed to creep back into the top 50. If he could maintain his form until the end of March 2002 he would be back at Magnolia Lane.

After his most lucrative season in professional golf, Daly felt it was high time he began to travel in a style that befitted his new-found status as a successful, high-profile sportsman. Tiger, Jack and Arnie all had their private aircraft to ferry them around from appearance fee to appearance fee, but Daly decided he needed something in keeping with his reputation as the PGA's aviophobic King of the Road, so he bought himself a new Prevost motor home, at 45 feet long, 460 square feet in area, 54,000lb in weight and 500hp in power the best money could buy. It took $300 of diesel to fill the tank, and you got six miles to the gallon, seven if you were going downhill. It looked like some kind of prototype NASA had been working on. It had a satellite navigation system, two 42-inch plasma TVs and a control panel that could have been ripped out of the *Starship Enterprise*. It boasted four air-conditioning units, mood lighting and front-door and rear-view video monitors. There was a full-size shower and bathroom, and two surround-sound stereo systems, one in the main cabin and another in the bedroom. It had granite floor tiles in the kitchen and two automatic awnings. It had a washer, a dryer, an intercom and Daly's favourite PGA 91 vanity plate. If you wanted one, it was yours for just $1.4 million. 'People get out of your way in that thing,' said Daly. 'Especially the way I drive.' Bettye Fulford had detested the drudgery of endless days on the road in his old American Eagle, but Sherrie and little Austin adored the luxury of the Prevost. With Donnie Crabtree sharing the driving with John, the Dalys hit the open road like latter-day Clampetts on their way to Beverly Hills.

Still, after the considerable success he had enjoyed on his European trips in 2001, Daly decided that much as he loathed flying he would now commit himself to playing more events on the European Tour. The victory in the 1995 Open had given him a ten-year exemption to join the European Tour whenever he wanted, and with four years left he opted to pay his £115 membership fee and pledge to play the minimum of eleven events that year.

It was an increasingly common policy among the game's top players to divide their time between the two tours. For the European players, it was the ideal way to enjoy the greater rewards of the US PGA Tour while still earning qualification points for the Ryder Cup team; for the likes of Daly, meanwhile, it was a more effective way of accumulating world-ranking points in his bid to win a place in the top 50. Of course, becoming a member of the European Tour meant Daly would no longer be eligible for the giant appearance fees he could command when he played overseas, but the fact that he was prepared to forgo such guarantees was a clear indicator that he was now taking his game more seriously than ever.

His first European Tour event, the Heineken Classic in Melbourne, began on the last day of January 2002, and his confidence was high. In his last US event before leaving, the Phoenix Open, his tie for fourth place had moved him up to 47th in the world rankings. 'It's nice that the hard work is paying off,' he admitted. 'I've made a lot of changes in my life that are for the better. I've got everything in my life the way I want it for the first time.' Prior to his departure, Daly's fellow players had told him how the Royal Melbourne course was ideal for his game. There was no need for the one-iron, they said, it was tailor-made for his driver. Daly took the advice on board and left his driving iron at home, but it was a bum steer. After only just making the cut courtesy of an eagle at the 36th hole, Daly took his two-iron to the club shop, had it placed in a vice, and then bent it until it had the loft of a one-iron. It made little difference. Hitting his new makeshift driving iron more often than his driver, he closed with two rounds of 71 for a tie for 39th, and then retired to the Crown Hotel for some light gambling – he now had a self-imposed limit of just $30,000 – while his caddie, Mick Peterson, stayed behind to do the drinking for the both of them.

Though Daly had once more failed to reward the huge Australian galleries with a performance worthy of their continued and fervent support, everyone had noticed the change in him.

None more so than Greg Norman. 'He has finally found peace in the world,' he said. 'He can take a double bogey now and shoot a 69 or 70. Before, he would take a double bogey and shoot 83. He has done a wonderful job in balancing his life.' It was a valid point. In the past, Daly's psyche had been so paper thin, so fragile, that if he did shoot a stinker he took it as a personal affront. Now he could look at himself in the mirror and, like other players, put it down to a bad day at the office. And if he left a few shots out on the golf course, well, he could always pick them up the following day. Moreover, that timeworn problem of his of starting well and fading had largely been eradicated; he set a new personal best of fifteen rounds of par or better, a run that came to an end only in the third round of the Nissan Open in mid-February.

His resurgence prompted countless new offers to land on the desk of Bud Martin. There was a three-year deal with building supplies firm 84 Lumber Company, and another with Nextel, the mobile telephone company. Golf firm Pinnacle was showing an interest, as was Titleist. With so many businesses fighting for logo space on Daly's bag and clothes, commentators were beginning to notice that he was taking to the golf course looking like a NASCAR driver. But then he always did have a bigger shirt than most.

In March, Daly claimed a tie for fifteenth at the Bay Hill Invitational in Orlando and in doing so cemented his place in the starting line-up at Augusta. He had even returned to the 'Tin Cup' hole and birdied it, taking some fourteen shots fewer than he had in 1998. All that was needed to make it a truly great week was for Austin to meet his hero and life would be sweet. But it wasn't to be. Daly did take his stepson and seven friends to the Magic Kingdom at nearby Disney World, but try as they might they couldn't locate Mickey Mouse. Austin was inconsolable; Daly was fuming. 'My two-year-old was dying to see Mickey,' he told the press. 'Couldn't find him anywhere. Nine of us go, we pay $381. Where in the hell is Mickey? We went to his house. We went to Tune Town. We went everywhere. We could not find Mickey Mouse. And my two-year-old is just dying because we couldn't get a picture.'

Back at Augusta for the first time since April 2000, Daly drove up Magnolia Lane with a smile as wide as his waist. As he sat in the cockpit of his mothership, he laughed as the fans walked alongside waving and applauding. The last time he had driven along this fabled road he had been travelling, at speed, in the opposite direction after missing the cut and storming away from the course with steam coming from his ears. Now he was back, with a new attitude and a golf game to be proud of.

On the Tuesday he sat down with the media to discuss just what being back at the Masters meant to him. 'It was tough sitting out last year's Masters. I look back when I went into rehab in 1997. I could have played then, but you know, I thought my life was a little more important at that time,' he explained. 'It's amazing. You get into these tournaments and you think you're going to be in them for the rest of your life. I always said, "Well, I've got next year." But that year runs out. It was pretty tough.' And it wasn't just the media who were making a big deal of Daly's return; there was widespread acclaim among the players, too, most notably from one of the game's legends, Arnold Palmer. 'The fact is, he has grabbed hold of the whole situation and is doing very well,' he said. 'I'm proud of him, and I hope he continues. The bottom line is, he's happier and the fans will enjoy watching him play.' Clearly, the Augusta patrons were overjoyed, too. The rapturous reception he received at the 1st tee on Thursday as he set off on his round with Mike Weir and Niclas Fasth was matched only by that afforded to the reigning champion, Tiger Woods.

Though his opening round on the newly lengthened (or Tiger-proofed) National course failed to live up to his or his fans' expectations, Daly nevertheless putted extremely well on the super-slick greens and it was only a combination of double bogeys at ten and fourteen and the slow play ahead of him – the round took over five and a half hours – that prevented him from shooting under par. On Friday, he went one shot lower and made the cut comfortably despite some wayward tee-shots. Daly had struggled with his driving ever since he'd grumpily lobbed his broken driver into the water at the Players' Championship in March; despite switching between three different models that week, he still couldn't get the same feel as he'd had with the one floating in the pond by the 14th tee at Sawgrass. Still, from the perma-smile on Daly's face that week it was apparent that he could have shot 100 in each round and it wouldn't really have bothered him that much. All that mattered was that he was back at the Masters and he had done it on his own, without the help of doctors, mind coaches or counsellors.

Daly was never really in contention. He recorded his lowest round, a two-under-par 70, on Saturday, then a tired 75 on Sunday left him some way off the pace in a tie for 32nd. Nevertheless, it had been a gratifying return to Augusta, and as he walked up the 18th fairway he was visibly touched by the standing ovation he received. As he crawled down Magnolia Lane that evening in the motor home he knew he would have to wait at least another year before he had the opportunity to slip on that size-52 green jacket he coveted so much, but for once he felt like a winner again.

Three days prior to his departure for some European Tour events, Daly was clambering out of his motor home when suddenly he felt the feeling drain from his left hand and left leg, and he lost his balance. He threw out his right hand to break his fall and eventually picked himself up, but he was scared. After all, his mother had suffered a slight stroke at the end of 2000 and he knew what it could do to a person, let alone someone who relied on his hands for a living. Six hours later the numbness still hadn't subsided, and as Daly was poked and prodded by medical staff he convinced himself he had suffered a stroke. It was only when he mentioned the diet pills he was taking that his ailment finally began to make some kind of sense. The doctors asked him what he had been eating prior to the loss of sensation. Daly told them he had had a banana and some cheese. They ran a few tests, and when the results came back they showed that Daly had not suffered a stroke at all, just a rare but temporary allergic reaction caused by a combination of his diet medication and the food. 'I was scared to death when it happened,' he said. 'It's even more spooky when you've lived the sort of over-the-top lifestyle I did when I was younger. You wonder if it's payback time.'

While the news was a relief to Daly, it was tempered by the doctors' concerns; with his weight creeping up again he needed to make some fundamental changes in his lifestyle if he was going to avoid further problems in the future. The increase in his weight, while not nearly as pronounced as in the past, was the inevitable result of too many long-distance flights, irregular sleep patterns and, of course, his fondness for hamburgers and 'a big ol' piece of chocolate cake'. He had also been enjoying the occasional beer as well, although now it seemed like he had finally mastered the art of knowing when to stop. 'I couldn't tell you how many days I've been sober,' he told the *New York Times* in April. 'People who count days spend most of their time thinking about drinking, and I don't even think about it.' Then there was the 40 to 60 cigarettes every day. 'I have to try and cut back the smoking,' he told a press conference at the Belfry, where he would finish in a tie for ninth, bruised hand and all, in the Benson and Hedges International. 'But if I do, my weight will probably balloon to 300lb. I'll be looking like Babe Ruth. Right now I'm about 235lb [sixteen and three-quarter stones]. At my heaviest, I was about 265lb. If I could zap my fingers, I'd love to weigh 200lb, but I don't see that happening.'

From the Belfry, Daly headed on to Germany for the Deutsche Bank-SAP Open, but it would be an inauspicious performance with a pair of 73s granting him an early flight back to the States. His on-course torpor continued when he got home. Take away his tie for 32nd at the Masters, and as the PGA Tour moved into the summer Daly had missed three out of four cuts and withdrawn in the other event. To the casual observer it seemed as though ever since he had confirmed his place at Augusta he'd merely sat back at home with his feet up in front of his staggering new 82-inch television (with porno channels) and rested on his laurels. Yet he was bingeing on practice as much as he'd ever binged on M&Ms. When he was at home he continued to work slavishly on his game, hitting hundreds of balls a day. He even had an additional two practice greens constructed in his garden, and his 124-yard hole had become 150 yards, so long as he played the shot from his garage. As usual, the dip in Daly's form did little to dampen the public's desire to see him in action, but playing well in one-off events such as Jim Furyk's Exelon Invitational, where he walked away with a fast $100,000, was rarely a problem; give him a four-day PGA event, though, and you still could not quite be sure which John Daly was going to turn up.

A desperate tie for 70th at the US Open at Bethpage in mid-June was followed by another missed cut at the Greater Hartford Open. A week later he tied for 75th at the St Jude Classic, and then made another early exit from the Open at Muirfield. It was free-fall time again. That said, at least Daly had an excuse for the Open. During his second round he had played a shot from some dense rough on the 5th which, he said, felt like somebody stabbing 'a knife through my finger'. The injury had left him in considerable discomfort for the remainder of the round and he was forced to play the last thirteen holes virtually one-handed. In the circumstances, a 77 was an astonishing effort, perhaps the round of the day, but not nearly good enough to avoid the cut.

On the Saturday Daly flew to Holland for the Dutch Open, and with the pain in his hand still bothering him he sought the advice of a local physician. When the doctor X-rayed his hand he discovered a small fragment of glass under the skin near his first knuckle. It had, apparently, been there for years; the shot from the rough at Muirfield must have dislodged it. All those years of punching TVs and wing mirrors, it seemed, had finally caught up with him. Daly had the shard removed, and after being stitched up he returned to his hotel. By Wednesday the stitches too had been removed, and he set about his first round confident that this latest medical mishap was now behind him. Eleven holes in, though, Daly looked down to see blood running down his hand. The wound had come open.

Faced with withdrawing and disappointing the nice folk from the Netherlands or patching himself up, Daly looked in his bag for something, anything, to stem the flow. All he could find was a tube of superglue. What the hell, he thought. After skipping the bit in the instructions about avoiding contact with skin, he squeezed a blob of the stuff over the cut. To the amazement of everyone, including Daly, the glue did the trick and he was able to complete his round. 'I don't care that it's unwise medically,' he said later. 'I'm not going to watch it bleed.' Impressed with his client's ingenuity, John Mascatello immediately began to think of ways to cash in on Daly's latest brainwave (in May, in the wake of Daly's 'mini-stroke', he had tried to cut deals with aspirin companies), but the glue world wasn't impressed. 'Our product is meant to be used to fix things and we don't condone its use for medical purposes,' huffed Terri Brown, spokesperson for Krazy Glue. The following day Daly opted for a large Band-Aid instead and recovered sufficiently to shoot a 70 on his way to an eventual tie for 53rd.

Entertaining though it was, the story of Daly's superglue surgery could not overshadow a slump in form that was up there with the very worst of his career. Yet unbeknown to the watching world, something had been playing on Daly's mind, something beyond constants in his life like ill-fortune and misplaced bravado.

In July, Daly had received news that his mother Lou had been diagnosed with lung cancer. It was in an advanced stage, and she had only months to live.

Clearly, his heart wasn't in his golf. With his mother gravely ill, the last thing he wanted or needed was to take his place on the Tour. At the PGA Championship at the Hazeltine National he shot 77–76, and at the Tampa Bay Classic on 20 September he took that final humiliating step into farce. Beginning his second round at four over par, Daly reached the par-three 14th (his fourth hole) and drilled his tee-shot some 50 yards wide of the green straight into a luxury Buick the tournament sponsors were displaying on a platform next to the 15th tee. He had never liked Buicks anyway. After double-bogeying the next, he made his excuses to his playing partners Billy Mayfair and Robert Damron and hopped into his Prevost, which, as luck would have it, was parked right by the green.

As his form crumbled and Lou's condition deteriorated, it would have been easy for Daly to seek some solace in the bottle again. Commendably, though, he avoided the simple solution and instead joined in with his family's efforts to find the best possible care for his ailing mother. It was a decision that perhaps proved that his own self-devised programme of leaving his options open when it came to drinking was working. Over the course of the year he had, according to close friends, enjoyed the occasional beer without ever falling back into the evil ways of old. He was, to all intents and purposes, a non-recovering alcoholic. Clearly, a settled home life with Sherrie and Austin, coupled with regular contact with Shynah and Sierra, had done much to placate Daly, as, indeed, had his return to form earlier in the year. He had also eliminated from his life what he called 'the hangers-on' and surrounded himself with people he knew and trusted. 'I don't need fifty people saying they can do this, do that, make me a lot of money,' he explained. 'I know who's sincere and who's a good friend of mine, who loves me and who doesn't. That's all I need.'

The one thing Daly still hadn't got a real grip on – apart from smoking, of course – was his gambling. Despite limiting himself to a mere $30,000 a night, he was still as keen as ever on the slots – so much so, in fact, that Donnie Crabtree was now refusing to go with him. 'I don't like to see it,' he explained. 'I've seen him lose $300,000 in a night.' Indeed, when Daly descended on Las Vegas for the Invensys Classic in October, it seemed like the golf tournament that was going on in town was just a pleasant way for him to help pass the daylight hours.

That Monday, Daly headed down to his favourite haunt on the Strip, Bally's, and commandeered a line of $500 slot machines. It was a hell of an evening, and after an all-night session he emerged at dawn a jaw-dropping $1.9 million richer. There was only one golf tournament in the world that could boast a first prize in excess of that, and even then you had to pay tax on it. Predictably, he pushed his luck and returned to Bally's the following evening to allow the slots to take their revenge; by the time the machines had sucked him in and spat him out again, he had handed back all but $400,000 of his winnings. Still, it was more than he had ever won in a golf tournament, and it was more fun. That said, it did his golf no favours. Exhausted from all those hours spent watching the spinning reels, Daly missed the cut and finished dead last. When asked about the story, Bally's, citing company policy, refused to comment.

With the PGA Tour over for another year, Daly turned his attention to some of his outstanding international commitments. Earlier in the year he had signed up for a mini-tour of the Far East starting in China, then moving on to Taiwan and ending at the Australian PGA Championship in Coolum, but with his mother's health on the wane Daly was having second thoughts about going. Indeed, as the family's concern for Lou grew, they decided to take her to Las Vegas to see a specialist at the Lake Mead Hospital. The prognosis was worse than they had initially thought: the cancer had now spread to her brain. When he heard the news Daly decided he wasn't going to get on the plane, but, dismissive as ever, his 65-year-old mother told him to go out and play some golf, just as she had when he was a kid getting under her feet in Dardanelle. After convincing her son that she would be fine through the holidays, Daly reluctantly agreed to make the trip to China.

The TLC Classic in the southern city of Dongguan was the richest-ever event on the Asian PGA-run Davidoff Tour, boasting mainland China's first $1 million purse. As one of the last untapped golf markets in the world, a host of top European Tour players had made the trip, including Colin Montgomerie, Lee Westwood and Michael Campbell. Daly had even been discussing the possibility of one day designing a course in China. But throughout his first round of 70 it was clear from his demeanour that Daly's mind was back home. In his second round he crumbled in time-honoured fashion, and having hit into the water three times on the par-five 14th he added a ten to his growing collection of double-figure scores.

From China, Daly headed to Ta Shee in Taiwan and another tournament he didn't really want to play in, the BMW Asian Open. Polite as ever, he smiled his way through a press conference and told everyone how much he was looking forward to playing in Taiwan, just as he had in China the week before. And, just as he had in Dongguan, he came home with a first-round 70. Afterwards Daly received a call from his brother, Jamie. It was the news he had been dreading: Mama Lou had passed away. Later that evening, Daly issued a statement: 'Before leaving on this three-week trip, I spoke to my mom, and her words and wishes were that I should play in China, Taipei and Australia ... I will grant my mom's wishes and continue to play here.' The following day he displayed admirable resolve and managed to shoot 74. After his round, he spoke fondly of his mother. 'Everything about her was great,' he reflected. 'She was a son's dream mum. That was what she was.'

It had been a tough trip, tougher than he could have imagined. As his mother lay dying at home it had been as much as Daly could do to look at his ball and swing a club at it. Still, as he waited to hear about the funeral arrangements, he did indeed fulfil the final obligation of the trip and took his place in the Australian PGA. 'I'd like to win it for my mom,' he told reporters on his arrival at the Hyatt Coolum resort course, 'and I'd like to do it here.' Despite a first-round 75, Daly played the best golf of his trip on the front nine of his second round and was four under par for the round when he reached the turn. But just as he began to entertain thoughts of making the cut, the predictable, inevitable implosion ensnared him. After bogeys at ten and eleven, Daly saw any hope of a strong finish sink beneath the surface of the water on the par-four 13th. He ambled up the fairway and shaped to drop a ball at the point where he thought the ball had entered the hazard. Trouble was, his playing partner, the Australian Craig Parry, felt he was stealing a few extra yards and suggested that he might want to take the ball back to where it had actually dropped into the water. Daly disagreed, so they called over the final member of the trio, Greg Norman, who concurred with his compatriot.

After the couple of weeks Daly had just endured, this was all he needed. Refusing to accept their decision, he summoned a PGA rules official, and after watching the shot on a television replay it was deemed that he should take his ball back towards the tee. Visibly incensed, he reloaded and smacked his new ball off the fairway with his driver, but when his next shot found the water to the right of the green it was as much as Daly could do to escape with a triple-bogey seven.

It was the cue for another meltdown. There was another bogey at fifteen, then a double bogey at sixteen, and by the time he reached the final hole you could almost sense that he was trying to think of the quickest possible route to the airport. Hacking his way down the 18th with all the finesse of an executioner, Daly dumped his approach in the bunker at the rear of the green. He then raced forward to his ball, hacked it out on to the green, and without marking it or cleaning it putted out for a triple-bogey seven and another ignominious early end to a competition.

After a year spent telling anyone who cared to listen how the John Daly of 2002 was a reformed character, Daly had once again pressed the self-destruct button. As Norman and Parry completed their rounds, he walked over to them, thanked them, then hurled his ball some 30 yards into the lake at the side of the green, followed soon after by his putter. As his incredulous playing partners set off for the scorer's cabin, Daly turned around and walked back down the 18th fairway, straight into an immediate disqualification and a $10,000 fine.

The following day, a diver retrieved Daly's ball and putter from the lake and someone had the bright idea of framing it and putting it on display in the Coolum pro shop. Later that day, tournament promoter Tony Roosenberg was asked about his star guest's latest fit of pique. It was, he said, 'vintage Daly'.

26. IF YOU CAN'T BE GOOD, SON, BE GOOD AT IT

'I cannot think of any need in childhood as strong as the need for a father's protection.'

Sigmund Freud

John Patrick Daly II came into the world on 23 July 2003. It was Daly's third child from as many mothers and the son he had always craved. 'We named him after his daddy,' he told the press, before adding, 'I don't know if the world can handle another one.'

Yet his son's future would soon prove to be the least of his worries. Just five days after the arrival of 'Little John', as the family Daly were adjusting to the demands of another permanently hungry mouth to feed, trouble once more came knocking at the door of John Daly. This time, though, it had come gunning not for Daly, but for the lady of the house.

When Daly had met Sherrie Miller at the FedEx St Jude, in 2001, he had thrown himself into the relationship with the same gusto that he once attacked the drinks cabinet. When they had married just 42 days after, the only real surprise was that John had opted to wear jeans to the ceremony. But if Daly had thought that Bettye Fulford's deception was a piece of work, then it paled in comparison to what he was about to learn about his new bride.

Under an indictment filed at a federal court in Oxford, Mississippi, Sherrie Miller, along with her parents Alvis and Billie Miller had been charged with involvement in a drug ring and an illegal gambling venture that had operated between 1996 and 2002. Moreover, the indictment also alleged that the three were part of a larger conspiracy to buy and sell cocaine, methamphetamine and marijuana and that they paid for them with monies earned from previous drug sales. For once, John Daly had nothing to do with it, the charges relating to a time before Daly even knew the family.

That said, it was still another hammer blow for Daly. Unbeknown to him, the woman he had thought was a car saleswoman, along with her parents, stood accused of laundering more than $1.2 million in illegal profits from drug deals. To his credit, Daly was determined to help Sherrie clear her name. 'I stand by her,' he said defiantly, before adding. 'Of course, if she gets twenty years in prison I'll have to end the marriage.'

With his game heading south again, the last thing Daly needed was another slice of marital strife and the strain of coping with the deception of another wife was soon beginning to tell. His mind, already battling the legion of problems that had accompanied him throughout his career, was now riddled with doubts about a marriage that he had thought was the final one. But while most everybody in the game knew that Daly's personal life was once more in chaos, nobody had really appreciated just how desperate he had become.

It was only as he teed it up at the 84 Lumber Classic at Mystic Rock, Pennsylvania, that the true extent of his turmoil finally surfaced. Having staggered through the first round in 75, Daly toiled manfully in his second round but it was clear that he was in no shape, be it mental or physical, to continue. By the fifteenth hole, he had had enough and just as in the US Open in 1997, Daly's hands began trembling so much that he could barely hold the club, let alone grip it and rip it. As he sat down on his bag, staring into space, a PGA Tour official arrived in a golf cart, helped Daly on board and then transferred him back to the clubhouse where he was attached to an IV drip for what was diagnosed as dehydration. 'He's a personality and talent we have to have out here,' said his fellow professional Rocco Mediate. 'He's a good man, but how many times can he go through something like this?'

Later, Joe Hardy, the founder of the 84 Lumber Classic, sent Daly a remote-control Hummer 4x4 vehicle as a Christmas present for his kids. It was his own way of letting Daly know that there were still folk that cared. 'When people are down, that's not the time you kick them out,' said Hardy. 'I'll do everything I can to help him.'

After the alarming turn of events at Mystic Rock, Daly's game descended into one of its all too predictable downturns. A week later at the Valero Texas Open, he dredged a putt in while the ball was still moving and didn't bother to mention it until after he had signed his scorecard, knowing full well that once it came to light he would be automatically disqualified. Then at the Southern Farm Bureau Classic in Missouri the following week, Daly six-putted one green on his way to a second round 83 and another missed cut, finishing the hole by slapping the ball into the hole like an ice-hockey player. It would be his last PGA Tour appearance of a season in which he had withdrawn, been disqualified or missed the cut, and which had seen him claim just $220,647 in winnings, his second worst showing on the Tour.

As his game, his marriage and his life deteriorated, it was inevitable that the whispering would once more begin. One New Jersey wire service, Sportsticker, even reported that Daly had been ordered to go back into rehab, or face censure from the Tour. Not so, said Henry Hughes, the PGA's Chief of Operations. 'There was no ultimatum,' he insisted. 'He's not in rehab. It is not mandated. None of that is true.'

Bud Martin, Daly's agent, was also quick to dismiss the reports. 'It is categorically false that he has entered rehab or even contemplated going to one,' he said.

For many observers, it was Mrs John Daly IV who was entirely culpable for his latest setback. Certainly, those in Daly's inner circle were not backwards in coming forwards on the issue. First, his caddie Mick Peterson called it a day, making it plain he couldn't cope with the ongoing drama with Sherrie and her family. Then, Donnie Crabtree, Daly's driver and old high school friend, made his excuses too. 'It is hard to watch someone you love self-destruct,' he reflected.

With his life unravelling again, Daly disappeared, opting to take up an offer of a decent appearance fee at the Korean Open in Seoul, South Korea, even though those that still purported to care felt he would be better served by staying at home. 'Everyone told me not to go,' he would admit, 'agents, players, people like Mark O'Meara, begging me not to accept. It was at the height of everything going wrong that could go wrong and they were worried about my wellbeing.'

The way things were going, a flight of several thousand miles seemed like a more agreeable option than heading home, even for a lifelong aviophobic like Daly. With his appearance fee tucked safely in his back pocket and with his personal problems half a world away in Arkansas, John Daly then did what only John Daly could do. He went and won the tournament.

The win in Korea would signal the beginning of a revival that would continue when Daly returned to the States. First, he took the title at the Callaway Golf Pebble Beach Invitational, a low-key event featuring players from the PGA Tour, the LPGA and the Champions Tour, before claiming the winner's cheque at one of his perennial favourites, the Wendy's Three-Tour Challenge, alongside his team-mates Tom Kite and Grace Park. After a prolonged absence, the smile was finally returning to John Daly's face. 'I finally like the way I'm swinging,' he grinned.

27. BLUE EYES CRYING IN THE RAIN

'Far better it is to dare mighty things, to win glorious triumphs even though checkered by failure, than to rank with those poor spirits who neither enjoy nor suffer much because they live in the gray twilight that knows neither victory nor defeat.'

Theodore Roosevelt

In January 2004, Daly signed a new, three-year deal with Dunlop, a manufacturer whose equipment was noted more for its value than for its Tour pedigree. For Daly, though, it was just nice that someone still saw him as an asset rather than a liability.

With a bona fide Tour presence, albeit one that came with more baggage than Heathrow's departure lounge, Dunlop announced that they had, with Daly's backing, given their star player a new range of suitably-monikered clubs to take on Tour with him. From 19 January, John Daly would play with Dunlop's LoCo clubs, their LoCo Pro golf ball and, hilariously, their Redneck putter. 'It should be a perfect marriage,' said Dan Murphy, the company's Director of Marketing, oblivious to the fact that the words 'perfect' and 'marriage' had never ever been used in the same sentence when discussing John Daly.

The following week, Daly made his first official outing with his new clubs at the Bob Hope Chrysler Classic in the West Coast Swing and continued with the promising form he had shown in the money matches at the end of 2003. During his fourth round,

Daly even had a rare double eagle on the second hole at PGA West, holing his second shot from 220 yards on the 514-yard par-5. It was precisely the kind of solid start that Daly needed to the new season and but for a level-par 72 in that penultimate round, he would surely have registered his first top-ten Tour finish in nearly a year. Instead, he would have to settle for a tie for 30th and a handy cheque for $27,337.

Happier and seemingly at ease, Daly attributed his run of form to the great strides he and Sherrie were making in trying to patch their relationship up. In the November 2003 issue of *Sports Ilustrated*, Daly had given an interview in which he confirmed that divorce proceedings were once more under way and that any chance of a reconciliation with Sherrie had long since vanished. 'I can't deal with it any more,' he said. 'The things that she has done to me in front of people. I've let her beat the living daylights out of me, just pounding me with her fists.'

But after a close season spent endeavouring to chart some kind of route out of their morass of problems, John and Sherrie had decided to make a go of it, regardless of whatever happened in the upcoming prosecution. 'The bottom line,' he said, 'is that we both just love each other, and we have two special kids to bring up.' He shrugged: 'It's worth fighting for, you know.'

With his game and his marriage in better shape than they had been in some time, Daly headed down to San Diego for the Buick Invitational at Torrey Pines. Tiger Woods, Vijay Singh and Phil Mickelson had also made the trip, making it the strongest field so far of the 2004 PGA Tour season.

He would make a fine start to the competition, registering rounds of 69 and 66 and after a third-round 68 in which he eagled the final hole, Daly, remarkably, held a one-shot lead over Stewart Cink going into the final day.

Now, as the final round loomed, there was every chance that John Daly, a player without a Tour win in 189 starts and floundering at a dismal 299 in the world rankings (sandwiched between such golfing luminaries as Henrik Stenson and Tomohiro Kondo) could actually go and win a tournament.

At times in that final round Daly would ride his luck, benefiting from the occasional lucky roll or ricochet, but buoyed by a crowd desperate to see him prevail, Daly arrived at the 72nd hole needing a birdie for the unlikeliest of victories. But he wouldn't get it, his 35-foot putt failing to drop and putting him in a three-way sudden death play-off with his compatriot Chris Riley and the young Englishman Luke Donald.

The trio went back to the tee on the 577-yard, par-5 eighteenth, Daly taking the honour. With the crowd on his side, he ripped a 300-yard drive down the fairway. When the trio reached their balls, Daly looked on as his rivals both opted to lay up with the second shots ahead of the pond that guards the front of the green. When Daly reached his ball, there wasn't a moment's hesitation. Out came his 3-wood. Cue spontaneous outbreak of hollering.

In a flash, Daly's ball had sailed over the water and found the bunker at the back of the green, some 263 yards away. Donald and Riley, meanwhile, would both hit their third shots within 6 feet, leaving Daly, faced with a devilish downhill bunker shot of around 100 feet, as the least likely of the trio to make birdie. His next shot, however, was sublime. Taking his sand wedge, he skied a lob out of the trap and landed it perfectly on a spot the size of a dinner plate. Six inches shorter and his ball would have held on the upper tier of the green. A foot further and there was every chance it would career through the green and bring the water into play. Instead, it crawled over the ridge, Daly yelling 'Go! Go!' as the ball trickled down to the flag, finishing just 4 inches from the hole. He tapped it in for his birdie before the screaming had ceased.

Clearly, Donald and the local boy Riley were fazed by the hullabaloo but with the din showing little sign of easing, the two eyed their putts. Donald was first up but read a break in his putt that simply wasn't there and slid his 6-footer past the hole to the right.

It was down to Chris Riley to take the contest to another hole. One of the most reliable putters on the PGA Tour, Riley had grown up in the San Diego area and knew Torrey Pines better than most players on Tour. With just 5 feet between him and another play-off hole with Daly, Riley was odds-on to make his putt. But, with the collective will of the Californian galleries behind the guy with the biggest gut, Riley watched aghast as his putt caught the lip of the hole, span 360 degrees around the hole and stayed above ground.

As the crowd erupted, Daly buried his head in his hands and began crying. Soon after, Sherrie Daly appeared from the wings and hugged her husband, the tears streaming down both their faces. With his first official Tour title since 1995 secured, Daly's relief was palpable, not least because there was the biggest single cheque of his career ($864,000) to help placate his three ex-wives for a month or two. 'It's the greatest. I've had a lot of ups and downs,' he blubbed, before running out of things to say. 'Geez, this is sweet.'

Ten years ago, John Daly would doubtless have marked his success by taking his winner's cheque and heading straight to the casino without passing go. This time, when asked how, as a recovering alcoholic, he would go about celebrating his victory, he simply said he would have a bar of chocolate – or three. 'This is the greatest victory,' he added later. 'I won two majors. Nothing can take away from that. But I've never won a tournament [when] Tiger Woods has been in the field. That feels good.'

Daly's Buick win merely served to re-emphasise the esteem in which he is held, both inside and outside of the ropes. While the fans in the grandstand genuflected, the players too were heaping praise on their colleague. The two men he defeated in that play-off were unusually generous. 'I take my hat off to Johnny. He's been through a lot and to see him win is great,' said Chris Riley, while Luke Donald added, 'He's had his troubles, and to come back to win, nine years without winning on this tour, you could never tell with him playing that last hole.' Even Tiger chipped in. 'He's had a lot of things happen to him. We've all read about it and seen it,' he said. 'It's great to have anybody who has gone through the things he's gone through and succeed.'

Across the world, the news of Daly's improbable win met with universal acclaim. The *Chicago Tribune* called his triumph 'a show stopper' while the *Los Angeles Times* suggested that the sight of the one-time hell-raiser bawling on the eighteenth green was probably 'the best breakdown Daly has ever had'. The praise was equally fulsome across the Atlantic, with the *Daily Express* saying 'Tearful Daly is as happy as a sandboy', and the *Sun* maintaining that Daly's victory completed 'one of the most remarkable comebacks in sport'. It was hard to disagree.

Since he turned professional in 1987, the Masters has been the one title John Daly has truly coveted. Often, like so many other players before him, he has dreamed of winning at Augusta, pausing only to wonder whether Hootie Johnson would actually have a green jacket in XXXXL or just what he would choose for the meal at the Champions Dinner. 'I don't know what I'd serve up,' he shrugged. 'Maybe Hooters chicken-wings. Whatever it would be, it would be greasy and fattening. That's for sure.'

Having failed to qualify for the tournament in 2003, Daly had squeezed into the 2004 line-up as one of the world's top 50 ranked players, despite missing most of the Tour events in March as a result of having shut his hand in a fast-food restaurant door. Presumably, they were trying to close early. As he rolled into town in his RV, the stitches in his hand long since removed, Daly was in his element. 'It's awesome,' he said. 'Everything's good here. I can forget about everything, because it's so serene here.'

As ever, though, serenity was conspicuous by its absence in Daly's life that week. On the Monday, Sherrie had finally pleaded guilty to the charges she faced. Under a plea bargain negotiated with US Attorney Paul Rogers, she and her mother would later be sentenced to five years' probation with six months of home detention – the equivalent of tagging – while her father would receive two years in prison. Bizarrely, Daly had told his wife: 'I know you're not guilty of anything, but you're not going to win. You don't beat a federal court, a federal judge and the FBI. There's no way.' So, rather than fight to clear her name, Daly and Sherrie decided it was best for all concerned if she just took the rap.

Going into the first major of the year, however, there were conflicting reports about just how seriously Daly had been taking his game. Some had him down the range, cigarette welded to his lips, gut spilling over his belt, working on his game until the sunlight faded. Others, most notably a story by Alan Campbell in the *Sunday Herald*, spotted him outside his van on Washington Lane selling John Daly merchandise to his adoring public until the early hours of the morning, as waitresses from the nearby Hooters brought him plate after plate of fried chicken. Indeed, Campbell reported that when a fan asked him why he wasn't resting when he had just twelve hours before he teed off, he snapped: 'Plenty of time to sleep when I'm dead.' Moments later, another fan asked whether he could win the Masters. 'Who cares?' he said. 'I don't give a f***.' Clearly, he didn't. He shot 78–71 and missed the cut by a stroke.

Still, at least he shifted some product, most notably his new CD. Entitled *My Life*, it was, according to the artist, a way for him to tell his many fans just how much he loves them. And, at $53 for an autographed copy, it was also a way for his many fans to show just how much they loved him.

Conceived in early 2002, it was an album that featured many of Daly's close friends, including the country singers Daron Norwood and Johnny Lee, and Darius Hooker from Hootie and the Blowfish. An eleven-track blend of rock, country and soul, it features 'Mr Fan', the song he wrote on the back of a pizza box after he missed the cut at the PGA at Valhalla, a bluesy number called 'I'm Drunk, Damn Broke and Ain't Got a Penny to My Name', and the highlight of the album, 'All My Exes Wear Rolexes', a playful dig at the lost loves of his turbulent life. It does not feature a cover version of 'Wild Thing'.

On reflection, the venture into music was a logical step for Daly, or as logical as any decision in his career has been. Over the years, as he battled alcoholism, marital strife and his chronic gambling problems, his life has often been likened to some tortured country-and-western song, or, given that he has had more ups and downs than most, a country-and-western album. Recently, he has even taken to performing the songs live, and his shows come with a refreshingly honest analysis of his musical aptitude. Not only does Daly confess that his guitar playing 'sucks', he also admits that his singing sounds 'like shit'.

Yet the sight of Daly cursing at his followers as he gladly takes their money for his autographed hats, cigarette lighters and God knows what is at odds with the fans' favourite image he likes to portray. While he frequently cites 'the fans' as the reason he keeps going (nothing to do with monthly alimony and child support bills running into the tens of thousands), Daly has been quick to seize upon his reputation as the man of the people. Indeed, his own online shop is a veritable Aladdin's Cave, albeit a rather disappointing one filled with junk. Quite why anyone would want to hand over nearly $2,500 for a John Daly pendant, for instance, is anybody's guess.

The missed cut at the Masters was Daly's first of a new season in which he had already earned more than five times his total for 2003. Moreover, he had played in just eight events. At times, his form was as impressive as at any time in his career. After the win at Torrey Pines, for example, he had claimed a fourth place at the Nissan Open at the Riviera Club, and a tie for tenth at the Bay Hill Invitational. He had nearly won again, too, beaten into second place by one shot by the player of the year, Vijay Singh, at the Buick Open at Warwick Hills Golf and Country Club, Michigan.

As Daly's world ranking improved, so too did his placing in the qualification table for the American Ryder Cup team, due to take on their European counterparts at Oakland Hills, Michigan in September. Having missed out on two Ryder Cup teams in the past (despite winning majors in the same years), Daly had remained off the Ryder Cup radar ever since, failing to gain either an automatic berth in the side or a place as a captain's pick.

As deadline day approached for the Ryder Cup team, there was a significant groundswell of opinion among the media and golf fans alike that it was high time that Daly was given a chance in the game's most prestigious team event. Certainly, the press, keen to see hostilities resumed, was in Daly's corner and the *Boston Globe*'s Jim McCabe was typical. Reporting on the battle for the two wild card spots in Sutton's team, McCabe suggested that 'truly the only guy who is generating any public interest is sitting in the twentieth spot: The one and only John Daly.'

It was an opinion reinforced by a fans' poll on the Golf Channel's internet site where some 87 per cent of the respondents answered 'yes' to the question: 'Do you think Hal Sutton should select John Daly for the Ryder Cup team?'

With the clamour to see Daly picked for the Ryder Cup escalating, however, the American team captain Hal Sutton appeared to be increasingly riled by the never-ending stream of questions about whether the Wild Thing would be a wild card. As the event drew nearer, though, Sutton's responses to the Daly question became appreciably less vague. Where once his replies had taken the line of 'everyone's still in with a chance', now they were all but declaring that Daly was no longer part of his plans. 'Right now,' said Sutton at the PGA Championship at Whistling Straits, 'if anyone picked John Daly based on anything, it would literally have to be because you just wanted to see him there and you wanted to spike the crowd . . . I never was going to play the popularity game and I'm still not going to play the popularity game.'

The PGA Championship, the event where Daly had announced his arrival in the professional game some thirteen years earlier, was the last qualifying event for the American Ryder Cup side. Going into the tournament, Daly was acutely aware of the need for a good showing so that even if he failed to make the team as of right, he would still give Hal Sutton a timely reminder of what he could do for him and his side. It didn't happen. A stinking 81 on the first day followed by an unsightly 76 in the second round left him twelve shots adrift of the cut mark and out of the Ryder Cup reckoning. The fact that he scored better than just six players in the field – five of them club professionals and the other a ring-rusty David Duval – merely confirmed Sutton's suspicion that Daly wasn't up for the battle at Oakland Hills.

Ultimately, it mattered not that Daly had posted five top-ten finishes – his best record since 1992 – and won again in 2004, Sutton instead plumped for the veteran Jay Hass and Stewart Cink as his wild cards, just two of a gaggle of dependable flat-trackers who represented a solid, unspectacular alternative to the inherent risk that was John Daly.

Daly, meanwhile, was philosophical about his absence from the team, suggesting that perhaps the principal reason he missed out was that his reputation as the People's Champion preceded him. 'They [the fans] kept on pushing for me to get a wild card, and in the end I think they might have pissed Hal off,' he told the press at the BMW International in Munich, Germany. '[But] I've created a couple of records. I was the first guy to win one major and not get on a Ryder Cup. And I was the first guy to win two and not be on a Ryder Cup.'

Certainly, the European team were delighted with Daly's nonappearance in the American team line-up. First, the European captain Bernhard Langer confided in Daly that he would have picked him had he been in Hal Sutton's shoes. Then, Colin Montgomerie, so long the stalwart of the European Ryder Cup team, caught up with Daly at the BMW. 'Monty said to me, "Tell Hal we said thanks for not picking you. It puts our team one up."'

Sutton's decision to overlook Daly has, perhaps, put paid to the last real chance he ever had of taking part in the Ryder Cup. In retrospect, though, John Daly was precisely the kind of player the USA team needed at Oakland Hills and their heaviest defeat on record was humiliating in the extreme, their performance hideous. Throughout the event, the home crowd, a crucial player in any Ryder Cup match, had no natural flag-bearer to rally behind. There was the rookie Chris Riley asking to be rested, there was Phil Mickelson looking permanently perplexed and then there was Hal Sutton in his Stetson walking the course looking like a little boy lost. Sure, Chris DiMarco tried his best with some energetic bouts of fist-pumping, but he was, perhaps, the only player willing to take the fight to the European team. In short, what the USA needed all along was someone to 'spike the crowd'.

At least the PGA Tour had the decency to recognise the strides Daly had made. Having won the most money ever in his thirteen years in the professional game, John Daly, a man who should really be dead by now, or, at the very least incapable of playing professional sport, gained official PGA recognition of his remarkable achievements over the course of the 2004 season. Despite the car crashes and the comas, the stomach pumps and the strokes, Daly was awarded the Tour's prestigious title of Comeback Player of the Year. The hick from Crooked Stick was back.

EPILOGUE

'I'm still the same . . . fat, out of shape, all that good stuff.'

John Daly, January 2005

When I visited the Open Championship at Royal St Georges, Sandwich, in July 2003, I chose to follow John Daly during his opening round. The first edition of this book had just been published and I had heard through the golf grapevine that Daly was none too pleased with it. As he reached the eighteenth hole, I walked ahead and took a seat in the grandstand to the right of the green, awaiting his arrival. With the coastal wind whipping up and conditions worsening, Daly carved his tee shot into the rough on the right.

Looking down the fairway, I could see a predictably large crowd gather round his ball, pointing at it as though it were an alien craft that had crash landed on a golf course in Kent. When Daly got to his ball, he took no time in pulling a long iron from his bag and smacking it in the vague direction of the green. It didn't find its intended target. Instead, it touched down within a yard of me in the grandstand and clattered round the seats. It was as if he was aiming for me and had it have been Tiger or Vijay playing the shot the chances are the result may well have been different. But this was Daly playing. Moreover, it was Daly playing it in the middle of one of his all-too-common troughs and his game, and his mind, were all over the place. Indeed, of the players that made the cut that week, Daly would come dead last again.

Then on Sunday, 15 February 2004, a remarkable thing happened. John Patrick Daly, a player without a win on the PGA Tour since the second year of the Clinton administration and a man with more ex-wives than majors, went and won a tournament. And it wasn't just any old tournament. It was the Buick Invitational, a proper, bona fide, big-time PGA Tour event, with Tiger Woods, Phil Mickelson and Vijay Singh all behind him as well.

The following day, I fielded several calls from radio stations in the UK, asking me about the seismic events at Torrey Pines and whether I was as stunned as everyone else by Daly's return to form. I told them I was mildly surprised but not entirely shocked. Daly had, after all, been making cuts (something he had only done in 8 of his 22 events the previous year) and shooting some very low scores. The only real surprise, I felt, was that he was able to string four decent rounds together and then do it in such a strong field.

In the pandemonium that followed his win, it was clear just what the victory meant, not just to Daly but to his supporters and to the game of golf more generally. As I watched the denouement at home on television, it was like some truly Messianic moment had been played out on the outskirts of San Diego. You could see grown men in the bleachers hugging each other, the CBS commentary team were beside themselves and when they finally cut back to the Sky Sports studio in the UK, I swear that it looked like their anchorman David Livingstone had been crying.

Older and wiser, well marginally wiser, Daly at last seems to be on something approaching an even keel. He has recently renewed his wedding vows with Sherrie, he has redoubled his charitable work and continued to be the best dad that he could to his kids, something he has always endeavoured to do, regardless of whatever personal crises he finds himself in. He even allows himself the occasional beer. 'Everybody has problems,' he says. 'I'm no different. But I've mellowed out.'

Certainly, Sherrie agrees. 'We are the most boring people that you've ever met. The party animal image that people have of us is completely untrue. There's no party till all hours. It's not what you might think.'

For the most part, it is this candour that has won Daly so many friends – and enemies – throughout his career, and it is undeniably engaging. I have sat in press conferences with Daly as he has openly discussed his myriad problems as if he were talking about the weather or the price of petrol. He is frank, self-deprecating and always amusing. If a golf course stinks, he'll say so. If he's played like a chump, he'll admit it.

He is, it seems, a golfer with a soul, a player who has always returned to his uncomplicated life at the foot of the Ozarks when every other professional has moved to Florida to avoid paying state income tax. He is not, and never will be, a golfing genius like, say, Seve Ballesteros, nor is he an automaton like Tiger Woods. In fact, the most accurate description of him was made by his PGA contemporary Fred Couples, who said, 'He's a freak. To be that long and have that kind of touch. He's one of the few players out here I'd pay to watch. I root for him to win more than I root for me.'

Daly has often maintained that the reason he remains so popular among the golf fans is because they can relate to the problems he has suffered. That is true, but only to a point. They can doubtless empathise with his raft of relationship problems and the battles he has fought (and lost) with his weight and his drinking, but can anyone really have an idea of how it feels to lose a million dollars at a slot machine in one evening, or know what it is like having to find $50,000 each month just to meet your alimony obligations?

It is too simplistic to view Daly as some real-life Rocky Balboa, forever picking himself up after another right cross sends him crashing to the canvas. Besides, the most difficult opponent he has ever fought is himself. Better to think of him as what he really is – a great golfer and occasional goofball with a rare generosity of spirit and a commitment to giving a little back. At the time of writing, for instance, Daly is actively involved in a variety of charitable causes, most notably the Make-a-Wish Foundation and the Boys & Girls Clubs of America, and he still donates 1 per cent of his Tour earnings each year to help fund the American Junior Golf Association, something he continued to do even when he was on the brink of insolvency.

But then his acts of generosity are legendary. In the past, he has stopped at a child's drinks stall and paid $100 for a cup of warm lemonade; he has bought friends cars and houses; he has picked up the tab for his fans on his way out of a diner; he has given the Pings he used to win the 1991 PGA to the University of Arkansas, and the Wilsons he used to win the 1995 Open Championship to friends in South Carolina; and he'll sign autographs until the sun sets. In an interview with *Today's Golfer* magazine in August 2002, Daly was asked what he was going to have engraved on his tombstone. 'Here lies John Daly,' he said, 'a man with a big heart.'

BIBLIOGRAPHY

Adams, Mike and Tomasi, T.J., with Kathryn Maloney: *Total Golf* (Carlton)

Alliss, Peter: *Peter Alliss' Golf Heroes* (Virgin)

Amende, Croal: *Rock Confidential* (Plume)

Concannon, Dale: *Driven: The Definitive Biography of Nick Faldo* (Virgin)

Conner, Floyd: *Golf's Most Wanted* (Brassey's Inc.)

Dabell, Norman: *Winning the Open – The Caddies' Stories from Four Decades of the Open Championship* (Mainstream Sport)

Daly, John, with John Andrisani: *The Killer Swing: John Daly's Guide to Long Hitting* (HarperCollins)

Davies, Laura, with Lewine Mair: *Naturally . . .* (Bloomsbury)

Donegan, Lawrence: *Four-Iron in the Soul* (Penguin)

Evans, Alun: *Virgin Golf Record File* (Virgin)

Feinstein, John: *A Good Walk Spoiled: Days and Nights on the PGA Tour* (Little, Brown & Co.)

Feinstein, John: *The Majors* (Warner Books)

Fodor's Special Interest Guides: *Golf Digest's Best Places to Play: 5,000 Public and Resort Courses in the USA and Canada* (Fodor)

Glover, Tim and Higgs, Peter: *Fairway to Heaven – Victors and Victims of Golf's Choking Game* (Mainstream Sport)

Golf Rules Illustrated 2002–2003 by the Royal & Ancient Golf Club (Hamlyn)

Levinson, David and Christensen, Karen (eds): *Encyclopedia of World Sport* (ABC Clio)

McWilliam, Rab: *Who's Who in Golf* (Hamlyn)

Montgomerie, Colin and Mair, Lewine: *Real Monty: The Autobiography of Colin Montgomerie* (Orion)

Partington, Angela (ed.): *The Oxford Dictionary of Quotations* (Oxford University Press)

Pegley, Rob: *The Virgin Book of Golf Records* (Virgin)

Riese, Randall: *Nashville Babylon: The Uncensored Truth and Private Lives of Country Music's Stars* (Guild)

St John, Lauren: *Fairway Dreams* (Mainstream Sport)

St John, Lauren: *Greg Norman: The Biography* (Corgi)

St John, Lauren: *Seve: The Biography* (Corgi)

Wartman, William: *John Daly: Wild Thing – Life on the Edge with Pro Golf's Bad Boy* (Aurum)

Woosnam, Ian, with Edward Griffiths: *Woosie – My Autobiography* (Collins-Willow)

INDEX